Pearl River County Veterans II: War Stories and Sea Tales

N. Christian Smoot

Rivercross Publishing
New York

First Edition

ISBN 0-944957-37-4

Library of Congress Catalog Card Number: 92-16350

Library of Congress Cataloging-in-Publication Data

Smoot, N. Christian.
    Pearl River country veterans II:war stories and sea tales/
N. Christian Smoot—1st e.
        p. cm.
    ISBN 0-944957-37-4 (HC): $18.95
    1. United States—History, Military. 2. Veterans—Mississippi—
Pearl River County—Biography. 3. Soldiers—Mississippi—Pearl River
County—Biography. 4. Pearl River County (Miss.)—Biography.
I.Title.
E181.S58 1992
355'.0092'276215—dc20   92-16350
                                                              CIP

Foreword

He could have been any boy from anywhere. He was graduated from high school in Small Town USA and, not long after that, got married. In 1968 he was drafted into the Army, and it changed his life forever. The Army sent him to helicopter mechanic school for his training in preparation for war. Then he got to go to Vietnam for a tour of duty. It was about 20 years later when his mother showed me his medals. I sent off a request of the Army "official" version of his life for 1968-70.

This boy, his name was Doug, started with a medal for expert marksmanship with an M-16. He went to helicopter mechanic school in December '68 and to Vietnam in January '69 as a helicopter repairman with Co. A, 228th Avn Btn, 1st Air Cav Div. In March he transferred to Co. C. From 21 April to 1 May '69, he earned an Air Medal on an assault support helicopter *(as a mechanic?)*. For his work over there he also received a Bronze Star *(valor as a helicopter mechanic?)*, the Vietnam Cross of Gallantry with Palm, and the standard National Defense Service Medal, Vietnam Service Medal, and Republic of Vietnam Campaign Medal with 60 device. On 27 February '70 he returned to CONUS (Continental United States). His mother also has another Air Medal with a "V" and a silver oak leaf, and an Army Commendation Medal. These are assumed to be battlefield awards that were not registered properly with the appropriate authorities.

i

The next time his family saw him, he was not the same person. Nobody will ever know what kind of scars he bore inside. He had to sleep between his parents when he got home; would sit up at night screaming and sweating, would walk around all night smoking cigarettes, wouldn't consciously talk about his overseas duty at all. We do know that, three weeks before he was to be sent home, he told his commander that he couldn't go up again. Doug got a letter as soon as he got home. His whole command got wiped out the day he left. *deathdeaTHDEATH* all around. Killing, torturing, mutilating death. Who can ever be prepared for that? What can one do? This man took his own life after taking that of so many others. How could a mechanic do that, you ask?

Well, the Army made Doug a door gunner in the 1st Air Cav as soon as he got there. He could never loosen up and talk about the horrors of war except to his brother, Jimmy, and that was only one or two times as best Jimmy can remember. There is no telling how many or what kind of lives a door gunner in Vietnam personally destroyed. According to other Vietnam veterans, he did what he had to do to stay alive. No hero. No hotdogging. Just staying alive. Jimmy knows this much of the story:

Doug's position was as a crew chief/ door gunner on a Jolly Green Giant. The Giant took a .50 cal. through the engine and went down in North Vietnam. Doug covered everybody while they scattered. Trouble was, they scattered so well, they ran off and left him by himself. He couldn't

ii

understand why the team would do that, but he knew he'd better catch up with them or be killed. Eventually, they were all rescued.

There was another trip up to North Vietnam from Pleiku. Doug was a door gunner again. This time the Giant got shot in the hydraulic system, and Doug was saturated with the spraying, flammable hydraulic fluid. Then a fire broke out in the back of the helicopter. Nobody else would help put it out. In fact, they locked Doug in the back with the fire even though he was saturated with the fluid. His crew locked him in the back! These bastards actually locked him in with the fire to die.

After that last episode Doug wondered what kind of animals he was over there with. He took all the locator equipment and survival gear and jumped out of the Giant when it went low enough. The chopper landed. Several men found Doug, and he helped them find the rest of the crew. Again they were rescued, but Doug never cared for his "buds" again because they had locked him in the back to die.

It wasn't long after that, Doug was walking around, talking with a friend he had made while in basic about not wanting to die. His friend stepped on a mine that blew off one of his legs, left his insides lying on the ground, and his head mostly severed. That was the final straw. Three weeks before he was scheduled to go home, Doug withdrew. He would lie on a ball on the floor and tell

his CO to shoot him if he wanted, but he wasn't going to go up again. He started in to heavy duty drinking. When that didn't work, he tried drugs. Nothing worked.
Doug told me he was going to commit suicide, but I couldn't talk him out of it. That was in October, 1975. In January, 1976, he succeeded.

Doug could have been anybody, but he wasn't. He was very special to his family and friends. I didn't get a chance to know Doug, but this book is dedicated to his memory and to what it stands for- the horrors of war.

Table of Contents

Introduction

The first book, <u>Pearl</u> <u>River</u> <u>County</u> <u>Veterans</u>, was more an "annual," where pictures and mugshots were the primary theme. There was a brief history section, but that was all. After the veterans' parade in November 1990 many of the participants told me that they had not been interviewed for the book. That has now been rectified. This book is the written part of <u>Pearl</u> <u>River</u> <u>County</u> <u>Veterans</u>.

A brief history of area participation in all the combat engagements is presented for Pearl River Countians. The story is given by first-hand interview where possible. An attempt has been made to keep families together, so there is some family lore involved. There are some 5-Star families, those who had at least five family members in the same war at the same time, no mean feat by anybody's standards. We have Burks, Lees, Stewarts, Laibs, Stockstills, Wheats, Cowarts, Ackers, Fords, Mitchells, Friersons, Strahans, Williams, Burges, Smiths, Flynts, McCormicks, Browns, Napiers, Lumpkins, Harrells, Casanovas, Dickersons, Whitfields, McLaurins, Martins, Nameths, Bilbos, and more.

I have gone to the history books in some instance to help clarify matters. After all, some of these guys fought a long time ago and their memories are like the old gray mare- she ain't what she used to be! In those instances, the script has been italicized. Any editorializing by the writer is also italicized.

1

Some of the veterans, such as the people employed by the Naval Oceanographic Office, were not from this area originally. They are now, so their stories are included. The writing is done in an attempt to match the style of the times and, in fact, gives representative jargon at the start of each engagement to set the mood. These buzzwords are not meant to offend anyone, only to reflect and restage that time frame. The pictures have been presented mostly by the veterans. Where I wanted explanatory pictures, such as newspaper headlines, pieces of equipment, etc, I went to the literature and tried to cite all. Where I wanted to put dates or to clarify time sequences, I used books from the Margaret Reed Crosby Memorial Library in Picayune. The histories of ships are all from the <u>Dictionary</u> <u>of</u> <u>American</u> <u>Naval</u> <u>Fighting</u> <u>Ships</u>, Naval History Division of the Department of the Navy, Washington, DC, 1976. This set is housed in the Maury Library at Stennis Space Center MS.

Only battles or participation in which Pearl River Countians were engaged (that I was told about) are listed. These stories were reported to me by individual veterans or the veteran's family. No attempt has been made to verify any of them, except where invited to, so we will trust everyone's integrity on the matter.

An order of priority of medals and attachments is included so the reader can evaluate some of the cited hero's records. Any veteran is a hero. When a person goes into the service, it is generally not known whether or not there

2

will be a wartime situation. That person just does their duty and hopes they can do some good for somebody somewhere and make a good accounting of themselves. A person armed against other armed people is in a war. Tell Custer surrounded by 5,000 Indians he wasn't in a war. The same holds true for Vietnam, the Mayaguez, World War I, or Desert Storm. A bullet is still a bullet. Some are just fatter and faster than others.

Here goes.

War of 1812

JACKSON-LAKE BORGNE-CREEK INDIANS-SPANISH
FLORIDA -REDCOATS-CHEF MENTEUR ROAD- DOM-
ENIQUE YOU-JEAN LAFITTE-PLAIN OF GENTILLY
-PEA ISLAND. *There were two major fronts
in the War of 1812 in the South. One was
the Creek War in 1812-13, and the other
was the Battle of New Orleans, 8 January
1815. The US won them both. We have one
documented veteran from that era, and we
have to assume he was in the Battle of
New Orleans. A brief history of that battle shows that there were actually two
battles. The first was when Jackson attacked the British at Villere Plantation
at night on 23 December 1814 and carried
the day with shock and surprise. Then
the British under General Sir Edward
Packenham brought more cannons up through
the mud and swamps. That gave Jackson
time to add to his defenses. On 1 January
1815 the redcoats attacked Jackson as the
fog cleared (near present day Chalmette).
Their artillery could not find the range,
and ours could. Bye-bye, British. On 8
January the redcoats made one last try
and failed again. Bye-bye Packenham. The
significance of that battle is that it
was absolutely useless. The Treaty of
Ghent had been signed on 24 December
1814.*

Daniel Burks was in Wilkinson's
Brigade, 2nd US Infantry, as a 7 year old
drummer boy. He came down from Kentucky
with Jackson. Daniel was captured by the
British after two engagements and put in
a prison ship on Mobile Bay. A British
general had been killed and his body

4

brought on board to be returned to England. Preservation techniques being rather primitive at the time, the general was deposited in a barrel of whiskey for pickling. Finally the British sailors ran out of booze and started drinking that! *(This was General Packenham, who was in charge of the British effort. He was packed in a barrel of rum! His wife witnessed him on the ship.)* Daniel escaped by pretending to be the son of a woman visiting on the ship. Daniel's brother, Roland, was also in the war. Daniel settled around Henleyfield and sired a long line of US patriots, starting withhis son, Joseph, in The War Between the States.

The War Between the States

REPEATING RIFLES-BLUEBELLIES-JOHNNY REBS-
STARS AND BARS-IRONCLADS-DIXIE-SUBMARINES
-SUNKEN ROADHORNET'S NEST-BLOODY LANE-
BURNSIDE BRIDGE-PICKETT'S CHARGE-STONE_
WALL-JEB-LITTLE ROUND TOP-CRATER. *First,
we need to dispense with one misconception. A "civil war" is between two groups of people in the same state (country). If you have one country with a capitol in Washington DC having its own President, Cabinet,etc., and you have another country with a capitol in Richmond VA with its own President, Cabinet, etc. and they go to war, it is a war between two states. The North American continent saw such a war from 1861 to 1865. Now, you can call it "The War Between the States," the "War of Northern Aggression," or whatever; but, by no stretch of the imagination can you call it the "Civil War." (The reason I even bother to point this out is that I have actually heard people using this phrase locally. They must have been damnyankees passing through!)*

The first shot was fired by South Carolinians at Fort Sumter in a squabble over States' rights. They fired the first shot in the Revolutionary War too. The right to secession was originally laid down in the Declaration of Independence and, subsequently, ameliorated by the founding fathers, particularly those from Virginia. New England was jealous of those fathers from the South. In 1803 Senator Plumer of New Hampshire said: "The eastern states must and will

7

dissolve the Union and form a separate government of their own, and the sooner they do this, the better." Senator Pickering of Massachusetts wrote: "I rather anticipate a new confederacy exempt from the corrupt influences of the aristocratic Democrats of the South... There will be a separation...The British provinces of Canada, even with the consent of Great Britain will become members of a northern confederacy." This was in opposition to the admission of Louisiana as a state just after Jefferson had sponsored the Lewis and Clark expedition. In 1814 New England held the Hartford Convention, which considered the withdrawal from the Union. In 1845 John Quincy Adams and fellow New Englanders urged the withdrawal from the Union because of the admittance of Texas as a state (from Facts Historians Leave Out by John S. Tilley).

To orient ourselves, the Appalachian Mountains split the Confederacy in a north-south direction. This meant there were always at least two fronts. The Armies of the glorious Confederacy were the Army of Tennessee *(western department)* and the Army of Northern Virginia *(eastern department)*. Most of our citizenry was in the western department, for obvious reasons.

This war raises many different emotions in many different people. More people were killed in this war, over 620,000,than in World War I, World War II, and Korea combined. I will show fully documented regiment histories from this area and include known veterans

8

(from county tax and pension rolls of the time) with their histories of participation and in which theaters they were. This will orient the reader as to the overall scheme of things so that we don't get bogged down in minutiae. Many thanks in this section to Josephine Megehee of the Picayune library, Rosemary Lovell and John Napier of Picayune for geneological and historical information. Vera Richardson of the State Department of Archives in Jackson was also most helpful and enligtening.

Beginning in 1862 the Confederates controlled a 600-mile stretch from Cumberland Gap through Bowling Green KY on to New Madrid MO in the western theater. Grant attacked the center of this line to gain control of the Tennessee and Cumberland Rivers. He won and moved on to Corinth MS to attack Albert Sidney Johnston's base of operations. Johnston made a surprise attack on Grant at Shiloh (6-7 April '62) and was promptly killed. Braxton Bragg took over his position as commander and decided to raid Kentucky at Perryville (8 October).

Even though Pearl River County was not a county then, several boys who would become Countians enlisted in the cause. James McLaurin Shivers of the 1st Batallion, Alabama Artillery, D.F. Archer of the 10th Mississippi, Albert Watson of the 3rd Alabama Calvary, and W. Calvin Stewart were at Shiloh and continued with the Army of Tennessee for a long time afterward. Shivers and Archer were at Perryville, and Shivers was wounded there.

9

The 3rd Mississippi Regiment was organized for coastal defense. The 3rd had companies called the Gainesville Volunteers (Co. G) and the Shieldsboro (Bay St. Louis) Rifles (Co. H). When it was realized that there was no threat from the Yankees on Ship Island, the 3rd was sent to Vicksburg (20 May 62) to reinforce General M.L. Smith.

VICKSBURG. They were there for the entire bombardment at Snyder's Hill. Then General Loring was given a command, and the 3rd went with him. During the campaign to take Vicksburg, Grant came in south at Bruinsburg. General Pemberton, Vicksburg Commander, did nothing as Grant took Port Gibson (1 May '63), Raymond (12 May), Jackson (14 May), but finally sent about 5000 troops to Champion Hill (16 May) to try to resist. Too late. Our lads had to retreat to the Big Black River Bridge to fight (17 May), lose, and retreat toward Crystal Spring and Jackson when the rest of the Army went to Vicksburg. One item on Vicksburg to clarify later matters. General Pemberton, CSA, was ordered by Pres. Davis to hold Vicksburg at all costs. A president in Richmond VA during that time would have had a hard time getting timely information from the front in Mississippi. In all fairness, Pemberton was caught between a rock and a hard spot. Lyndon Johnson would try the same tactics 100 years later *(If you watch throughout the book, you will be able to pick up many references to politics and war as bedmates.).* Grant circumvented Vicksburg to go to Jackson first. Pemberton

10

disobeyed his theater general, Joe Johnston, by not trying to cut Grant off until too late. Likewise, Johnston would not come to help Pemberton during the seige. We know he at least had the 3rd in reserve to force Grant in a pincer movement. Wouldn't it have been better if the two generals had worked together for the common good?

Hardy Smith and Carlos Alexander were with the 3rd Mississippi at Baker's Creek (Champion's Hill, 16 May '63) just before the Battle of Vicksburg with John C. Pemberton. This was one of the bloodiest battles of that campaign. Alexander was in several more skirmishes, presumably associated with the Vicksburg seige. He was captured and later paroled at Mobile.

Washington Sampson Ford joined in 1863 presumably after his brother was killed in Virginia. We are not given his unit, since he was from Alabama before he settled here, but we are told he fought in many major battles. He lost his hearing at Vicksburg when he was 16 *(this information courtesy of Beth Windham, granddaughter)*. Apparently "Whistling Dick" (a cannon) played too cacophonous a tune. After Vicksburg the army was so poor they resorted to following the horses and picking up droppings. They would get the kernels out, clean them, and parch them for food *(Now I don't know about you, but to me that's hungry.)*.

STOCKSTILL

We learn that the Stockstill family. Brothers David Warden, George W., B. Franklin, and William E. and their cousin William Alonzo Stockstill were all with Co. G of the 3rd Mississippi Regiment.

They fought at Biloxi and Pass Christian MS. They went on to Vicksburg (Snyder's Mill 4 February '63) and Jackson MS, Demopolis and Decatur AL, and to Resaca (13-15 May), New Hope Church (31 May '64), Kennesaw Mountain GA (27 June), Peachtree Creek (20 July), the trenches around Atlanta (September), the Chatanooga and Atlanta railroad (October), and Decatur AL (26-29 October. Later they moved to Franklin TN (30 November), Nashville TN (15 December), Augusta GA (February),Newberry SC (25 February), and surrendered near Durham NC (26 April '65) after participating in the battles of Kingston (10 March) and Bentonville (19 March). Dave Stockstill was sent home on one occasion to "requisition" food for his unit. He found a man with some cattle in the Honey Island swamp; however, the man gave him such a "hard luck" story that Dave stampeded his herd into the swamp and went back empty handed *(from the Picayune Item)*. Also in the same unit with the Stockstills, Carlos Alexander, and Augustus Beall were several Burks brothers, Roland and William *(family outlined later in WWII section)*, Morris Blackwell, Orlando and S.C. Mitchell, and G.W. Young *(information from Rosemary Lovell)*.

The 38th Mississippi Regiment was newly formed in 1862 when it was sent to Corinth (May '62). It went to Columbus, Saltillo for a long layover at Camp Baldwin, the Battle of Iuka (19 September), and back to Corinth (3 October). Then the commanders apparently got lax according to State Department records. The County had many soldiers in this

12

FORGET, HELL!

13

Detail from base of Mississippi monument at Vicksburg.

This sillouette epitomizes the war- the Southern calvary against the northern artillery (from Arms and Equipment of the Civil War by Jack Coggins).

Marker for line of 38th Mississippi Infantry Regiment at Vicksburg.

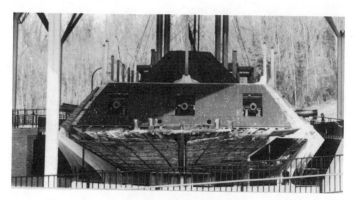

Remains of ironclad USS CAIRO.

regiment, with most of those in Co. C, the Hancock Rebels. Joseph Burks was there for roll call in August '62. He deserted from Baldwin on 23 September '62, was carried on the rolls until November-December '63, and placed on AWOL. His brother, Andrew, died in camp at Saltillo 15 August '62. Joseph Wheat deserted from Baldwin 26 September '62. William Smith, W.G. Wheat *(grandfather of the fighting Wheat boys in WWII)*, J.W. Rogers, and John Madison Stewart were there. Stewart was put on the lost roll in October 63. John Penton had seven sons in the 38th. Their histories from the Archives really leave something to be desired and, in fact, leads one to question the very records themselves. This is what is there *(Since I didn't make it up, I can't apologize.)*. Emmanuel deserted from Camp Baldwin September '62 and was struck from the roll October '63. John J. did the same. Alfred E. was killed in the trenches at Vicksburg *(date uncertain)*. Davis was AWOL from September '62 through all of '63. George deserted 26 May '62. Thomas deserted 6 August '62 and was struck from the roll October '63. W.A. Penton was AWOL from March '62 through December '63. The records are incomplete after 1863, so there is no record of any of these gentlemen after what is shown. One would hope they may have joined another unit and continued in the glorious cause, but they missed Iuka, Corinth, Vicksburg, and any other engagements the 38th took part in during '62 and '63. For this state that is disastrous. *(In defense, I noted that the rolltaker for the 38th seemed harsher that any of the other companies that I looked at as far as desertion went. I talked with the resident expert, Vera Richardson. She told me the boys would go home to help with the spring planting and the fall harvest. But, 15 months at a stretch seems like a bit much "leave" to me.)* The 38th was then sent to Vicksburg and stationed at Snyder's Bluff, along with the 3rd Louisiana. They defended the Jackson and Graveyard roads (17-18 May '63) at Vicksburg where they underwent strafing by 10 inch columbiads (11 June), were charged repeatedly, mined and exploded (25 June), suffered hand-to-hand combat, and were mined and exploded again (1 July). They caught it bad, to say the least. After the 38th surrendered the unit was "detained" until the new year, at which time they became a cavalry unit. The 38th was at Tupelo (July '64) and Harrisburg (14 July), where they were pretty well shot up. After that the 38th combined with other units to take part in Concord Church (1 December), Franklin (2 January 1865), Wilson's Raid in Alabama, and broke up at Brewersville at the end of the war *(these histories from Military History of Mississippi 1803-1898 by Rowland).*

The 7th Mississippi Regiment was also formed for coastal defense and contained two companies from the northern part of the county, the Jeff Davis Sharpshooters (Co. D) and Marion's Men (Co. F). John M. Hill was with the 7th. He was shot through the hip, neck, and face and was held prisoner at Camp Douglas. William Calvin Stewart was in Co. D of the 7th. He had a rough time of it in the early going at Camp Clark, Bay

St. Louis. He lost his musket and accoutrements in '62 because he was too sick to take care of them. Sometime later he was listed as a deserter, but he reported back for duty 28 February '63 and was placed "in arrest." Cal went on to make a most excellent account of himself. The 7th was sent from the coast to Jackson TN (26 February-2 March '62). It was recalled to Corinth MS and placed under the command of General Chalmers.

SHILOH AND CORINTH. At Shiloh the 7th made the first charge through the Federal camp (6 April '63) and fought all day both days. During the seige at Corinth the 7th manned an outpost on the Monterey Road. When a Federal force moved into a swamp near them (28 May), the 7th pushed them back out.It then took part in the Kentucky campaign at Munfordville (14 and 16 September), Perryville (8 October), skirmished at Lawrenceburg, and went to Murfreesboro (November and December '63). Then they fell back to Shelbyville until July '64.

Occasionally life presents us little unexpected pleasures, lagniappe, you know. This was one such occasion for us. I was talking to my racquetball partner, Marvin Foxworth, about this book. He is not a veteran, but someone in his family is, one Lt. Jobias "Job" M. Foxworth, late of the Jeff Davis Sharpshooters, 7th Mississippi Regiment raised in Holmes-ville, Marion County *(Remember, half the County was Marion County back then.)*. Job was college educated and kept an extraordinary diary, which now rests in the Department of Archives. We get to watch the man's ideology evolve in the

19

time before Shiloh, and we start at 12 February, 1862:

"Since I began my diary in 1861, many important and serious events have transpired. My brother George has been carried to that bourne from whence no traveller has ever yet returned. He died in Richmond VA. He went in August with my brother Franklin...12th Mississippi Reg.. He and they first belonged to this company but became dissatisfied with it. He died far away from home, no kindred, no friends near to soothe his parched brow, or to hear his last precious words. His remains were brought home and inter- red near my mother's and father's."

Camp Lovell. The Colonel had ordered all the officers to wear uniforms on Mondays and Thursdays, but at least half of them didn't. Job seems to have been rather jocular at first, citing incidents such as the killing of an "obstreporous rooster" *and the* "little reptiles known as mosquitoes."

"We are having bad news from Virginia and Kentucky. It is rumored that the Yankees have taken Columbus...We can not expect to win every battle. We must suffer reverses, and that too, sadly, heavy ones. Still I apprehend that this will be a terrible blow to our interest- it will prolong the war and cause many a Southern hero to pour out his patriotic blood like water in the defense of his principles and government...We have been fearfully underrating the strength and number of our foe. We have not calculated the power and immense resources of the old government to which we belonged. Though the trunk is full of corruption in its heart...its branches are green and flourishing... Before our company started out...all were boasting that one Southerner could cope with ten Yankees...This belief is now, of course, out of date... that one Yankee was fully a match for a Southerner. If the people of the north continue or become unanimous in principle and policy, we need not expect a speedy cessation of hostilities."

In late February a boat in this service fired on a schooner trying to enter the Jordan River. It turned out to be a boatload of Spaniards who could not speak English. Later a patrol attacked a skiff, where the man fled and deserted the rest of his family. That created a lot of laughter.

"Tomorrow the 14th of February is St. Valentine's Day, the day sacred to women- to Cupid and his equally blind followers *(This is neat: I just realized I'm copying this on Valentine's Day 1991, 129 years later!)*...How idle! How frivolous! How absurd! How very foolish! How shameful it is for young men and ladies, who are old enough to have gathered some sense...

"Col. Mayson drilled the battalion for about an hour and a half, practicing them to march in the line of battle...(Job tells about David Tanner in the Mexican War. Tanner and three others were hunting when they spied five Mexicans coming. The Mexicans surrendered and their captors"placed them all on their horses and tied their ropes, fastened to their necks, to limbs under a tree...Who would drive out their horses...Tanner stepped forth...The poor, unarmed, unoffending creatures were hurled into an unknown world to gratify

21

the sport of American soldiers."

His description of the Gulf Coast:
"I have not seen a bird or anything of a
wild nature...It seems to be almost a
barren land, productive of nothing except
potatoes and a few garden plants.

*His camp gets news of the battle at
Roanoke:* "That an attack was made at 7
o'clock in the morning by the enemy,
fifty thousand strong, under General
McClelland- our forces commanded by Gen.
Pillow. We had driven them back at the
point of the bayonet- had taken all their
batteriesvictory decisive- loss heavy on
each side. Our forces amounted to about
twenty thousand...Thank God for the
success...To him the praise is due."

*Job has prayer meetings every day,
visits with other camps, and reads Virgil
and Homer at night, suffering camp life
in the pouring winter rain. The news of
the loss of Fort Donelson disturbs him
greatly, as does the loss of Columbus and
Bowling Green KY. By the end of February
he is griping more:* "headache, which I
suppose was caused by the diet we have
now, that consists of pickled beef- this
no one can eat with any relish- and
molasses with cornbread, constitutes what
I eat." *He plays chess with someone in
camp:* "Thus it goes in war- we surrender
one post, the enemy loses one. It depends
in good measure upon the same rules. But
its final issue does not depend on such
rules, but the Justice of a righteous
Ruler and God."

*By March '63 Job is in Camp Beaure-
gard at Jackson TN. About the Tennessee
girls he writes:* "...have cheeks that
look the color of a newly opened rose. I
have fallen in love with them."

day much larger, perhaps double.

"It was the hardest fought, most destructive and important battle ever fought on this continent (100,000 troops committed). When our troops, a good many, were scattered through the forest and worn out with fatigue and hunger, and the enemy, with reinforcements, did not dare to pursue, some of the idea of the blow administered may be gathered.

"Many a hero fell in this bloody attack...Gen. Albert Sidney Johnston was shot in the leg while leading on a regiment which had wavered a little before. The ball cut the artery, but he seemed not to perceive it...

"We must have confidence in our leaders(?).. "In this battle Gen. Gladden was wounded fatally in the arm by a shell which made amputation necessary. He did not survive long...they admit a loss of between fifteen and twenty thousand, while ours is said to be between seven and ten thousand...Our march back to Corinth was dreadful. In every mud-hole there was left a wagon, and in some a or horse or mule had sunk so far in the mire as to not be able to escape. There they perished. Wounded men were strewn along the wayside, some in houses, some in the woods. It was sickening in the highest degree.

"Our army was very much demoralized, scattered all over the woods...and though papers claimed a great victory, it would have seemed our soldiers were very elated with success."

4 May: "With merry hearts and cheerful visages we set out in a northern direction...very slowly for about four hours, when we suddenly halted...on the

The company is preparing for war when the men are informed that General Price has killed 5,000 or 6,000 Yankees and captured the Division, some 20,000. This really raises their spirits: "Such a victory now...will do incalculable good to our cause, arouse a number from despondency total and others from the discouragement induced by the reverses at Fort Henry and Donelson.

"These indeed were severe calamations to us but still have the reflection left that it was the cowardice of our leaders that caused it...Had our generals possessed half the moral courage of their men, we would have driven them back and ultimately triumphed in each case. But they evidently were guilty of shameful, ignominious cowardice or villainous treachery..."

In the middle of March the Yankees left some provisions near Jackson, and several units went out to steal it. While the boys back at camp were drilling, the wagons returned. They got 40,000 pounds of meat. The company is now under the command of General Bragg and itching for a fight. The men hear about railroads being torn up around them and Yankee movement. Other units report back after skirmishes. Still Job's unit is drilling and spreading rumors. On 14 March they were ordered to be ready to move.

On 19 March the company was ordered to board trains to go to Bethel, where the unit joined the 8,000 to 10,000 troops under General Cheatham. They were sent to Corinth MS and reached there that night, which they spent on the railroad cars: "If the Lincolnites do attempt to take the place, they will have their hands more than full. They can not whip us with triple our number; they may bring force enough to overwhelm us, but never, never, NEVER can they conquer us until the last man ceases to breathe the breath of life. We do not intend to yield another inch of ground.

"The people of Miss. are very different from those of Te. *(nnessee)*, especially in regard to the war. They are lukewarm to the cause, halting still between two opinions...the people are frightened with the gloomy prospect before them and waver in their opinions ...have we not a far better right and reason to secede from the union than our fathers had when they rebelled against the English laws?

"I must by all means take along my journal, as it is the only real entertainment I have...

"Our guns were loaded nearly a week ago; they ought to be discharged...Yankees have entered Perdy...They are advancing with a large force, and it is said "To Corinth or Hell" is marked on their caps and baggage...savor strongly of Packenham's remark when he said he would eat his dinner January the eighth, 1814, in New Orleans. He was killed...I do not desire that their souls should be lost, but I desire that their wicked devises may be turned upon their own heads..."

About the generals he wrote: "... they have no business in houses. Their proper places are with their men, with their commands, where they should know the conditions and perhaps feel the sufferings which they endure...But, alas! I fear, I know we have no *(George)*

Washington...the more I think of the w the worse I make it out." *Later on, a moving to the front:* "...the dirt i be thrown up six feet high, ditche tolerably wide and deep. The w consist of trees felled on the side small creek, the road running up th the middle of the hills where breastworks are thrown up."

23 March: "Fighting has been on at Island No. 10 for three days some heavy loss to the enemy and o lieutenant. From last accounts th had not accomplished any thing Polk came in town on yesterday w whole command; that Johnston command was expected to be he them come *(Yankees)*. I hope s they will come. Though I am by anxious to get in a battle- I h shrunk from the horror of it- s willing that they should come a I should march against him w even cheerfully..."

We lost Island No. 10 Johnston withdrew and decided attack at Shiloh against Gran diary is confused as to times tried to reconstruct the actu events in their proper hist spective.

The results of the bat recorded on 8 April: "It se of our generals was to atta Grant's army before reinforced by Buell's colu begun sooner. But Buell's Sunday night, time to retreating and demoraliz available force was about theirs thirty thousand fi

wrong road. Instead of going to Monterey, we were on the Perdy route *(This is in preparation for the battle at Corinth.)*...There we were, about three o'clock, in sight of Corinth after travelling eight or ten miles...reviled the General for not knowing where he was going...yet to go six miles before we could camp...A great many fell off by the way, exhausted with fatigue. It was not in the power of any officer to keep them going.

"In the morning we received orders to move back two miles...reached Monterey that day about six o'clock and slept on the ground without any thing to shelter us. After midnight it commenced raining. This aroused us...

"...flew to arms in an instant. The brigade started off, thinking the Yankees were near...halted...ordered to load... torrent of rain poured in on us for over ten minutes...put on the march...halted about two miles off, were ordered to form a line of battle behind the fence of a small enclosure...Gen's aides came up and pronounced it all a mistake and failure...picket duty...somewhat disappointed ...marched directly until we came to a place called Pea Ridge...ten minutes couriers came in hurredly and announced that the battle had already commenced. In an instant our regiment flew to arms and marched off about two hundred yards and stopped. Our guns had all been wet by the rain...stood up in line of battle for half an hour in mud six inches deep, expecting every minute to see the enemy, but none appeared. Our cavalry had charged their advanced pickets and after a short fire drove them, killing several

and capturing a few prisoners who, when
brought in, created some excitement among
us to see real, live Yankees...moved back
to our quarters and halted, and presently
the hail poured in upon us dreadfully,
striking our naked ears. Here was another
picture of suffering for soldiers. We had
to stand until it ceased.

"...ate our scanty dinners, our
provisions being nearly all gone. I
filled my canteen with molasses instead
of water to eat with my few biscuits. I
divided it with those who had
none...Tomorrow will commence the
dreadful work of carnage between
brothers. How strange, how revolting..."

7 May: "All who had any thing to eat
made speedy use of it; most had none...In
a moment we grasp our arms and stand in
ranks. We advance by the right of
companies towards the river, easterly. Up
hill and down hill, some of us double
quicking...heavy, incessant firing of
musketry on our left. Soon it was nearer
and nearer...top of a hill, on the next
we saw tents and what was more exciting,
a regiment of real Yankees. Down in the
hollow we went and nearly up the hill we
stopped, when on the left of our brigade
fired a volley at them...bullets now and
then went whizzing over our heads.

"The order was to charge. The right
wing of our regiment went ahead with loud
yelling. The order was halt; they heard
it not...men followed one another, no one
noticed the officers... formed a line
again and forward through their camp...I
threw away my overcoat, as I did my
blanket some time before...enemy's
battery before us would now and then cast
a shell or ball, tearing down large tree

28

tops...formed a line across a small stream...lost their shoes...moved on... came to a house on a side road...halted. ..thinking no Yankees were near. Suddenly a startling volley of muskets were heard on our left...enemy ceased firing. We marched straight ahead to the front, through a creek, fallen trees, and thick briars...old field to a fence on the other side...balls pouring over very thick...The boys were some bolder; some laughed and joked...I was so exhausted with fatigue, etc., I could move no farther. A sickness seized me...About two o'clock news was brought that the enemy's whole line was in full retreat...taken near ten thousand prisoners, drove as many in the river, and completely routed them. They abandoned in their camps a large amount of provisions, ammunition, guns, besides many other articles such as clothing."

8 May: "They found everything in nice order: cakes, candies, cheese, figs, and every thing good to eat...

9 May: "Early the next morning the enemy, heavy with reinforcements, came against us, while our forces were very much demoralized, half of the men scattered in every direction so as to be unavailable, unmanageable; but those left stood firm until they were forced back by overwhelming numbers. About two o'clock our army began to withdraw in tolerable good order. The enemy did not pursue us farther, but returned well satisfied with what they had done.

"Our retreat was by no means hasty, but slow and orderly, but very disagreeable on account of the bad state of roads from the rain Monday night. Our brigade came back to Monterey a little before nightfall, tolerably wore out."

Job's diary goes a little further, complaining about how the draft is only for one year, and not even that if you can buy your way out. This gives a pretty good slice of life during that war. It also shows Job Foxworth's ideas of fun and games devolve into the horror of war while showing his immediate grasp of the epitome of the situation from rumors that have been proven to be historically accurate: Shiloh and Corinth could not be described any better than by a Johnny (Reb)-on-the-spot.

Joseph Burks' father, Daniel of 1812 fame, appears again. It seems as though the damnyankees were about to do some foraging around Picayune. Daniel and John Wheat put a torch to Burnt Bridge to keep them out (from John Napier, Picayune Item).

In 1863 Rosecrans started moving towards Bragg's army of brave lads, the Army of Tennessee. Shivers, Watson, Stewart, and Archer fought with him at Mumfordville, Murfreesboro (Stones River 31 December-1 January [except Stewart]), Shelbyville, and whipped him good at Chickamauga (19-20 September). Archer was wounded at Chickamauga. B.L. Spruell joined them there fresh from Gettysburg. Cal Stewart was captured and placed in a hospital at Glasgow KY, detained 60 days at home, and then rejoined the war. Jesse L. Herrin was with the 27th Mississippi Regiment at this time, being wounded by a minie ball at Chickamauga. He was in the hospital at Chattanooga by the surgeon's order 1 July '62 and rejoined the unit by the July-August muster. After this the Confederates were routed from Lookout Mountain (24 November '63) and Missionary Ridge (25 November) to Dalton GA, where they encamped for the winter. Herrin was shot through the neck at Missionary Ridge.

Sherman, in 1864, took command of the army of northern aggression in Chattanooga to begin his infamous march on Atlanta. "Old Joe" Johnston replaced Bragg and reorganized the Army of Tennessee from its demoralized condition. This was a reunion of sorts for Johnston and Shivers, who had collaborated for a sweet victory at First Manassas (Bull Run) in July 1861.

ATLANTA. From 5 May to 1 September 1864 Johnston, Shivers, Watson, and Augustus Beall of the 3rd Mississippi fought battles along a 100 mile front at Dalton, Resaca, Kingston, New Hope Church, and Kennesaw Mountain destroying the railroad facilities while trying to delay Sherman's approach to Atlanta. Johnston had a tough row to hoe and was subjected to a severe backstabbing campaign, especially by Bragg and John B. Hood, who were really lying to President Davis about the state of the army. They retreated from Dalton, Hood left his post at Resaca too early and lost that, Hood moved his troops and changed the plan of attack at Kingston for another loss that he credited to Johnston, got flanked at New Hope Church, and Hood replaced Johnston on 17 July. The reader is reminded of Johnston's role in the seige at Vicksburg when evaluating this (see *outline of 3rd Mississippi above for that campaign).* After Hood took over, he abandoned Atlanta only to move north to try to attract Sherman's forces from Georgia. Hood's plan backfired and left the women and children of Georgia to Sherman's mercy, which obviously was nil. On 30 November at Franklin TN and on 15-16 December at Nashville, the glorious Army of Tennessee which still had in it Shivers, Stewart, and Beall, was finally destroyed *(Essentially the end of the western Confederacy with the loss of this Army in December '64. Virginia, the Carolinas, and a few isolated pockets were all the resistence left until April '65.).* We lose Beall from the record at this time, but Shivers fought again at Spanish Fort and Mobile (12 April 1865), three days after Lee's surrender.

SHIVERS

In all Shivers was wounded at First Manassas (21 July 1861), Perryville (October 1863), and Atlanta (20 July 1864). During one of the battles he fought in, a yankee soldier shot down the standard bearer in Shivers' company and took the Confederate flag away from the boy. Shivers ran up to him and started a fist fight in order to get the flag back. He succeeded and carried the flag home. It is now preserved in the state capitol in Montgomery *(Pearl River County History, Vol. 5).* The descendents of James McLaurin Shivers certainly have every right to feel proud of this ancestor. But then, he had it in his blood. His great-grandfather was in the Revolutionary War, his grandfather was an Indian fighter in Florida, and his father

32

raised a company to go fight in the Texas revolution in 1831.

Meanwhile, let's get up to date on events of the eastern front. B.L. Spruell was at Lewisburg, Sharpsburg (Antietam 17 September '62, the bloodiest one-day battle ever on American soil, and 1st and 2nd Fredericksburg (13 December '62) with Robert E. Lee and the 18th Mississippi as part of the Army of Northern Virginia. They opposed Burnside and kept him out of the Southern capital, Richmond VA. Interestingly, Spruell apparently was captured after the battle of Fredericksburg and imprisoned at Washington City. He was paroled at Stafford Heights on 4 May '63, just in time to rejoin Lee and fight at Gettysburg (1-3 July '63), the second invasion of the north. Truly a fine, upstanding Southern Gentleman and our only reported veteran ever to fight on damnyankee soil.

I personally have good feelings about Albert Watson because he turned out to help prevent Aiken SC from the yankee scourge in February '65. I lived in Aiken in February '65, although it was 1965!

Thomas Jefferson Kendrick enlisted in Pike County KY. William R. Newell served 4 years with the 14th. He was taken prisoner three to four months before war's end.

After the regular army-infantry and cavalry came the militia cavalry, such as Wirt Adams Regiment, and with the partisans last. The Seventeenth Battalion-

33

Cavalry Commanding Officer was Abner Steede. This group was actually CO'd by an officer in the real army and fought in several campaigns attached to several groups. Frederick Alexander and Thomas J. Stockstill seem to have made a good accounting of themselves. A muster roll *(provided by Josephine Megehee of the Picayune Library)* from 10 May 1862 gives the local company, Company B *(J.M. Poitevant commanding)* of the Lovell Rangers Mounted Partisans. In 1862 Jefferson Davis forbade the formation of partisan ranger units. He then tried to draft them into regular army units after they went against his orders. Most of the conscriptees ran off rather than be drafted; however, the Poitevant company is the only partisan group to have submitted a roster to the Secretary of War. Apparently, this company of men was placed in the 17th Battalion-Cavalry under Steede. They were reorganized in February '63 and were left at Jackson 3 May '63 where they were ordered to operate against Grant's supply trains during the Battle of Vicksburg. They became part of the 9th Regiment-Cavalry in 1864 during the Atlanta campaign as Co. B. The record gets pretty fuzzy here as far as keeping the Countians together. As is popularly thought, these men are not the Gainesville company: Isaac Attaway, Robert Allen, D.V. Breland, H. Bridges, Samuel E.F. Byrd, Elijah Byrd, E. Batson, J.W. Carroll, W.M. Crawford, B. Cooper, C. Cooper, J.E. Cooper, H.F. Davis, Charles Frazar, E.H. Frost, L. Favre, John Grantham, A. Hartfield, John Holloman, Allen Hood, J.A. Kennedy, J.A. Kinnone, Johnathan Lee, J.M. Lee, Jesse

Lott, James Land, John Martin, T.A. Mitchell, Eugene Moran, Natall Moran, Thomas Murphy, Madison Newman, J.H. Odom, H.L. Pearson, J.T. Shelton, Joseph B. Stewart, R.C. Windham, and W. Warden.

I was able to find some information concerning Isaac Attaway. He was captured 3 July 63 at Jackson and sent to Camp Morton, Indianapolis IN. On 22 March 64 he was sent to Camp Delaware DE. On 7 June 65 he signed the oath of allegiance.

Many of our troops were diverted during the war to go back home take care of the "jayhawkers." These worthless scum in any time would be from anywhere, but generally the same region. All they did was to prey on defenseless women and children by stealing their food and needlessly raping and pillaging the area. The jayhawkers would swoop down on our area and steal cattle. They would herd them around The Big Spring to get them ready for the move out. You've already heard about Daniel Burks and Burnt Bridge. Well, a bunch of the local men caught some of that worthless, less that human scum and made them pay- BIG time. "They shot five of them and buried them out here. Colonel Redding Byrd caught them. Some of the others they captured tried to escape. They hung them in a big oak up on River Road." *(courtesy Jerry Bertucci, who happens to own the land now)*.

In all 753 Pearl River Countians enlisted in this glorious event, and 153 died as a result of killing, diseases, and wounds *(from John Napier for the last time. Thanks, John.)*

SPANISH-AMERICAN WAR

1898-SANTIAGO. Ten Countians went into the service, but no natives left the state.

Medals

An order of priority is given for the US military medals so that the reader may be able to judge for him/herself the degree of gallantry performed by our veterans. This is by no means to be used as a "scorecard." Given that politics sometimes rears its ugly head in any undertaking, so it may have occurred in this book. Who is to say? Just as we are assuming that all of the stories are more or less correct, so shall we go under the assumption that all of our battlefield decorations have all been earned, no questions asked.

Before World War I, medals were not presented to Mississippi veterans. There was no decoration for Confederates during The War Between the States other that to have been recognized as valorous.

During the 20th century the highest military honor has been the Medal of Honor. The next group can be earned only for extraordinary heroism in connection with military operations against an opposing armed force: the Distinguished Service Cross (Army), the Navy Cross (Navy, Marine Corps, Coast Guard), and the Air Force Cross. Pearl River County is honored to have several in that category. Next comes the Defense Distinguished Service Medal, Distinguished Service Medal, and Silver Star for gallantry in action against an opposing armed force. Again, Pearl River County is honored by the presence of several of these, and I am equally as honored to have been able to interview them. The next two are not action awards: the Defense Superior Service Medal and the Legion of Merit. The Distinguished Flying Cross is for heroism or extraordinary achievement while participating in aerial flight. Then come the life-risk medals not associated with war: the Soldier's, Navy and Marine Corps, Airman's, and Coast Guard Medals. The Bronze Star is awarded for heroic or meritorious service not involving aerial flight in connection with operations against an armed force. Pearl River County has many Bronze Star recipients

The Purple Heart. One has to sacrifice blood for this one. The Purple Heart was the only award given before the War Between the States. George Washington himself presented a cloth purple heart for any single meritorious action. Only three men got it. Then the award fell into oblivion until 1932, when General Douglas MacArthur revived it as the Purple Heart. It is now awarded for wounds or death as a result of the action of any opposing force. Pearl River County has shed much blood and suffered much death in the wars. We have one veteran who earned 19 Purple Hearts. He's in this book.

After that the order of awards continues with: Defense Meritorious Service, Meritorious Service, Air, Aerial Achievement, Joint Service Commendation, Army/Navy/Air Force/Coast Guard Commendation, POW (no time limit), Combat Readiness, Good Conduct, the Reserve Medals, World War I, Haitian, Nicaraguan, China

Service, American Defense, American Campaign, Asiatic-Pacific, Europe-African-Mediterranean Theater, World War II, the Expeditionary and Occupation Medals, the National Defense (50-54, 61-74), Korean Service, Antarctic and Arctic Service, Armed Forces Expeditionary, Vietnam Service, Humanitarian, Armed Forces Reserve,United Nations Service, Inter-American Defense Board, United Nations, Multinational Force and Observers Medal, and the Republic of Vietnam Campaign Medal. These are the campaign medals, and our Pearl River Countians have won them all. Our boys- and now young ladies- have been there when called. They have done their duty all over the globe.

There are various devices worn in conjunction with the medals, such as battle stars or oak leaf clusters denoting additional awards. There is also a "V" for valor and arrowheads for initial assault landings.

World War I

BOCHE -MAXIMS- ZEPELLINS- MUSTARD GAS-DOUGHBOYS-AEF- BLACK JACK PERSHING-SPRINGFIELDS- BIPLANES- LILI MARLENE-MADEMOISELLE FROM ARMENTIERES- TANKS-BROWNING AUTOMATIC RIFLES (BAR)-LOGISTICS REFINEMENT. *World War I going on for quite a few years with both sides jockeying back and forth in the Alsace-Lorraine area of France. As a result of the trench stalemate, poison gas and tanks were introduced to the arsenals. It was German U-boats that finally brought the United States into the war in 1917. We had no draft, so it took a while to build and train an army. Each man was supplied with a backpack, one blanket, a carton of hardtack, a water canteen, and a pup tent (luxurious accommodations for a vacation in France!).*

We went "over there" in the Spring of 1918. The Germans made a series of drives aimed at taking Belgium and France during early 1918. The third German drive, the Aisne Offensive, was into an area between the French and British troops where it was thought there were no reserves. This attack was planned with the utmost secrecy. The American intelligence service tried to warn the French of the impending attack at Chemin des Dames, but the French generals, Petain and Foch, ignored it. Sure enough, the Germans advanced for three days and made it all the way to the Marne at Chateau-Thierry, only 37 miles from Paris. The French had to ask the Americans to come in, and our participation started with the capture of Cantigny on 28 May

40

H.L. Bagley
WWII
Navy

Johnny Baker

Marines

Julian W. Bennett

Navy

Darrell A. Boyd

Marines

James L. Carbonette
WWII
Marines

Vernell Cowart
WWII
Army

Benny Crocker
Korea, Vietnam
Army

Johnny Crocker
Desert Storm
Army

Alex "Buster" Fisher
WWII, Korea
Army

Elmo D. Flynt
WWII
Army

Gregory E. Flynt
Vietnam
Army

James W. Flynt
WWII
Navy

Robert C. Flynt
WWII
Army

Dallas C. Grant
WWII
Army Air Corps

Ernest H. Grant
WWII
Coast Guard

Harold Jackson, Jr.
WWII
Navy

James Ladner
Korea
Army

David Lee
890th Engr. Bat.

Wm. F. Leaumont,Jr.

Wm. Jude Leaumont
Army

Theodore G. Lewis
WWII
Navy

Arnold Matthews
Korea, Vietnam
Marines

John A. McDonald

Navy

Darwin A. Mitchell

Marines

Donald D. Mitchell
WWII
Navy

Melville Mitchell
Korea
Air Force

Michael L. Mitchell

Army

Norvell R. Mitchell
WWII
Army

Roland E. Moore

Air Force

Stanley Neal
WWII
Navy

Elvis Odom
WWII
Coast Guard

Shawn Palmer
Desert Storm
Navy

Granville Pearson
WWII
Navy

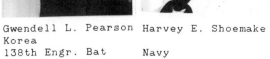

Gwendell L. Pearson
Korea
138th Engr. Bat

Harvey E. Shoemake

Navy

Clinton Smith

Delbert Smith

Navy

Haskell Smith
Korea
138th Engr. Bat.

Q.C. Smith
WWII
Navy

Richard Earl Smith

Air Force

R. Terence Smith
WWII
Army

Arthur E. Stockstill
WWII
Army

47

Honorable Discharge from the Army of the United States

TO ALL WHOM IT MAY CONCERN:

This is to Certify, That _Henry F. Welborn_ (2132044) *Corporal of Company "C", 367th Battalion, Tank Corps National Army_, as a TESTIMONIAL OF HONEST AND FAITHFUL SERVICE, is hereby HONORABLY DISCHARGED from the military service of the UNITED STATES by reason of ‡ _acceptance of commission per telegraphic instructions W.D. May 13, 1918 and S.O. 64 Hq Camp Colt, Pa May 15, 1918_

Said _Henry F. Welborn_ was born in _Ellisville_, in the State of _Mississippi_ When enlisted he was _24_ years of age and by occupation a _mechanic_ He had _brown_ eyes, _black_ hair, _dark_ complexion, and was _5_ feet _5¼_ inches in height.

Given under my hand at _Camp Colt Pa_ this _13 th_ day of _May_, one thousand nine hundred and _eighteen_.

DD Eisenhower

Capt Infll Arc.
Commanding.

Wellborn discharge papers signed
by Eisenhower after WWI.

Form No. 525, A. G. O.
Ed. Aug. 30-17—500,000.

* Insert grade and company and regiment or ci termaster Corps;" ¹Sergeant, First Class, Insert "Regular Army," "National Army," case may be.
‡ If discharged prior to expiration of service, gi

department; e, g., "Corporal, Company A, 1st Infantry;" "Sergeant, Quartermaster Department."
"Regular Army Reserve," or "Enlisted Reserve Corps," as the number, date, and source of order or description of authority therefor.   2—3164

49

50

and Chateau-Thierry on 1 June.

The fourth German drive from 9-13 June created a salient at Noyon-Montdidier and one at Soissons, where the French losses were light and the German losses heavy. We had some Pearl River Countians in this action. The fifth and final German drive of the war came 15-17 July. The Germans came under the influence of the worldwide flu epidemic like everyone else and couldn't muster much strength. By then the US involvement had increased to the point that the Allies could consider going on the offensive themselves. The Germans tried to take Reims and failed.

The Allied offensives were aimed at reducing the German salients. The first to come under attack was the one at Aisne-Marne from 18 July to 6 August. The Germans had created this encroachment on their third drive. Eight American Divisions were in the fight. The Allies reduced the salient for the first significant victory of 1918. The second step was to reduce the Amiens salient, which was established during the first German drive. That objective was accomplished with a little help from one American division from 8 August to 3 September. The third was the St. Mihiel Offensive 12-16 September. The Germans had taken that area and controlled and fortified it since 1914.

General Pershing was in charge of this assault, although Foch divided the Americans into three groups. The 1st Army attacked St. Mihiel on 1 September, and, by 13 September, the salient had been reduced. This was not a hard fight, but it set the stage for the Meuse-Argonne

campaign. *For the final drive there were
42 American divisions available at full
strength on the Southern pincer. From 26
September to 31 October the Americans
drove the Germans behind the Sedan-Mezi-
eres rail line. The American assault met
four German Divisions and advanced five
miles along the Meuse River, but only two
along the Argonne Forest. The drive kept
going, and on 1 October, fresh troops
were brought in.*

*The Americans kept up a steady
pressure on the Germans, and Pershing
launched an offensive across the river to
alleviate pressure on his own ranks. By
31 October he had progressed only 10
miles beyond the starting point, and the
going was mighty rough. By 1 November the
Allied position had solidified, and ammunition and supplies had caught up with
the men. On a cold, wet front, the Americans attacked the Germans at Bourgogne
Wood. They hooked up with the French and
took Montmedy and Longuyon. After the
Armistice, the Americans occupied
Coblenz.*

Doughboys, so named for their uniform buttons that looked like dumplings,
from Pearl River County were there: James
Smith, Francis Rufus Frierson, Hobart
Walker, Byrd Mitchell, John A. Bennett,
James Frank Allen, Stephen Gary Leonard,
Henry Jack Frierson, Henry McKissick, and
Robert Reid Keaton. Henry G. Welborn was
in with the 326th Battalion, Tank Corps.
Interestingly, Henry's discharge papers
were signed by a Captain in the infantry,
one D.D. Eisenhower. Allen Bounds was
rushed into the Muese-Argonne battle with
no training. Melvin Wheat Stockstill was
32 when he was drafted and sent to the

Argonne Forest. He was wounded in the groin by shrapnel.

I was able to interview Jesse Wells (dec) at the Poplarville Nursing Home one week before his 101st birthday. I wrote the questions and he gave me this story:

I was in WWI. My unit was sent to Brest, France. I fought in France. Then I fought up to Belgium and got to within a few miles of Germany. I was in my 20s *(born 1890)*. I saw Woodrow Wilson on the battlefield. He went out on the battlefield and told 'em "Boys, we're going to win it, but I don't know when." We fought one more big battle, and the war ended for me a few miles from the German border. I still don't hear too good because of all the guns. Like all grunts then, I didn't know what we were doing or where we were, just the country I was in. When I got home the Army sent me to Spanish Honduras to work a sawmill, because that's what I done. Later I got drafted for WWII, but I didn't do nothing. Family? Oh yes, my son was in WWII. In the Navy.

In the interest of history I have tried to reconstruct Mr. Wells participation in the war. The Germans made a successful invasion to within 37 miles of Paris. The French had to ask for American help. Americans had been used to reduce the St. Mihiel and Marne salients in July and August at Verdun and Pont-A-Mousson and September at Chateau Thierry, and were brought in on the south pincer to close in on the German army. This was probably Mr. Wells route according to his

53

*description, which would be the 1st or
2nd US Army.)*

Several interesting veteran stories
were gathered by various people
working during the era of the Works
Progress Administration in the late
1930s. These accounts were collected
first hand at that time, and are now
housed in the Crosby library in Picayune.
They are catalogued under <u>Pearl River
County History, Vol. 5.</u>

Magnus Moody was in the 20th
Engineers, 7th Army Corps. When his ship
was on the way overseas, it was attacked
and sunk by a German U-boat between
Scotland and Ireland. Magnus eventually joined up with the troops in England
and went to France for the St. Mihiel
offensive. On his return trip after the
war, his ship backed into a tugboat,
causing several deaths.

The Marne campaign with Houston E.
Stockstill:
...In the trenches and on all the
battlegrounds were spies who could
speak every language. Our officers
wanted to get a message across to
another section. This was somewhere
near Aimes *(Amiens?)*. We had liquid
fire on us all day, and the trench
telephone wires were tapped by the
Germans so the officers couldn't
talk. These two Indians from Oklahoma saved the day. One crawled
through "No Man's Land," those
barbed wire entanglements, and got
safely to the American trench where
the message was delivered. The other
Indian then talked to this Indian

...even though the Germans had
tapped the lines, they could not
understand a word

...night of July 14th, on which
night the Germans made their big
drive and fought us in a bloody
battle...lost 45 men in our company
from shell and gas...ordered across
Marne River on pontoon bridges on
anything the engineers could
get...only one man could cross at a
time...on to Lar-Charmal where we
had horrible battle which in
history is known as the second
battle of the Marne, and is said by
many to be the bloodiest battle
fought *(This was the turning point.
With their morale restored, the
Allies remained on the attack the
rest of the war.)*...French on our
right but suffered heavy loss of men
and gave way. That let the Germans
come in on us from the right and had
us in a trap. My outfit, Company A,
38th Infantry, realized our position
and sent runners...other part of the
Army had travelled back with the
French leaving part of the outfit as
a sacrifice so the main company
could get to safety. We kept up
firing until night- we knew we were
completely surrounded. A few of us
made an attempt to get to the linesI
do not know if they made it or not.
When daylight came, there were only
7 of us alive, one of which was a
captured, wounded German soldier.
Six Americans alive- three of us
badly wounded and begging piteously
for water. I got a canteen and
started for water for my wounded

comrades. Airplanes were still over us, and I dodged in and out among buildings looking for water. I had rounded a building and was within a few feet of a pump when a German cook halted me and yelled something. Instantly I was surrounded by Germans with fixed bayonets on me. I thought they were going to kill me, but instead they made me a prisoner of war. This was on July 23rd...weighed 220 pounds when I was captured, now I weighed 110.

Eddie McFadden Mitchell and George Mitchell were at Chateau-Thierry with the 163rd Infantry. On 14 July the German artillery began firing and hit their dugout. Eddie recalled:
A shell exploded near us and covered us so we could not get out. A piece of shrapnel cost George part of his hand and a wound in his side. It cost me a leg. We remained buried in the dugout from midnight until 9 or 10 a.m. Our lieutenant came and dug us out.

Grover C. Barrett in the Argonne Forest:
We landed at Brest, France, and went right on to the Argonne Forest. Fighting was going on when I got there. I fought for seven days and got a flesh wound on the 6th. ..there were many things too horrible to tell. There were times when we had to advance over bodies infested with vermin. One of the most horrible things I saw was at the Rhine River *(Marne?)*. We were on

the lines, waiting to cross. The Marines and the 136th Division Engineers were trying to put up a pontoon bridge. On the other side was a long, high slope. The Germans were on top of this shooting our boys down in the valley. So many were killed while making this bridge that the heavy machine guns, etc., crossed on the bodies of the dead men. It was impossible to get a pontoon bridge built. The river was not so deep, but the machine guns could not cross without something under them. They would bog down. 22,000 soldiers were killed there.

Jesse T. Smith was with the 304th Ammunition Train, 79th Division, AEF:
The ride that night and the impression made upon us will never be forgotten. The congested traffic on the roads, the flashing of the sky ahead of us, the ever increasing rumble of the guns, and the whole adventure of our first trip had indelibly imprinted itself on our minds...the heaviest artillery barrage of the war opened the Argonne offensive. Conditions were very trying here, the roads were knee deep in mud, and shell hole followed shell hole in rapid succession caused by a terrific barrage on the night of 25 September. Rain fell almost continuously, keeping the men soaked to the skin at all times and never giving the road time to dry up.

Floyd W. Seals ended up in the 102nd

Infantry, 26th Division, Company D. He
was quoted as saying:

>We relieved the 13th Marines between
>Soissons and Chateau Thierry in open
>warfare. We lost down to 15 men and
>were sent back of the lines. By 12
>September we had a full company
>again and began the drive on St.
>Mihiel. We lost 16 men in an air
>raid and captured an immense
>quantity of pretty good beer, some
>horses, and a large number of German
>prisoners. We went on to Verdun and
>entered a large wheat field on the
>way. The woods around us were
>fortified with German machine guns.
>I crawled out of a dead furrow,
>started to flank the German machine
>guns, and received a gun shot wound
>in my left leg 26 September 1918. I
>ducked and slid back in a shell hole
>where I was picked up about two and
>a half hours later. I had a painful
>ride because the stretcher bearers
>would get scared of the falling
>shells and dive for the ground.

Floyd met a bunch of guys from Pearl
River County on the way back home.

Samuel L. Spinks was in the Rainbow
Division at Alsace-Lorraine, Chateau
Thierry, St. Mihiel and the Argonne
Forest. He got pneumonia (7 Jan '18) and
also was gassed (15 July) once. He went
back to the hospital 2 November, and was
there at the war's end.

Joseph M. Wheat "was wounded at
Argonne Forest (St. Mihiel)-shot in the
right leg while out patrolling at night
and sent back to base hospital. I went

over the top three times. I was in the hospital when armistice was signed recovering from shell shock and the wound in the leg. I had trench feet and am now a nervous wreck."

Henry Elbert Holcomb was in the 42nd Rainbow Division. He saw three major offensive battles and remembered:

In one battle we were entrenched on one side of a double railroad track. The Boche were on the other side 150 feet away. The railroad embankment was about 10-12 feet high, and we had to cross it. About 4 a.m. our heavy artillery concentrated on them *(around Metz)*. At 5 a.m. a light artillery barrage hit them. Then we went over the top to take the enemy trench. Of the 57 men in our platoon sent over, 16 reached the enemy trenches. We were in rest camp when the war ended.

Jim Stockstill joined the 32nd Division at Jonesville, France, and went to the front 26 September '18. Jim stayed on the front for 20 days, enduring the most horrible hardships, including being gassed and not being able to change clothes for the entire time. He helped capture 82 Germans at Romagne. When he went back to rest camp, the air raids at night and the constant shelling during the day chased him back to the front on 10 November. The war ended the next day, but his company kept on going through Germany for a few months.

Frank Allen. France. Hell:
I was detailed to a French

detachment for special instructions
as an expert rifle grenadier. Later,
when demonstrating to the Captain
and Lieutenants, I shot my hand all
but my right thumb and forefinger
away. We moved on...shells were
raining from every direction. We
were all scared with no place to
cover...crevice...sniping from our
enemy...duty October 10th. Our
mission that night was to go across
"No Man's Land" to the German
trenches and bring back a live
enemy. We had certain times and
places in our front line we could go
out through and certain places we
could return through. Every few
minutes the enemy illumination
flares would light up the ground
light as day...marched to Cericeaux
16 October where we came under shell
fire...near St. Mihiel we were back
under shell fire...
...took a little town named
Moranviller. About 3 o'clock a
German plane circled over us and
shot out some signal rockets. The
Germans then centered their
artillery barrage on us. It began to
rain shells. We could see men on all
sides that shells had made direct
hits on. There were parts of bodies
such as legs, arms, heads, etc.,
falling on us- like a stump that had
been dynamited. On all sides were
wounded men hollering or begging for
help, but we couldn't do anything
but try to look out for ourselves.
One boy asked me to shoot him to end
his suffering. I took a gun away
from a dead soldier nearby and

handed it to him. I advanced about
fifty feet furthur, helped load four
men into a field ambulance, and saw
it, the mules, helpers and all blown
to bits when only thirty yards away.
November 11. 6:00 a.m...We started
the drive again...covered with frost
and ice. We had not advanced but a
short distance until we met heavy
resistance. We had given up hopes of
peace...we were mowed down with
machine gun fire. We were advancing
across an old wheat field...8:20
o'clock we came to heavy barbed wire
entanglement and had lots of trouble
getting through. I took my pack off
and threw it down. I was lying half
in and half out of a shell hole with
my rifle pointed out...shrapnel hit
the rifle stock and broke it off
smooth...We were within 40 feet of
the Germans who seemed to think they
had to use all their ammunition at
once. Some of our shells were
falling short on us, which did not
help us any when every moment seemed
like it would be the last. The
firing ceased at once.
For Frank Allen and all the rest of the
men, the war ended right there at 11:00
o'clock, 11 November 1918.

John "Hollie" Blackwell was at
Picayune High and lied about his age to
join up. Hollie made it to France and had
to train for a year before seeing any
action. Then he really hit it a lick.
Hollie was among the first Americans to
set foot on French soil, and he went in
with the 1st Division under "Black Jack"
Pershing. He said that he spent some time

in the trenches, and that his friend was killed by mustard gas *(courtesy Dee Ann O'Niel story from Picayune Item 11 November 1981)*. Hollie also made it to Germany with the 28th Infantry Regiment for the Battle of Tantiganey. *From his list of medals I have tried to reconstruct his war. His Victory Medal included campaign ribbons (like our battle stars) for the (1) Aisne-Marne, where he was wounded in the left thigh by shrapnel at Soissons (received Purple Heart). This battle was fought 18 July 1918 as part of the three-day 2nd Marne Campaign, and the victory restored Allied morale and put them on the attack for the rest of the war. (2) Montdidier and Noyon campaigns, which were fought during August. At Noyon the British surprised the Germans with 400 tanks and fatally undermined the morale of the German leaders. (3) St. Mihiel and (4) the Muese-Argonne. This campaign was from 16 September to the end of the war. Apparently Hollie made it over into Germany during this offensive. He also earned the Silver Lapel Button (Star) and the French Croix de Guerre Fouragguerre.* His son, John Hollie, Jr., is chronicled in World War II with the Furr family.

We were supplied information on Hailey White. Most of the information contained in this book is first hand when possible *(Unfortunately, most of the WWI veterans were dead at the time of the interviewing process.)*. Hailey was 17 when he went to Forts Leavenworth and Knox for training for the Army. He was sent to France in November 1918. On his third day of marching to the front, an armistice was declared *(plain old luck)*. While Hailey was making his way to the front marching down this muddy road, it was rainy and cold. His unit passed a Red Cross station where coffee and doughnuts were being sold . Since this outfit had not seen a pay table to collect thei wages in over three months, nobody could get any coffee because the Red Cross was charging. Little did they know, but fortunately soon discovered, that a few miles down the road was a Salvation Army coffee booth. They all got coffee there free. For that Hailey never gave to the Red Cross for the rest of his life.

Later on, some of the guys from the outfit went to town for a little R and R. One of them was from New Orleans and spoke French. He did the ordering in the cafe. The wine they drank was good, and they had a nice evening. A couple of weeks later Hailey had leave to go to town again. He asked the Cajun what it was he had told the waiter. He said he had ordered "vin de neuf." Hailey order- ed the same thing when he got to the cafe, and the waiter brought him just what he asked for: nine glasses of wine! *(We were told Hailey enjoyed them all because he was by himself.)* We were also told that Hailey never had hair on his legs again because of the wrappings they wore in that climate.

"Mademoiselle from Armentiers, parlez vous?
"Mademoiselle from Armentiers, parlez vous?
"Mademoiselle from Armentiers "hasn't been kissed in forty years. Rinky, dinky, parlez vous."

*A note of explanation is warrented
here because this will happen throughout
the book as I digress or divert from the
main path to tie in families. In this
case it is the Beth Windham connection.*

You've already met her great-grandfather, Washington Sampson Ford, in The
War Between the States. Now you've met
her father, Hailey. Hailey's brother,
Charlie Ford White, also was in WWI in a
different unit. Beth's husband, Joe,
retired from the Army. As part of the
Army of Occupation in Austria, Joe always
wanted fresh vegetables. He found a man
on the edge of town with whom he could
trade chocolates and cigarettes for let-
tuce. It must have worked because Joe was
big and healthy. Joe, by the way, earned
the Legion of Merit, WWII Victory Medal,
American Campaign Medal, Army of
Occupation Medal, and the National
Defense Medal with oak leaf cluster.
Beth's two sons served in the Army. Joe,
Jr. is out and Hailey is stationed in San
Antonio.

James M. Smith was in the Army in
the Dixie Division. He went in right
after Belleau Woods and was gassed
(chlorine) in his first battle. Then he
got in the way of a shell that broke his
leg. He was in the hospital when the war
ended. He also had a daughter while he
was "over there." James is the progenitor
of Connis and James in World War II,
and the reader will find them in that
section.

Joseph MeGehee got there in the rain
and sleet just in time for the armistice.

His company was assigned guard duty of the prisoners while the front was being cleaned up.

***** BILBO *****

The sons of A.J. "Sug" Bilbo made their mark. They went from Caesar to France and back: Clarence, George, Carr, Troy, and Brutis Bilbo.

Orville Carver was killed when a U-boat torpedo destroyed one of the firerooms on the troop transport, USS MOUNT VERNON.

Rosyma Ladner died of pneumonia in France.

Whatever it took, that did it. The Germans surrendered on 11 November 1918, and that is the day we celebrate as Armistice Day. Over 500 Pearl River County soldiers were involved in every campaign in which Americans participated. 132 of them were black.

Interregnum

The US policy of the Monroe Doctrine was the reason for most of our extracurricular involvement in other people's affairs since The War Between the States. In keeping with that theme, we first occupied Nicaragua from 1912-34. Woodrow Wilson had us intervene in Haiti from 1915-33. Claude Whitfield was there for Haiti *(see WWII Section)*. All this time we were protecting the western hemisphere from outside interference and doing a fine job of it, too. A.W. "Goofy" Stockstill and William W. Parker were on the USS LEXINGTON in the early 1930s. Goofy tells us that the Depression was so hard in Picayune that he had to join the Navy to be able to make a living, much less eat.

Hitler and the Germans started making their move in the late '30s.

World War II (Pacific)

TINCANS-PIGBOATS-FAT MAN and LITTLE BOY-
BANZAI- KILROY- BLITZKRIEG- BATTLEWAGONS-
OVENS-LIMEYS-AUSSIES-RATIONING-AXIS SALLY
-TOKYO ROSE-BETTY GRABLE. *On 7 December
1941 the Japanese bombed Pearl Harbor. On
the same day they attacked Bataan and
Corregidor. The "day that will live in
infamy" brought the U.S. kicking and
screaming into World War II. There is
some conjecture that President Franklin
D. Roosevelt let the Japanese pull off
Pearl Harbor to solidify America's
resolve to beat the Japanese. The Japanese Ambassador reportedly told him there
was going to be an attack. The Americans
sunk a Jap mini-sub that morning just
outside Pearl Harbor. Our radar picked up
the low flying Jap planes coming in to
the island and followed them through the
gap. Our hierarchy seemingly didn't feel
like listening to the warning. Indeed,
there seems to have been nothing surprise
about the attack at all in retrospect. In
May 1942 the American Navy defeated the
Japanese in the Coral Sea to open that
prong of attack. The USS LEXINGTON and
YORKTOWN were there. The battle was
fought entirely by planes against planes,
planes against ships. Not one ship fired
on another for the first time in history.
The LEXINGTON was lost here. Another
group also defeated the Japanese on Midway, and they never won another battle in
World War II. The YORKTOWN was lost here.
The Japanese were stretched to four
fronts by the Allies, and Pearl River
Countians were in every one of them. An*

attempt has been made to keep the stories in chronological order as well as by service.

William Whiteford "Bill" Parker (deceased) figured prominantly into the early action *(information from A.W. Stockstill, Ed Parker, and Navy commendation letter).* First, Bill was one of the deck gun crew members on the USS ARIZONA at Pearl Harbor. The ship took a bomb down the stack. In fact the ARIZONA took one torpedo and eight bombs in all during the not-so-surprise attack by the Japanese, and the ship was left on the bottom as a memorial. Bill's citation for a Navy Cross from the Secretary of the Navy, Frank Knox:

> "For distinguished service in the line of his profession, extraordinary courage and disregard of his own safety during the attack on the Fleet in Pearl Harbor, Territory of Hawaii, by Japanese forces on December 7, 1941. When the enemy strafing became severe, despite orders from his gun captain to take cover, Parker remained at his station on anti-aircraft gun No. 1 of the USS ARIZONA with two other members of the gun crew, and assisted in keeping it in operation against the enemy until he was blown overboard by an explosion."

Bill Parker, being of stocky constitution, was blown clear of the gun turret and into the water. He made it to shore and lived to fight another day. Bill's clothes had been blown off, but he did have a quarter in his hand. In February '42 Bill was sent to the USS LEXINGTON.

We know he was there at the Battle of the Coral Sea *(7-8 May '42; The LEX was struck by a torpedo at 1120hrs on 8 May. Seconds later another hit her on the port side abreast of the bridge along with three dive bombers. Fires broke out all over. By 1300hrs she was under control again, but an explosion on board took care of that. At 1707hrs the Captain ordered the men to abandon ship. All the men who jumped overboard were saved. Our Navy destroyed the ship with two torpedos at 1956hrs.).*

Bill Parker survived that sinking too. In all, he had now taken 3 torpedos, 11 bombs, and a gas explosion on two different ships. After a 30-day leave at home, he went back to the Navy and war. Norman Stockstill saw "Willie" in May 1942. Norman was just going in. He saw Willie had a cast on his hand and asked him if he had gotten that on the ARIZONA or the LEX. Willie said "Neither. I got it in a barroom in Miami." Nothing else is known of his career by my sources, although his brother, Ed, did say he'd seen Bill's picture in Life magazine a year or so later *(see Ed's story in the Aleutians Section).*

In the interest of history, through a vicarious connection to Pearl River County, I have found a veteran of Pearl Harbor- none other than my uncle, Carey M. Smoot. Unc was in the Navy from 1939 to 1941 on the SARATOGA. He got out in August 41, got married, and went to work for the Civil Service. What a plum! Uncle Carey recalls:

> We were living in quarters outside the gate at Hickham. My job was on

69

Ford Island at the N.A.S. During the first attack, all hell broke loose. We were called out for firefighting duty at our work stations as the Japs were strafing the streets. I found myself standing with Roy Wilson, a reporter from The Cleveland Plain Dealer, and another reporter from The New York Times at the 1010 dock. There were somr boiler plates stacked up in an A-frame arrangement. The other three guys said they were going to get under them for shelter from the attack. I told them I was going to stay right where I was to see history being made. There was a beautiful rainbow over the whole harbor outlining the Jap attack. I was standing beside the minesweeper, OGLALA. It was blown all to hell and right up the chute made by the boiler plates. It made hamburger out of the other three guys. I didn't even get a hangnail!

I watched them turn the NEVADA loose. The Navy was trying to get her out of the harbor before she got hit. It beached in a sugar cane field by Hospital Point (The NEVADA was hit several times, once while leaving the harbor, and the Navy decided to beach it instead of having it block the channel.). I watched another battleship come in and drop the hook. They dropped the hook, too! Somebody had forgotten to attach it to the ship. It was all confusion.

I finally sought some cover in a building. In there they had brought in the first dead Jap. He had on civvies under his flightsuit, and his pockets were filled with RTA tokens and American dollars. He was apparently going to try to mix with the civilian populace if he got shot down. About that time the Civil Defense ordered our wives up into the hills.

My Aunt Betty was there for that:

We were told to take canned goods and blankets and move up into the hills. I guess they thought there was going to be an invasion. People were digging bomb shelters in their yards. One man even took his piano in the ground with him. Some of the ladies just made it out with armloads of booze. My matron-ofhonor came to get me to evacuate, so I left Carey a note that I had gone up to Aunt Alice's. We had a blackout, but Carey got there somehow. We heard a radio broadcast that the Japs had invaded Manoa Valley and were wearing red uniforms. One of the ladies said "What am I going to do? My husband's out at sea, and I don't have a black dress to wear." Another girl picked up her flashlight, shined it in her own face, and said "Oh, there you are." It was terrible.

Pearl Harbor was not the only point of attack. James P. Mitchell was with the Marines on Wake Island in 1941. He was an escort for 1400 civilians. We pick up his story there:

We were the civilian's defense. They were on Wake to cut out a lagoon to

71

bring ships in and to fix a landing
field. There was nobody on the
island but us. The Jap ships came in
and we had to surrender to them.
What would you do standing in a
corner with 40 guns aimed at you?
I spent 45 months as a prisoner of
war between China and Hokkaido,
Japan. We had a few get out, but
they were recaptured and sent to
another camp. We were treated
rotten. We got boiled rice once or
twice a day. Sometimes they gave us
boiled this or that, so we ate
anything we could find. You know,
viper tastes pretty good! I weighed
200 pounds when they got me. I
weighed 85 pounds when I got out. It
gets cold in China. All the Marines
were over 5'9" and all their clothes
were for a people whose tallest men
were 5'8". Yeah, we got cold.
The US dropped the A-bomb, and the
Japs didn't know what to do. They
just disappeared. We got on a radio
and started calling anyone we could
raise. An aircraft carrier was in
the area. They "bombed" us with food
and clothes and everything. I was
freed on 16 August 1945, and the US
flew us to an airfield in Guam.
I just got back from a reunion. Of
the 411 of us that were on Wake, 180
of us are left.
(The 1st Defense Batallion, Fleet Marine
Force, went to Wake Island on 19 August
1941. Two months later they got "reinforcements" of two 5-inch 51-cal. guns,
12 3-inch anti-aircraft guns, 24 .50-cal.
machine guns, and some .30-cal. machine
guns. The Marines were equipped with

Springfield rifles, khaki uniforms, and WWI steel helmets.

On 8 December the Japanese Fourth Fleet attacked. It destroyed our eight planes and killed a number of Marines and civilians. Wake is a 21-foot tall atoll to give you an appreciation of where you could hide in an air attack. On 11 December the Japanese fleet got there. The Marines sank two of their destroyers–FROM THE SHORE no less. Their two Wildcats downed two Japanese bombers, antiaircraft guns got a third, and a fourth flew away smoking. Never again did coast defenses stave off an amphibious landing. That's not all, though.

Our Navy made several tries at getting help over there from Hawaii. They sent the SARATOGA. Unfortunately, the Admiral decided to play it safe, and was still refueling 600 miles from Wake when disaster struck. On 21 December the Japanese threw against our Marines 2000 of their own Marines, three light cruisers, a minelayer, a seaplane, six heavy cruisers, a fleet of destroyers, a seaplane carrier, and two aircraft carriers with 54 planes. The Marines were overrun, while the Navy stayed out of range. A change of Admirals in mid-stream did not help, even if it was to bring Nimitz to command. He was in Washington. Admiral Fletcher did not want to risk the SARATOGA. When the island was taken, there were three American task forces within eight hours of Wake. All were recalled, sacrificing the Marines who were trying to hold such a valuable piece of real estate. This is from History of United States Naval Operations in World War II, Vol. 3: The Rising Sun in the

Pacific 1931- April 1942, Samuel Eliot Morison, 1961.)
The Navy sacrificed their own, just as they would do with the PUEBLO 27 years later. The Navy would not even attack the Japanese Navy even as it had split up and was going in 40 different directions. What a turkey shoot! Wake was sacrificed 23 December '41, and so was James P. Mitchell.

The first order of business was to take care of the home front and protect our interests. We put our Navy out to protect the shipping and our Army to such strategic points as the Panama Canal. After being away from New Orleans for several years and coming home to start his life as a bachelor, Paul Lagarde was there:

I picked up my tux for the Carnival season on 4 December. When I got home I picked up my letter from the War Department saying I was being called to active duty for one year as of 3 January 42. Everyone knows what happened December 7th, so I took the tux back.

I completed radar classes and was told to put down on my dream sheet any place I wanted to go, so I picked England. A short while later I received orders to go to "Mercury" at a New Orleans port of embarkation. I was puzzled because that didn't sound like England. That's when I found out I was going to Panama.

After arriving in the Canal Zone, I was assigned to the 615th Anti-Aircraft Regiment at Fort Clayton under

the Pacific Defense Command as S-2.
We were apprehensive because we were
still afraid of a Japanese carrier
task force attack on the canal
locks. Anti-aircraft batteries were
moved into the jungles. Malaria
cases went out of sight because the
men had to sleep in tents by the
guns. The 615th was composed of
three battalions with the first
having four batteries of 90mm guns,
the second having 40mm automatic
weapons, and the third of searchlights. The evolution of weaponry
precluded the need of searchlights,
and our Battalion was reorganized
into Gun and Automatic Weapons
Groups. I finished the war as S-3
and came home in 1945.

Paul had a very interesting career in the
Canal Zone. His future wife, Polly, was
there as a secretary at the base. She had
been safely employed in Washington DC
when the call came out for that field in
Panama. Being the adventurous soul she
is, Polly volunteered. Because she was
tall and so was Paul, they were
introduced on a blind date only to get
married *(Now where is that tux Paul got
rid of?)*. Paul was made Trial Judge
Advocate on two occasions even though he
was a radar officer. He has some other
interesting stories to tell about that.

We had to protect our shipping
interests on both coasts, and we had some
incidents happen there. Things were
rather active; in fact, downright nasty.
Our shipping off the East Coast suffered
from German U-boat attacks before we
actively started war in the European

Theater. George S. Johnston, Navy engineman, was killed on the USS JACOB JONES in February 1942. *(A U-boat, 578, fired a spread of torpedos. The first torpedo struck just aft of the bridge and apparently exploded the ship's magazine. That destroyed the bridge, chart room, and the officers' and petty officers' quarters. Then a second torpedo struck about 40 feet forward of the fantail and carried away that part of the ship. Only the midships section remained intact. It stayed afloat 45 minutes while the remaining crew got on the lifeboats through oily decks, twisted wreckage, and fouled lines. As she sunk, another explosion by the depth charges aboard killed even more men. Twelve men were eventually rescued, one of whom died en route.)*. George Johnston was the first man from Pearl River County killed in World War II.

WILLIAMS

W.T. Williams and his family served their country as they were asked. W.T.'s brothers, Richard and J.C., were in the Army in WWII. W.T.'s sons, Walter S. and Aurelius, served in the peacetime Army. W.T. himself was in from 1941 through 43 helping train engineers. W.T.'s feelings on the Gulf War:

> I'm glad this war is over *(interviewed 14 March 91)* and happy for the soldiers coming home. But, I don't think this war is really over. We keep messing around, Saddam will keep on 'til he kills a bunch of our boys.

MacArthur led an amphibious drive

starting at Guadalcanal (Aug '42) moving north through the Bismark Archipelago (Jul '43) to New Guinea (Jan '44), the Philippines (Feb '45), and Okinawa (Apr-Jun '45). During this prong of attack Pearl River County was represented in all branches of the service. Graham Graves was there with the 112th Calvary. Fred Lumpkin was on Bismark Archipelago and New Guinea. He was a construction machine operator and won the Asiatic-Pacific (A-P) Medal with two battle stars. Louis Dawsey, 417th Light Bomb Group, saw action in New Guinea, South Philippines, Luzon, and Tokyo. Louis earned the Asiatic-Pacfic (A-P) Theater Ribbon and the Philippine Liberation Medal. Paul Varnado, Marines, saw action on Okinawa. William P. Huffman earned the A-P Theater Ribbon with two battle stars and the Philippine Liberation Ribbon with one bronze battle star. Harry Arnold served with Company E, 20th Infantry in New Guinea and the Philippines, where he was wounded. He earned the A-P Theater Medal with oak leaf cluster and campaign service medals. Incidentally, Harry married his Army nurse. B.I. Mitchell, a Navy man, was in the battles of Leyte, Lingayen Gulf, and Okinawa. James Allen Boutwell was wounded in the Philippines. Cullen Bounds served three and one half years in the Navy. Virgil Lewis served 37 months in Company E, 155th Infantry, and G.W. "Buster" Moody three and a half years in the Army. Joseph Arnold was stationed on Midway and wounded in the Battle of the Coral Sea. Joe Seal served aboard an LST from 1944 to the end. William Gaspar was on the LCI(L)96 at Okinawa. Claude E. Singleton was in the

Coast Guard and participated in nine invasions of the South Pacific. Thomas J. Stockstill, Navy, earned the A-P Campaign Medal with two battle stars and the Philippine Liberation Medal. Walter David Croas, Marines, was at Okinawa. He earned the Navy-Marine Corps Medal for saving the life of a pilot he pulled from a burning plane. The plane had a bomb and was about to explode. George E. Stockstill was wounded in the South Pacific. Bill Roche was stationed on a ship landing troops on Admiralty Island, New Guinea, and the Philippines. He also survived Japanese air and sub attacks and earned five battle stars. Alfred Aultman Mitchell, Jr. saw duty in the Pacific.

OUR FIGHTING MEN

A Marine told his buddy, on Guadalcanal
"The Army is coming. Think of it, pal."
His Corporal answered him "Alright then,
Let's build a nice club for our Fighting
Men."

"They can have entertainment, and maybe a
play,
Recreation advisors from the W.P.A.
USO hostesses and movies galore,
For the Army gives morale a very high
score."

"One thing," said the chow hound, "We'll
eat better now.
Depend on the soldier to drag in the
chow.
They will start Post Exchanges, have ice
cream no end.
Life has to be pleasant for our Fighting
Men."

A Seabee rolled up and asked "What's the
score?"
The Wagons and Cruisers are laying off
shore,
With scads of Destroyers a-sweeping the
bay.
Is the Army finally landing today?"

They dashed up the beach when the boats
hit the sand.
Steel helmets, fixed bayonets, and rifles
in hand.
Marines washing clothes asked "You lads
going far?
What the hell is your hurry, have you
heard of a war?"

"Shut up!" said their Sergeant. "Go
limber your legs
And swap that Jap helmet for a case of
real eggs.
This barking at soldiers must come to an
end;
You must be respectful of our Fighting
Men."

"Their Generals outrank ours, so they'll
take command;
New rules and new orders will govern the
land.
They'll have some M.P.s to shove us
around
When the Army takes over it shudders the
ground."

"We can take it," said the Raider. "It
won't be long
Til the Admiral bellows, and we'll shove
on.
And a little while later we'll be landing
again

To make Bouganville safe for our Fighting Men."

-a Marine on
Guadalcanal

***** BURGE *****

R.B. and Marvin Burge were on different aircraft carriers during this prong. They met at Rabaul, New Guinea. Let's keep the Burges together. Mr. and Mrs. Randolph Burge of Henleyfield had eight sons in the service, seven of them at one time in WWII. The Burge boys must have been the entire eastern flank of--no. R.B., Marvin, and Garland were in the Navy; Lester and Hershel were in the Army; Hubert was a Marine, and Bernard was in the Merchant Marines. These guys were all over the place. R.B. was stationed on the ARIZONA in Pearl Harbor. He got transferred to Pensacola just before the action started. Marvin was on an aircraft carrier escort. Lester fought in North Africa for 30 months before his outfit was cut off for two weeks. He had nothing to eat during this time, and his stomach is still messed up. When the war ended in '45, Hubert and Marvin were stationed in San Diego. R.B.'s ship pulled in and they were all together for the first time and for the whistle blowing. All seven made it home, and R.B., Hubert, and Marvin went on to retire from the service. What can you say about such a family!

AFTER RABAUL IS OVER
After Rabaul is over,
After the close of day.
Count up the Japs and zeroes
But just let me get away.

80

Take all your Navy Crosses,
Medals and ribbons too,
Along with my orders and stuff them
Right up your avenue.

After Rabaul is over,
After Bull Halsey's day.
MacArthur can have the credit,
Just send me home to stay.
I don't want to be a hero,
So take your wings of gold,
To hell with the southwest Pacific,
I just want to grow old.

Now that Rabaul is over,
None of them got away.
Fifty four Japs is the record
Shot down in a single day.
Give Douglas our Air Group's story
To claim in his Army bunk.
Give me that bottle of whiskey,
I just want to get drunk.

Now that Rabaul is over,
I want to spend my days
Back with the wine and women
Reading Army communiques.
I'll take the stateside duty,
A desk job and what is more,
Take all the Admirals and Generals
To hell with the god-damned war.
*   -Anonymous*

Lewis Kilbourne, a Marine combat
intelligence officer with the VMF 114
Squadron, was in on the landings at
Bouganville, Green Island, and Pelilau.
His group still has yearly reunions.
Lewis reported:
        I grew up with a kid who came to
        Quantico as a PFC when I was being

commissioned. The kid went on to
earn his commission and become the
four star general Commandant of the
Marine Corps.
Because of classes, I missed Tarawa.
Most of the guys I went in with did
make it, though, and 70 percent of
them were killed there.
One time on an island invasion we
caught one of our 15 year sergeants
with another male. We sent him home,
and he was discharged the next day.
We didn't put up with that kind of
crap back then like they do now.
Once some of our guys had to go to
Vanuatu to pick up a dozen or so new
Corsairs. On the return flight
everyone was following the leader,
not paying much attention to the
route, when they got lost
(Conjecture has it that, if there
are no railroads to follow, Marine
pilots can't fly!). Finally, a
rookie pilot spoke up and said that
he knew the way home and that the
group was going in the wrong
direction. The leader gave him
permission to go his own way, and
the rookie was the only one to make
it back. The rest of the planes and
men are still missing.
One of our jobs was to keep bombing
the Japanese air strip at Rabaul. We
hit it every morning. They finally
started writing WELCOME YANKEE on
the strip (see photo).
Senator Joe McCarthy came to visit
us. He had a photographer, so we
gave him a hat, goggles, and a bag
to use as props. He took some really
nice pictures sitting in a dive

Marine F-4Us (Lewis Kilbourne).

Jap runway on Rabaul with bomb
craters and daily message for
Yanks (Lewis Kilbourne).

A restful flight over Mt. Fuji
before August 45 (Lewis
Kilbourne).

Marines rest camp at Eumia near
New Caledonia (Lewis Kilbourne).

85

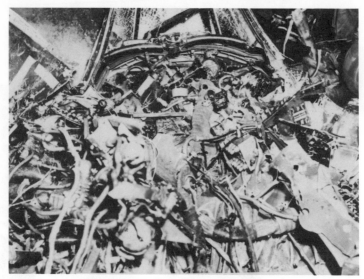

Remains of a Corsair (Lewis Kilbourne)

Lewis Kilbourne, intelligence officer extraordinaire. You would never guess by the uniform (or lack thereof!).

bomber on the ground. We had the first Marine ace, Jack Conger, in our squadron, so we volunteered Jack to take the senator up for a ride in an SNJ. You won't believe what he did to McCarthy, but we never saw the pictures his photographer took when he got back on the ground again. I do know the bag was full!

Lewis says that one of his jobs was as a duty beer runner. He'd fill up the TBF's wing tanks with ten cases of beer on Guadalcanal, fly up over 10,000 feet to cool it down, and take it to the troops on Green Island *(Very resourceful, those intelligence officers! They didn't have ice.).*

"We are poor little lambs who have lost our way,
Baa, Baa, Baa
We are little black sheep who have gone astray,
Baa, Baa, Baa
Gentleman songsters off on a spree,
Damned from here to eternity.
God have mercy on such as we,
Baa, Baa, Baa."
                    -theme song of a Marine
                    Corsair group

Joe Wise, Army "Dixie Division," went to New Guinea for jungle training, and the Japs attacked. Joe recalls it this way:

We fought up to the top of New Guinea to the Erinomor River, 'bout like Boley, and dug in. We stayed there 60 days fighting the Japs, mostly banzai attacks at night. I remember catching catfish in that river and cooking them to relieve the boredom of mutton and rabbits from Australia. Then we had a 30 day rest before going to Morotai Island in the East Indies. We took it and stayed there seven months. We helped set up airstrips to begin attacks on the Philippines. We lived in bunkers. Good thing, too. We got air raids by the Japs from Halmahera *(next island to the SW)*.

Mostly B-24s and 25s took off from our strips, escorted by P-38s and 40s. The small planes had to carry extra tanks full of fuel. We'd watch them come home. Got to see a "Black Widow," which could fly by radar. They flew at night and had 37 mm guns. I saw many dogfights, and these planes would wipe out the Jap Bettys.

We went on to Mindanao on LSTs. We went ashore against no opposition because of the previous softening by the airplanes. We got to Tadabula and went up the river at night. Just before dawn we got to a logging road. We could see the Japs ahead of us. They were using '37 Chevy trucks to haul equipment, and they had really obsolete weapons. It took us 60 days to get to the end of Mindanao. When we had been there about a month, we heard the war had ended in Europe. We thought maybe we'd get some relief forces. There were no buzzards in the place, so it got really ripe with the smell of dead Japs.

Reminded me of New Guinea all over. Just before we got there the Aussies

had pushed the Japs all the way 300
miles across the island. There were
no ships to take the Japs off, so
the Aussies wiped them out to the
last man. We buried the Aussies, and
left the Japs to rot. They called it
"Maggot Beach," and you could smell
it two miles out to sea.
I never saw an atheist over there.
Nobody laughed at anyone on his
knees.

Joe earned the A-P Theater Ribbon with
three battle stars.

Burt Pearson spanned several wars in
his career. In World Wat II he was a
Ranger, which was the forerunner of the
Green Beret in Vietnam. Because he was so
active during two wars, I'm splitting his
coverage between this one and Korea.
Burt's WWII exploits go like this:

I am the sole surviving member of
the 7th Ranger Battalion. In 1941 (3
December) I was on my way to the
Philippines when the Japs attacked
Pearl Harbor. We put ashore on Oahu
and set up a defense perimeter until
the 20th. Then we went to Australia
for jungle training. Our mission in
the war was to take little two-bit
islands (3-4 square miles) that the
Japs had communication stations and
the like on. My war action started
on Borneo, then New Guinea.
I got captured on Kwajelein in '43.
The Japs kept me as a guest for 9
months, giving me all kinds of mis-
treatment. I ended up back on Luzon
in a forward prison camp. The Navy
and Royal Australian Air Force would
drop fire bombs at the ends of the

prison camp barricades, and the
Philippine Scouts would be waiting
in the jungles to help us if we
should be able to escape. My "job"
was to work the camp water wheel 12
hours a day *(One can imagine the
start of the Conan movie of a few
years ago!)*. One day, about 9:30 or
10:00, in the morning the fire bombing started. My guard was a young
man. He got scared and threw his
rifle down. He made a crucial
mistake. I didn't. I took care of
business and left with nobody to
follow me. Eight of us escaped from
camp that day. I had had jungle
training, so I suggested we take off
in that direction. The others wanted
to head straight to the beach to get
picked up by the Navy. I went my
way, and they went theirs. When the
Philippine Scouts picked me up in
the jungle, I told them to go find
the others. They told me it was too
late, they had already been found.
Unfortunately it was by the Japs.
All their heads had been cut off.
I went down to Luzon and spent 14
days hiding in a cave until I could
get back to Australia. I had to
finagle my way back into the war.
Because the Japs had tattoed my name
on my arm, in Japanese, I was not
supposed to go back into action
against them. No f--ing way. I got
back to the 7th Ranger Division on
the Philippines, where I assisted in
the liberation of Manila. MacArthur
wouldn't let us attack several of
the hotels very vigorously. Later we
found out he owned them! Then I went

to Okinawa and on to Korea in '45. I participated in the liberation of that country from the Japs, helped set up a military government, and became guard sergeant of the palace guards.

That was not the end of Burt's career. For this segment of it, he earned the A-P Medal with 4 battle stars, 2 Bronze Stars, and a Silver Star. He says he still won't have anything Japanese in his house. We'll pick him up again just before Korea.

William J. Wilson, H.Q. Detachment, 531st Quartermaster Battalion, led a varied career. We listen:

I was trained in jungle warfare, of all places, at Fort Huachuea, Arizona! I put that to good use at Port Moresby, New Guinea, after the Battle of the Coral Sea. Then we went on to Melody Bay and engaged in bloody battle after bloody battle up to the Dutch lines. After that, I was captured and spent 28 days as a guest of the Japanese. I escaped and made my way back to the unit. We then went to Mindanao, Philippines. After that I joined the Army intelligence corps, and that's about all I have to say. I did run into Joe A. Wise and George Patterson from home.

STEWART

Alvin Stewart ended up in the 24th Infantry Division, after graduation from ROTC and MSU. Here's how he recalls it:

After training, I went to Hawaii in the winter of '42. We were put on

91

beach position because we did not
know if the island would come under
attack again. Then I went to
Australia and trained my way north.
We practiced beach landings and went
to Goodenough (Don D' Casteaux)
Island, where we staged for New
Guinea. I landed at Hollandia. My
job was cutting off troops and doing
some fighting in the Dutch part.
From there I went to the Leyte
campaign. I fought on Mindanao, Marinduque, and an island to the west
of that. I was fighting in the front
line in this campaign- foxholes,
guys getting killed all around me.
Our unit had a lull in the battle on
one of the islands, so I was sent
back to Marinduque to help the
guerillas as a liaison officer. I
spent a lot of time helping them
clean up, got in a few fights, and
helped with the paperwork. I never
got a scratch.
The war ended after I had 36 months
over there with not enough points to
go home. I spent a few months in the
occupation of Japan, which was nice.
I never would have been able to on
my own.
I got out of the service to get my
Master's Degree and was called right
back in for Korea. I spent that at
Fort Ord and extended for a tour in
Europe. There, I spent three months
with the Corps of Engineers in Paris
in an outfit called the Joint Construction Agency. We built facilities for the US and NATO. Then I
went to San Lazare to build a
pipeline from there to Metz. After

that, I came back to teach at Oregon
State for a year and muster out.

Alvin earned the Combat Infantryman's
Badge, the Bronze Star, the Philippine
Liberation Medal, and the A-P Medal with
3 or 4 battle stars. We've already met
his grandfather, Cal, in the War Between
the States. His brother, Wynon, was in
the ETO with the Army:

I was in the 87th Acorn, Infantry. I
went to Scotland in 43 on the QUEEN
ELIZABETH. It was a lot of fun and a
free trip. We had 21,00 people on a
ship built for 3200. One time we got
an "All Hands" call on the intercom
announcing that 20,000 of us were
seasick. Fortunately, I was not one
of those.

From Scotland we went into battle
between Paris and Metz. Then I
crossed the border and went to the
point of the Bastogne spearhead. We
fought through there, and I ended
the war a few miles inside
Czechoslovakia.

Wynon earned the Combat Infantrymans
Badge and the EAMETO with 3 battle stars.
"Actually," he says, "I earned every
medal they've got, they just didn't give
them to me. I almost got my upper lip
shot off, but it had scabbed over by the
time I got to help. No Purple Heart
even." First Calvin. Then Alvin and
Wynon. What a bunch of fighters!

H.I. Harris was in the Navy on the
USS BRACKEN as a reluctant signalman.
H.I. went to three different schools
learning all about signalling, but he
didn't want to be one. Finally an Admiral
said "You will learn signalling:"

I could send, but I couldn't receive. One day I was being sent a *(flashing light)* signal, and something just snapped. I have been able to read signals ever since. I served on a troop transport ship (Apr 43-Apr 46) and was in on the invasions of the Solomons, Philippines, Midway, China, Okinawa, and Japan.

SMITH

James R. and Mable Smith provided three sons for America's war effort in the middle of this century. Oldest, Robert Lamar, was in the Navy for eight or nine months. Then he joined the Army, Calvary, and was sent to Panama before WWII started. The youngest, Lloyd C., was in the Army Air Corps in WWII. Lloyd flew 31 missions over Germany. Then he volunteered to stay on and teach how to be a tail gunner in England. Lloyd flew a few more missions, including some on the "Memphis Belle. James R. Smith, Jr., provider of the above information, was in the Navy, and he tells this story:

I put the NEW JERSEY in commission in May (23rd) of '43 and stayed on until the Navy took it out of commission (30 June '48). I was a gunner's mate. We had 3300 officers and men on board. The living conditions were okay. The food quality was debatable. We had three racks to a tier. I was in Hawaii once for R and R and in the States just before the war was over. We went to relieve the MISSOURI for the surrender because we had seniority in the Pacific, but we didn't make

94

it.
I had one confirmed hit, a Betty,
with a 40-mm gun. It was at night,
and the radar didn't pick it up. We
had two or three near misses by
kamikazes. Our only hit was from one
of our own tincans. The shell hit us
and went down a few decks into the
cook shack. It knocked the toes off
one of the cook's feet, Me and
another guy went down and hauled the
shell out.

*(From 29 January to 2 February 1944 the
NEW JERSEY screened carriers from enemy
attacks at Kwajelein and Eniwetok. She
then became Admiral Spruance's flagship
at Majuro and struck against Truk in late
February. Next came a strike against the
Palaus, bombarding Woleai. From 13 April
to 4 May she supported the invasions of
New Guinea, Truk, and Ponape. On 12 June
she downed a torpedo bomber [probably
James' Betty] and battered Saipan and
Tinian. NEW JERSEY provided air cover for
a task force at the "Great Marianas
Turkey Shoot" on 19 Jun, struck at Guam
and the Palaus, and went to Hawaii for a
rest [9-30 August 1944]].*

*The NEW JERSEY set up base at Ulithi
as Halsey's flagship of the 3rd Fleet,
striking airfields, shipping, shore
installations, and invasion beaches at
the Philippines, Okinawa, and Formosa. In
September she joined the fleet for the
Battle of Leyte Gulf and shot down
someplanes in Octoberr. During early 1945
the battleship was in on strikes at Formosa,Okinawa, Luzon, the coast of Indo-
China, Hong Kong, Swatow, Amoy, Formosa,
and Okinawa again. Halsey moved on, and
Admiral Badger took over. From 19 to 21*

February she helped at Iwo Jima. From 14 March to 16 April she fought off air raids, rescued downed pilots with her seaplanes, and defended carriers against kamikazes by shooting down at least three. She went back to Bremerton for an overhaul and missed the surrender. She did transport troops home.)
James earned 9 battle stars on the NEW JERSEY in WWII. He also served during Korea off the coast on a cargo ship. Salty.

James J. Brown, an armed guard with the Navy on merchant ships, was all over the Pacific, even "returning" with Mac-Arthur to the Philippines. One of the big problems in WWII was the lack of sufficient maps, especially reef location. Jim helped chart any of those discovered by his ship with sketches. Once they went through about two days of yellow seas. An Indonesian on board told him it was fish eggs. On another ship, Jim had a Russian captain who would not fraternize with any of the crew. In Jim's words:

> One night I was asleep on deck by my gun when I felt the ship stop and back down. I hustled to the bridge to find out what the trouble was. The Captain kept screaming about running up on a shoal. I took a look over the side and ordered a bucket to be lowered. The Captain thought I was crazy, but it turned out to be the same fish eggs again! After that we became good buddies.
> I also had a brother, Herman, in the Army Air Corps. One time I was in New Hebrides and got a letter from Mom. Aside from the fact that it had

96

been censored, it contained Herman's APO address-you guessed it, New Hebrides. I blinked over to his camp, found out his whereabouts, and went on over. He was busy interrogating captured Japs, so I just sat on his bunk. When he finally finished, he came to talk to the others around us while sneaking an occasional look at me. Since I had a beard, I figured I had better say something. Boy, did we have a reunion!

Clifton James (C.J.) Harrell, a gunner's mate aboard the USS SABINE, won nine battle stars and campaign ribbons between 1942-45. The SABINE was a "seagoing service station" and supported carrier task forces against Wake and the Gilberts and many others. She was with the USS HORNET for General James Doolittle's stirring raid.

What was the HORNET doing that was so significant? She was helping pull America up by her collective bootstraps and get going again. *(The HORNET was supposed to get within 400 miles of Japan for the raid, but it only got to 600. The HORNET made Midway [4 June 42], the Solomons [17 August-24 October], and the Battle of Santa Cruz [26 October]. The HORNET suffered a severe Japanese torpedo and dive bombing attack that left her crippled. She had to be abandoned. This was HORNET number 7.).* Joe Brown was a pilot on B-25s. Joe Brown was one of the pilots responsible for psyching up the American war effort, picking up morale, after the Japanese bombed Pearl Harbor. You see, Joe Brown was on Doolittle's

Raid. Essentially Army bombers were carried on the USS HORNET in a task force. When the carrier got to within 600 miles of Tokyo, the planes took off. Never mind that the planes did not have enough fuel to return. Never mind that they couldn't land on a carrier. They took off. The first few were touch-and-go, as the planes lumbered off the flight deck only to drop to the water before getting up a full "head of steam" and taking off. We'll listen to Joe's war:

I was the number seven plane to take off. We bombed Yokohama, Tokyo, Osaka, and Kobe before heading for China. One of our planes ditched in the water, one on the beach, and the rest of us bailed out over the mainland. Chinese guerillas picked me up and hustled me to safety in Chunking. We regrouped in Karachi, and ships brought us more planes, equipment, etc. (May '42). My new plane was called the "Jap Exterminator." We had no squadron number, but flew missions over China and Burma using General Claire Chennault's "Flying Tigers" for cover. When they disbanded (Jul '42), 80% of those civilians joined the Air Force and stayed on to fight. We were flying out of Kunming, China. We flew strikes against the Japs in coastal China and Rangoon, Burma. I spent 13 or 14 months doing this. Then I returned to, of all places, Gulfport to teach others our tactics.
Once while flying a strike against Mandalay, Burma, my plane got hit. I had to bail out about 40 to 50 minutes later. A Brit patrol picked me

up and got me to safety. That was the end of '42.

Our group still has a convention every year on 18 April because that is the anniversary of our bombing Tokyo. The group is made up of the "CATF" Doolittle's Raiders Flying Tigers Inc.

For my service I received a Distinguished Flying Cross (Doolittle) with one bronze oak leaf cluster, Purple Heart (hit over Mandalay), Silver Star (over Rangoon), Air Medal (completion of 10 missions) with five oak leaf clusters (54 missions in all), American Defense Medal, A-P Medal with 3 battle stars and a Chinese Army-Air Force-Navy Medal.

(This is one of the instances I talked about at the start of the book. A fellow named Lawson wrote the book Thirty Seconds over Tokyo. In Doolittle's Tokyo Raiders by Glines, "all" of the personnel involved with the raid on Japan are listed. Joe is not in that book. I went to the Naval Aviation Museum in Pensacola and saw all the memorabilia from the HORNET and Doolittle's raid, including signatures. Joe was not represented there either. I wrote to the museum curator and told him he had made a mistake, and that the history books were wrong. Joe Brown flew the number 7 plane off the HORNET in Doolittle's raid; he told me so himself. Lawson said he was pilot of the seventh plane off, the "Ruptured Duck." Joe says that Lawson was number six. In fact, Joe says that for historic accuracy about five or six of the names on that raid are wrong. I wish we could have gotten our

hands on some documentation. That would have really created a stir among the historians- or readers.)

Emile Williams ran a Navy dock crew at Pearl Harbor from 1943 to the summer of '45. When he came home on 30 days leave, the war ended and he was discharged. Emile adds this to our WWII lore:

I had to keep '45 men working, clearing the docks. One of our jobs was to raise the OKLAHOMA *(one of the sunken battlewagons)*, repair it, and send it back to the States. *(We were actually able to salvage all but three of them from the attack on Pearl Harbor, but it was a monumental undertaking. One of the "Victory at Sea" tapes shows this routine perfectly. The OKLAHOMA was moored outboard of the MARYLAND. She took three torpedoes even as the Japanese bombs were falling. Two more hit her while she was capsizing, and there were strafing runs. Water depth prevented her from sinking, and she rested on her port side and masts with part of the keel and the starboard side exposed. The salvage job began in March '43, and the OKLAHOMA entered drydock in December.).*

I had the job of keeping the Admiral's (Nimitz) gig in good working order. One day we were taking it out of the water when something happened that never made the news. We had a mini-Pearl Harbor all over again. We had about 10 or 12 fully loaded LSTs ready to go to Guam. They went off. It was just my luck that I got off the gig when I

100

did. I looked and saw the side of an LST going up in the air. The sailor I was running with ducked one way, and I went another. That piece of metal chewed him up like hamburger when it hit because it was spinning. Those explosions tore up our waterfront, buildings and all. My next job was to find all the missing pieces of the dead sailors and get them back together to send home for burial. We spent a few days pulling pieces out of the water and off the LSTs, but we never found them all. They *(the press)* never reported that.

Emile's crew saw Prentis James at the sub base on Pearl Harbor and told him about Emile back at his dock, always looking for a homeboy. Prentis and Emile got together right then and there. Emile also saw Roger Cain.

Bill Spiers (deceased) was drafted into the Navy in August 1943 and returned home in 1945. Bill was a barber on the LST-719. *(Bill may have been the barber, but he also participated in the A-P theater landing on Palawan Island in March of '45 and the Mindanao Island landings during April and May '45. He earned a battle star for that.)* Bills's son, Kenneth Wesley Spiers, was in the Navy from 1964 through 1968 *(courtesy of Bill's wife, Monie)*.

Talk about patriotism, it seems as though the entire senior class at Picayune High dropped out to join the war effort and got sent to the Philippines. Some were on Bataan and lucked out by swimming to Corregidor four miles away. Even though they were captured, they avoided the Bataan Death March. Clyde Sumrall (Army), Carl Holloway (Marines), Kenny Smith, and Lawrence Thames were all made POWs. Meanwhile, William R. Seals, a sailor, was waiting on dock with supplies for a ship. The Japs came instead. He got away and joined forces with other Navy men to form an infantry batallion. He was subsequently captured with the rest of the Countians. Sumrall lost weight down to about 80-90 pounds. One day he got mad and attacked a guard. He was knocked to the ground. As the other Americans were made to watch, he was severely beaten by a host of guards before being put in a sweat box for 30 days. Sumrall, not to be broken, made it home. This camp was losing about 300 people per day to dysentery, malaria, scurvy, and other diseases.

Carl Holloway described the early fighting in the Philippines. The Japs attacked Subic Bay sub repair base where seven or eight PBYs were sitting in the water. Zekes made strafing runs, setting fire to and sinking the planes. Carl left Olongopo for Manila, and the Japs bombed there. Then he went to Bataan peninsula with MacArthur, found it indefensible, and made it to a small fortress on an island, Corregidor. Winston Churchill said of that place "Acre for acre and bomb for bomb, Corregidor was the most bombed place in the world." From Carl's book, Happy, the POW:

> Every man in my Company of 300 was wounded or killed except one by the Japanese attack before the actual surrender. Almost half the Bataan-

102

Corregidor captives died in the first five months. That's about 3000 out of 6500 by the end of '43. Everyone who was alive had diarrhea, dysentery, and two kinds of beriberi. Most also had malaria and hepatitis. To add to that, we had large rats and bedbugs. We were given no meat and very little else except grain *(rice, millet)*. We were lined up facing each other and forced to slap each other. If we didn't do it hard enough, the guard would eagerly give a demonstration.

I was on a burial detail at one of the camps. We were dying so fast that it would be possible to be on a burial detail one morning, help dig a hole in the afternoon, and be buried in that hole the next morning. Because of the crude burial methods and constant rains, corpses all over the area were constantly exposed. This caused an unbelievable odor at all times.

(I will attempt to put these men's feelings about the Japanese in the proper perspective right now in case we have any bleeding heart, pinko liberals reading this book.)

Escape. They kept us from trying to escape by a very simple means. They gave us numbers and put us in groups of ten. If we escaped, the rest of the group was executed. So, we always had in the back of our minds (1) eluding the guards, (2) surviving the jungles and disease, (3) avoiding being turned in by some Filipino for the reward, but also (4) knowing we had killed nine other

103

men. That could be very hard to live
with.

One time 996 of us were put into the
hold of a ship for transportation to
Japan. We spent 21 days there with
very little food. Not all of us
could even sit down at the same
time. There was so little water that
we tilted our heads to catch water
running off the decks or rain. But
it got worse. These "Hellships" were
unmarked, so the American Navy
started blowing us out of the water.
They had no way of knowing.

About the only good news I had while
in there was smuggled in by a Filipino boy. It was an English newspaper. It said that Admiral Yamamoto's
plane had been shot down while he
was on an inspection tour of Truk
and Rabaul.

Carl was weighed after he had been a
captive for about 1000 days. He says he
only weighed 81 pounds, which was about
half his normal weight.

Morris E. Megehee was with the 27th
Army Air Corps on the Philippines. He did
not surrender 8 April, even though he had
participated in the Bataan and Corregidor
campaigns. Morris turned up with the
Philippine Guerilla Forces as the radio
operator. (These were the type of Philippine Scout that found and hid Burt Pearson.) He and another guy found a caraboa
and loaded it with rice, the radio, and
.30-cal ammunition before leaving San
Jose to the Japs. His group of refugees
made "home" in the jungles. On 5 May Morris received a radio message saying:
"This is Corregidor. We are surrendering.

You are on your own." Megehee's group then moved on to a coastal town and was reported MIA 7 May 1942. He apparently fought with the guerillas against the Japs until his death 28 January 1944. A Purple Heart was awarded his mother, but his family never got the A-P Medal with at least 2 battle stars .

Admiral Nimitz's forces began amphibious assaults at the Gilbert Islands, continued to the Marshall Islands, the Marianas (Jun '44), split to attack Iwo Jima and Leyte (Oct '44), the Philippines, and Okinawa (Apr-Jun '45). It's a good thing for Nimitz that Pearl River Countians were with him. There were enough to have had a quorum and a hometown election it seems! Because of these men and men like them, Admiral Nimitz was able to charge across the ocean. Hayward Mardeece Mitchell was at Okinawa with the Navy. Leo Henry Reyer, Navy, earned the A-P Ribbon with two stars. John H. Horne was in the Pacific with the Army 63rd Ordnance Group. Archie Dickerson was on Okinawa with the Army Air Corps. Red Jones was on Okinawa with the Infantry. Woodrow Whitfield was in the 4th Marine Division at Iwo Jima as a rifleman. After six days on the job, he had received five wounds, so he was evacuated. He did get to see the flag raising from the ATO 196. Cully C. Lee was in the South Pacific in the Coast Guard. Toxie Pigott was on New Caledonia. Carl Boutwell was in the South Pacific. Edward L. Bankston was a machine gunner with the Marine Corps Third Division on Guam. Theodore Lyonell Spiers was on LST 555 while participating in invasions of

Palau, New Guinea, Leyte, Luzon, and Okinawa. Odis Carroll Spikes, Navy, served in the Asiatic-Pacific and European-African theaters.

"The girl of my dreams has bobbed her hair,
And dyed it a flaming red.
She drinks, she smokes
And tells dirty jokes,
And she hasn't a brain in her head.
She thinks rotten gin makes the world go round.
She can drink more that you or I.
Oh, the moonlight beams
On the girl of my dreams,
She's the sweetheart of six other guys."
—Anonymous

WALKER
Hobert Walker was in WWI. He was on the way over when the war ended. Hobert had three sons serve in WWII. Billy C., a Navy coxwain, served in Dutch Harbor, Alaska. Jack was in the Air Force and switched to the Army. In all, he was in Korea, the Philippines, the occupation of Japan *(he had heart surgery there)*, and back to Korea. Jack made Porkchop Hill and several other battles in Korea. Then he went to Geneva for the peace signing. Richard D. Walker (dec), Navy, served aboard the USS HORNET. He, too, could write a travel guide to the western Pacific islands: Yap, Ulithi, Volcano and Bonin Islands, Palau, Mindanao, Cebu, Negros, Morotai, Welea Strait, Davao, the Philippine strike, West Sula, Hollandia, Truk, Marianas, Ryukyus, China Sea, and Tokyo harbor. Walker earned numerous campaign ribbons and battle stars, a

106

Presidential Unit Citation, and a Purple
Heart *(this courtesy of wife, Jeanette)*:

> The HORNET got separated from the
> fleet one time and ran out of
> everything to eat except beans and
> biscuits. They finally got back to
> 'em. They had some horse's patooties
> as commanders on that ship. They
> wouldn't do no way right.
> Richard went up to Tokyo Bay. There
> was so many dead Japs in the water
> and the smell was so bad, they had
> to back out to sea to get out of
> there.
> Richard used to tell people he got
> hit on the head with a coconut.
> Actually, he was in a suicide plane
> attack on the HORNET. He was sent
> home on a hospital ship, I can't
> remember the name. The day after he
> left the hospital ship, it was sunk
> by enemy fire.
> He was on the ship one time when
> Roosevelt visited. Otherwise, he
> didn't see anybody he knew. He did
> meet a streetcar conductor in New
> Orleans once who was on the HORNET.

*(This is the 8th HORNET and not the one
in Doolittle's Raid. This HORNET made New
Guinea and the Caroline Islands May '44,
Tinian and Saipan 11 June, Guam and Rota
12 June, Iwo and Chichi Jima 15-16 June,
the Marianas Turkey Shoot 19 June, and
generally wreaked havoc all over the
Pacific until 7 July '45. Then she was
overhauled and became part of operation
"Magic Carpet.").*

Richard's son, Herman, was in
Vietnam with the Army *(see that Section)*.
Billy's son, Jimmy, was in the Army in
Vietnam.

FURR

Jesse Ryals and Ruby Thornhill Furr provided us with an interesting way to get a 5-Star family- through their five daughters! In fact, they gave us a 7-Star. First, though, their grandfather, John James Thornhill, fought in The War Between the States. Then, I list this family here because most of them were in the Pacific:

(1) Daughter Jesse Mae Furr was married to Robert Chester McMullan. He was in the Navy Seabees in the Philippine area. After he died in 1961, Jesse Mae remarried, this time to Joe F. Scoggin. Joe had served in WWII in the 498th Engineer AVN Battalion, Army, on home soil while earning the National Defense Service Medal.

(2) Blanche Christine Furr married Thomas O. Metcalfe, Jr. He was a bombardier-navigator on a B-17 Flying Fortress with the 457th Bombardment Group, Army Air Corps, flying out of Glatton, England. On their 19th mission their plane was shot down and the crew captured. While he was at Stalag Luft 1, Metcalfe met a close friend from Picayune, Norman Stockstill *(see his story later)*. They were liberated by the Russians 2 May '45. After Metcalfe died, Christine married another WWII veteran. Robert A. Carsley was the Regimental Surgeon of the 361st Engineer Special Service Regiment from '43-'46. He served in France from Omaha Beach to Rhiems; th regiment built general hospitals

and airfields. In June '45 he was sent to Clark Field in the Philippines. In September he was sent to Osaka, Japan, as part of the Army of Occupation.

(3) Iva Loy Furr married Clarence Edward Tolar. Tolar was in the Army, Company E, 179th Infantry, 45th Division. While engaging the enemy in Morocco and Algiers, at Anzio, the invasion of Southern France and Germany, Tolar earned the Purple Heart with 2 oak leaf clusters, a Bronze Star, and the Combat Infantryman's Badge. Tolar saw "Sonny" Lane about one month prior to his death in Italy. He also saw his cousin, Earl Loftin, in Italy.

(4) Ruby Thomasine Furr married John Hollie Blackwell, Jr. *(We told his father's story in the WWI section).* Blackwell was an airplane crew chief with the 333rd Bomb Group, 8th Air Corps, at Kodena, Okinawa. There he visited Wesley Patch, who was his neighbor in Picayune.

(5) Lastly, we get to meet the lovely lady who made this section possible, Charleen Furr Schrock. She called me about a possible 5-Star female side, and it sounded perfectly reasonable to me. Her husband, James L. Schrock, was on the destroyer, USS STORMES, in the Pacific Theater. *(The STORMES sailed 22 April '44 for Pearl Harbor. On 1 May she sailed escort for the LOUISVILLE and joined the 5th Fleet at Hagushi anchorage. On the morning of 25 May during nasty weather a Japanese plane sneaked through cloud cover*

and was heading for the ship in front. At the last minute the kamikaze pilot veered into the STORMES's aft torpedo mount. Its bomb exploded in the magazine under the number 3 5-inch mount. By noon repair parties had plugged the holes and put out the fires. Twenty-one of the crew were killed and 15 injured.). Schrock went all through boot camp with J.P. Buckley, Billy Page, and M.D. "Maxie" Stevens, all now deceased.

Pat Holcomb sailed on the USS ELECTRA. The two of them sailed to Eniwetok to supply boats and equipment for the initial landings (18 February '44). Pat earned a Bronze Star for that one. The ship then carried troops to Saipan (15 June) and embarked casualties for a return to Pearl Harbor (20 June). They went to Guadalcanal to stage for the Palau invasion, and made a feint assault on Babelthaup to divert attention from Peliliu (15 September). After a brief break the ELECTRA landed troops on Leyte (20 October), lifted troops from Guam (23 November), then went in for a layup. She made the next invasion at Lingayen Gulf, Luzon (9 January '45), under air attack and offloaded her supplies and troops (17 January). Then she embarked Army troops from New Guinea to Mindoro. Pat and his ship then took the 5th Marines to Iwo Jima (18 March) and went back to Pearl Harbor (15 April. The ship finished the war by carrying fresh troops to Japan and taking a load of the veterans home to the US *(You could get seasick reading about all this jumping around.)*.

Speaking of taking the 5th Marines to Iwo Jima, Johnnie Walters (deceased) did the same on the USS WHITLEY as a Navy gunner. He had a very interesting experience. The WHITLEY was strafed by the Japs *(On 27 January '45 the WHITLEY, an attack cargo ship, left Pearl Harbor for Eniwetok, then went on to the Marianas. On 14 February she disembarked the 5th Marines on Iwo Jima. On the night of 23/24 February two Japanese planes attacked her. This was her only action, so this must be where the rest of Johnnie Walters story took place.)*. Johnnie got shot up pretty badly, was put in the body pile, and was being given the last rites. The chaplain realized he wasn't dead, so he extricated Johnnie from the dead pile and offloaded him to a hospital ship *(courtesy son-in-law, Jan Depner)*. Johnnie got patched up and sent back out on another ship to finish the war. This was in 1945. In the 1980s his daughter, Sharon, was at a party at the University of Mississippi in Oxford. A man came up and asked her if she was kin to Johnnie Walters. She said "Yes, he is my father." He said "It must be a different Johnnie Walters. The one I knew was killed in WWII on the WHITLEY." Sharon told him that her father was the same man, and the stranger almost fainted. He couldn't believe he was seeing Johnnie's female spitting image after almost 40 years, and that from a "ghost!"

Granville E. Smith served on board the battlewagon, USS NEW YORK, at Okinawa and Iwo Jima *(This NEW YORK, BB-34, was left over from WWI. She participated in*

the preinvasion bombarddment of Iwo Jima
and fired more rounds than any other ship
just to prove she could still do it. Then
she went to Okinawa for 76 days and
preinvasion and diversionary bombardments
among other things. She got a kamikaze
hit on 14 April, but kept on fighting
until 11 June.).

JARRELL

Harlon P. Jarrell (deceased) and his
brothers created quite a stir during
WWII. Lonnie was a torpedo operator on a
PT boat in the Pacific. Toxie was one of
the last to be called up. He had just
made it through basic training when the
war ended. Harlon I was able to pin down
a little more:

I helped commission aircraft
carriers. We gave shakedown cruises
and made up operations sheets for
the real crew. I helped on the USS
WASP, TICONDEROGA, SHANGRI-LA, and
the HANCOCK. We had a problem with
that one. No relief crew was sent
for the HANCOCK, so we had to take
it to war! It was the last of the
big ones, and I was a plank owner on
it.
We went to the Pacific outfitted
with teachers and instructors and
the first IFF radar on planes. We
should have been in great shape, and
we were. We could shoot at night as
well as during the day. Our biggest
problem was that we never had a good
PR man (!), and I'll tell you why.
We were in both major battles at
Leyte, the Straits of Mindoro,
Eniwetok, Midway, Saipan. We shot
down something like 246 Jap planes

and sunk 226 ships. The HANCOCK was responsible for damaging more that a third of the Japanese fleet and planes by herself. I was a machinists mate, in this case a catapult operator. I got hurt after Leyte. I was working on a catapult when a Jap bomber hit us. It broke me up. I came home on a hospital ship after a stop on Guadalcanal. I was discharged on V-E Day and got a Navy Commendation Award.

(In the interest of all concerned, I again went to the American Naval Fighting Ships *dictionary. The HANCOCK was laid down as the TICONDEROGA but renamed 1 May '43. She sailed from Boston and went through the Panama Canal to Pearl Harbor and joined Halsey's 3rd Fleet. She went to Ulithi and to the Ryukyu Islands on 10 October. On that day her pilots destroyed 7 enemy aircraft on the ground [Okinawa], a sub tender, 12 torpedo boats, 2 midget submarines, 4 cargo ships, and a number of sampans. On 12 October her pilots destroyed 9 planes on the ground and downed 6 more, 1 cargo ship definitely sunk, 3 probables, and several others damaged. I mean, this ship was awesome! Totally outrageous! A one-man-gang! Every other day is like this. She survived bombings, strafings, torpedoes. She attacked Formosa. On 18 October she struck the northern Philippines. On 23 October she went back to Samar, missed the battle, and made up for that at the Straits of San Bernardino. She shot down a suicide bomber on 25 November, then returned to Ulithi. She fought all over the Philippines, even riding out a severe typhoon 17 December. To show how squared*

113

away this ship was, and instance serves. On 20 January '45 one of her planes returned from a mission, made a normal landing, taxied to the control island, and promptly blew up. Thew explosion killed 50 men and injured another 75 - not to mention setting the flight deck on fire. Next morning she was back on formation - launching strikes on Okinawa. She struck airfields near Tokyo in February. On the 16th her pilots downed 71 enemy planes. She hit bases at Chichi and Haha Jima. She provided tactical support for the invasion of Iwo Jima. The ship led a charmed life, to be sure. HANCOCK was refueling the HALSEY POWELL 20 March when a suicide plane cartwheeled across her flight deck and crashed into a group of planes. Its bomb hit the port catapault and caused a tremendous explosion. Sixty-two men were killed and 71 wounded. This was where Harlon Jarrell got hurt. The ship sailed on and Harlon sailed home.)

Harlon thinks the HANCOCK did not get all the credit it deserves because of those rookie PR men. I didn't add up the actual kills, but his figures seem to be about right. The HANCOCK was a horse! On top of this, we are presented three more Jarrells, all of them Harlon's sons. George served two six-month tours in Nam as a fighter pilot. George was trained for refueling planes in the air, and he ferried A-7s and A-10s to Nam; later, he ferried F-16s. He taught fighter pilot tactics for a while after the war and also flew cover for the Grenada invasion. Son Mike was in the ROTC at State and went into the Army Reserves for 5 or 6 years. Fred is in the Bogalusa National

Guard motor pool. This is another heavy duty family from Pearl River County. *This is also another instance of just barely getting there. I interviewed Harlon in June '91, and he died the next month. I'm sorry he did not get to see his ship get credit in print.*

Charles Aubrey Baxter was on an Essex class flattop, USS BENNINGTON, with "Bull" Halsey's Third Fleet off the coast of Japan *(This BENNINGTON joined the task force 8 February 1945. She took part in strikes against the Japanese homeland, the Volcano Islands, and Okinawa. On 7 April her planes were in on the force that sunk the YAMATO. In July-August she took part in the final raids on Japan.).*

STRAHAN

John H. "Buster" Strahan was in the Navy Seabees. He went from here to Virginia to Gulfport to Port Hueneme. In April 1943 he shipped out for Guadalcanal. He remembers:

> We stayed in the New Hebrides for 3 days waiting for an escort to take us to Guadalcanal. I was on the SS BRASSTAGGE, a Dutch ship that had gone through the raid on Rotterdam. Man, were they gunshy! Anyhow, we got four destroyer escorts and some battleships and went on. I helped build the bomber strip at Coley Point. While we were there, fighting was still going on. I went through several air raids. We stayed there 18 months and saw many interesting things. We had one guy whose brother had been killed on Guadalcanal. One time he got ahold of a Tommy gun and

got into our Jap prisoner stockade.
He killed eight or ten before he
stopped. We were working with the
3rd Marines. They were on the front
line, but would come back to our
area once a week or so for a hot
meal and a shower. One guy told me
the reason he stayed so fired up was
that he had found a Marine bayoneted
to a tree with his genitals stuffed
into his mouth. One time, the Japs
got so hungry, they stole some GI
clothes and were actually caught in
our chow lines! The native women
over there, they didn't wear tops.
That took some getting used to
(*Fortunately, the missionaries
showed up and taught them they had
been living in sin since time
immemorial. They got them to put
tops on.*). Oh, yes, we also
maintained Fighter 1 and 2 air
strips.
After that we went to New Zealand
for a 30-day R and R that turned
into a 9 dayer when the Japs attacked Bouganville. We were sent to Russell Island south of the Solomons
and spent 5 or 6 months there main-
taining camps. From there we went to
Erimau, south of Truk, and built an
air strip. Erimau was only four
square miles, so the runways were
short. Some of the bigger planes
couldn't take off and ran right into
the ocean. We went back to Russell,
and then to Milne Bay, New Guinea.
There we waited for a really big
convoy to build up, 2 to 300 ships,
and we went to the Philippines (late
'44). The forward ships full of

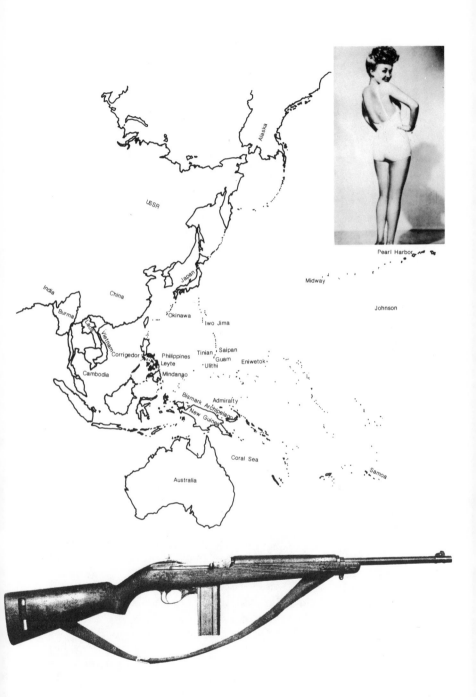

USSR

Alaska

India

China

Japan

Burma

Laos

Okinawa

Vietnam

Iwo Jima

Corrigedor

Philippines

Tinian

Saipan

Cambodia

Leyte

Guam

Ulithi

Eniwetok

Mindanao

Bismark Archipelago

Admiralty

New Guinea

Coral Sea

Australia

Samoa

Pearl Harbor

Midway

Johnson

117

Trying to build a runway on rain-soaked Leyte (Buster Strahan).

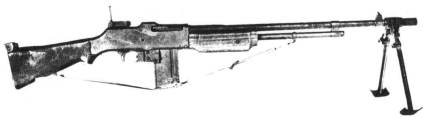

Jap equipment captured on Leyte (Buster Strahan).

All right, guys, let's go get
'em (Buster Strahan)

Seabee camp on Samar (Buster
Strahan).

The calm before the storm on
Emiru (Buster Strahan).

Marines went in, and we landed the
next day on Leyte. We were camped in
a rice paddy between the artillery
and the front lines. Heavy duty. The
Japs were parachuting in on us, and
some others were attacking from the
other side of the island. There was
a really big sea battle that took
care of those Japs landing. We had
to do some fighting here. One night
we shot a Jap, and he moaned all
night. We found him the next morning, and he was covered with booby
traps *(see photo)*. The Jap planes
were coming in so low, you could see
the rip cords hanging out the doors
and the machine guns. We had to put
up with a lot of bombing and
strafing, not to mention the constant wetness of the rice paddy.
Both us and the Filipinos left the
dead Japs out to rot.
Tales? The US government gave the
Filipinos one rifle for every Jap
head they brought in. One morning I
saw two guys coming in with a pole
across their shoulders. I counted
seven heads hanging from that pole.
We had an air alert this one time
and a movie camera going. There was
a guy trying to use the latrine, but
he had to get up and run to a
foxhole every now and then. That was
funny! I just got that put on video.
Anyhow, it was so boggy there, we
went north of Leyte to build an
airstrip. We found an island with a
lot of coral, Samar. Last tale. That
island. A plane was taxiing down the
runway. There was a guy out packing
it down. The pilot didn't see him,

121

and ran right over him. Cut off both his legs. When the pilot realized this, he jumped down and put tourniquets on his legs. Now, you won't believe this. The pilot died of shock, and the other guy lived. I couldn't believe it!

I saw Purvis "Junior" Hall on Leyte several times. He is my neighbor in Crossroads now.

The war ended with Buster Strahan on that island. His father, John H. Sr., went to France in WWI with the Army at the Argonne Forest. Buster's sons, Jimmy Wayne and Jack Ray, were in the Navy. Buster's four brothers were also in the military, three of them in WWII: W.H. "Bill" was in the 73rd Seabee Battalion. Bill and Buster got together on Guadalcanal. J.E. was a stevadore in the Navy. George E. was in England as part of the Air Corps ground crew. Joseph Farrell enlisted in 1955 in the Navy and retired from that branch. Truly a patriotic family.

James Charles Spikes (deceased) was a storekeeper with the Navy. He was stationed on an island in the Pacific and worked in the accounting department. The troops arrived there before the Seabees, so they had to open all their supplies that were packed in wooden crates. When they found the typewriters, they made desks out of the crates, set up a tent, and opened shop *(courtesy Jean Frisby)*. Spikes also walked by some native huts and saw a Sears Roebuck sewing machine. That made him feel nearer to home.

Leon D. Mitchell served aboard the

USS ATR 50. When asked what an ATR was:
An ATR was an ocean-going tug rescue boat about 270 feet long. There were three of them in the war with 80-man crews, armed to the teeth. We had to pull LSTs and other landing craft from the beaches during invasions. I saw some of the most beautiful islands in the world before we got through with them. AND, I got paid to do it-$58.00 a month plus $5.00 hazardous duty pay for diving *(nothing like a satisfied swabbie)*. We kept ourselves refreshed on Gobel beer. I was there from '43 to '46. I saw Charles Metzler from Nicholson on Tinian. My brother Jackie B. was in Korea. My grandson, Wayne Tucker, is on a battleship in the Gulf right now.

Leon was in on the invasions of *(get ready)* Johnston Island, Eniwetok, Samar and Leyte in the Philippines, Ulithi, Saipan when the bomb hit, Tinian, and Guam when the war ended. He earned the A-P Medal with 6 battle stars.

Edrow Lee rode the USS GAMBIER BAY down for the count. *(The GAMBIER BAY essentially carried replacement planes until it got in a task force for the Marianas invasion late in the war (June '44). She gave close air support to the Marines and turned back all but a handful of 47 Jap planes sent against her. GAMBIER BAY remained in Saipan until she moved to Tinian (19-31 July) and then on to Guam. She then became part of the task force to attack the Philippines, that being "Taffy 3" at Samar. Remnants of the Japanese fleet hit her hard 25 October.*

Planes from the ship dropped torpedos and bombs and strafed until they ran out of ammo. They then made dummy runs and threw up smoke screens, but to no avail. The GAMBIER BAY was reduced to a 5-inch gun at the end against three cruisers. She deep sixed 25 Oct '44. The ship received 4 battle stars and a Presidential Unit Citation.). Edrow Lee spent a couple of days in the water fending off shark attacks while trying to keep the others going. He made it out, and the survivors still have reunions. Edrow is almost deaf, so I couldn't get the entire story from him. He did say that he and several others had stayed in the water for about three days, while many of the seamen were rescued earlier. That would have been quite a story!

David M. Brock, Navy, was there too. Dave was on LSC USS 75. His sea tales include these:

Our boat was launched in Portland. We took it down the Columbia river and into the war as part of the amphibious assault group. We were a gunboat and would be the first to the beach to launch rockets before major assaults. We went to the Marshalls, shooting our way up to Saipan. We went to Okinawa and assisted in a smoke screen. We went to Leyte Gulf and then back to Okinawa when peace was called for. We were supposed to guard the battleship, PENNSYLVANIA, when it was torpedoed. We had some smuggled beer on board and were enjoying the sunset when a plane came up with fire and smoke shooting out of its exhaust. All of a sudden, it got straightened out and we got nervous. It dropped a torpedo that ran just across our bow and hit the PENNSYLVANIA. It killed 149 quartermasters. Then it dived into a Liberty ship that was unloading. We went over and assisted it, but we didn't give them any of our beer.

We had a daily allowance of two beers. I bought out seven other guys rations, which gave me 16 per day. I sold 8 of them to pay for mine and came out pretty good. Of course, I never had that many in one day.

My gun trainer *(he makes the gun go around while I do up and down and shoot)* copped a plea that his wife was pregnant. Our CO *(a young lieutenant)* believed his story and let him go home. Can you believe that!

After the war we got sent to Japan and China. Once while in China, we were surveying the Yangtze River. We could make 8 knots, and the river made 8 knots. That was interesting. Anyhow, the Communists came screaming in and we went out in 1945. I got the A-P Theater Ribbon and Japanese and Chinese ribbons. By the way, this is a nice way to handle Saddam *(I talked to Dave at 2100hrs 16 January)*.

Dewey "Smitty" Smith was a Navy pharmacist mate on LSTs and PT boats. True to his home state, Smitty was on the USS MARION COUNTY. Smitty's war went something like this:

I was in the Nimitz Theater going wherever he sent us. At different

times, I was in on the invasions of
the Philippines and Okinawa. I
hauled the 2nd Marines to Nagasaki
and took an Army group to Hiroshima.
I even hauled a USO group from
Mindanao to Luzon. Now, that was a
trip. We all got these stars on deck
to pose for pictures. Only trouble
is, we had run out of film months
before! We got some nice poses
though. The worst I had it was being
attacked by kamikazi planes toward
the end. They were dropping all
around us but never hit my ship.
Smitty says he ran into H.I. Harris in
Pearl Harbor one time. He earned the A-P
Theater Ribbon with two battle stars and
was activated for Korea.

Ira Dale Watson was at Pearl Harbor
for the bombing party. Then he served
aboard a PT boat throughout the Pacific
trying to pay them back. He had
reasonable success at the Battle of
Leyte. He knocked a Zeke out of the air
with a set of machine guns he had
salvaged from a drowned American plane
and installed by his boat station. The
significance here is that Dale was a
radioman. It was also early in the war
and his boat had not been armed yet. In
this war of give-and-take, he then lost
his boat to a tracer bullet from a
Japanese cruiser. To add insult to
injury, Dale lost all his belongings,
including $300.00 in back pay (ouch).
Dale then transferred to the Aleutian
Islands for the Battle of Attu. He lost
his second boat there when it collided
with a sister craft during an Arctic
storm.

SMITH

The County is fortunate in having plenty of Smiths. They certainly made their presence felt. The Henleyfield branch provided brothers Q.C., Clinton, and Delbert in different theaters. Delbert was in the Navy and never left the States. Clinton was in the Army in Europe. We'll see his story at the Bulge. Q.C. was all over the Pacific islands with the Navy:

I went over in 43 to Windy Island in New Guinea and joined a tender for a motor torpedo squadron for the first six months of my tour. I got to be real good friends with the Chief because I was one of the few torpedomen who could go inside the fish and know what was going on. The Chief tried to get me to stay when I got transferred to a PT boat. I wanted to get the R and R to Australia after six months, so I went on. Two weeks later a kamikaze hit the tender right in the torpedo room and killed the Chief *(another charmed life in the making here).* The boat was 80 feet long and 20 feet wide. At slower speeds it had about a 5-foot draft. It was supposed to do 55 knots, but we were always loaded down with four torpedoes, a .40-mm gun on the rear, and 17 men. We could do only 45 to 48 knots. At that, we'd still leave the Jap ships behind. We'd blow right by them! Our hulls were made of plywood so they wouldn't attract mines. Our squadron had 13 boats and two planes.

127

While I was on PT boat 188 I had many experiences. We got to Leyte Gulf just after the fight. Then we escorted a convoy up to Mindoro. We went all the way in to Luzon at night within ten feet of the beach and took depth settings. Then we ran 200 miles south to set up a mock invasion before the real one. After that we went to Zamboango two or three weeks before the invasion and stayed there until it was secured. We ended the war patrolling rivers in British North Borneo.

We'd go out every afternoon, seven days a week, about 4 o'clock because we were a "bastard" outfit. Since our missions were mostly secret, we were just given a course and speed to make. After two hours, we would open our orders. One time, we were listening to Tokyo Rose for a laugh. She came on and told us where we were, what we were going to do, and that it would be very hot for us there. Sure enough, we ran into a lot of fire! It made you feel funny. One time we were under attack, and our CO took a .50-cal. across his shoe top, and it only cut his shoestring. He put himself in for a Purple Heart and got it! I was trying to unjam our .40 when I cut myself. I didn't notice it, so blood ran all over my side. The CO tried to put me in for a Heart, but I told him there'd be no days like that. I might get my head blown off tomorrow! I saw Raymond Allen. He was an officer on a tincan we were getting fresh water from. He grabbed

128

me like a lost brother. I also saw
Purvis Hall.

Julius Kellar, Navy, served in the
Pacific theater. I mean, he served all
over the Pacific. On the good ship USS
BILOXI Julius participated in 13 battles
including Iwo Jima *(BILOXI was a cruiser.
She screened fast carrier attack groups,
bombarded shore installations, and
covered amphibious landings at Eniwetok,
Truk, Marianas, Palau-YapUlithi-Woleai,
Hollandia, Truk-SatawanPonape, Saipan,
Philippine Sea, Bonins, Guam, Chichi
Jima, Luzon, Leyte, Iwo Jima, and
Okinawa. BILOXI was a real workhorse!)*.
When the BILOXI was hit by a kamikazi
plane, Julius transferred to the USS
GENERAL S.D. STURGIS. Julius was on board
in Tokyo Bay for the peace talks and the
Japanese surrender. Julius was there!--to
the tune of 13 battle stars, Julius was
there *(almost as prevalent as Kilroy)*.

CASANOVA
The exploits of the Casanova family
(NO, not THAT Casanova family), appear in
the annals of Naval history for several
mid-20th century wars. I talked to W.R.
"Bob" about his war:
I was in the service fleet on the
tanker, AO-49, the USS SUAMICO, in
the Pacific. I made eight invasions
on her from Eniwetok to Tarawa,
Kwajelein, and Ulithi. I was in the
fire room at Okinawa when the war
ended with the 7th Fleet. *(The USS
SAUMICO had an illustrious history.
From his islands he mentions, Bob
must have set sail 18 January '44
with Task Force 52 for the Marshall*

129

Islands invasion. She made Kwajelein in February, then to the New Hebrides, back to the Marshalls, and on to Saipan 23 June.. The SAUMICO was in Eniwetok for the month of July. After a yard period in the US she went to Hollandia, New Guinea 16 October. On 26 October she was attacked in the Leyte Gulf. After cruising around she supported the Lingayan invasion. In January '45 she shot down a Zeke off Mindoro. After that, the tanker made Ulithi, the Carolines, and the Volcano Islands where she watched the flag being raised on Mt. Surabachi. The ship beat off two more attacks in February. Next she was sent in for the invasion of the Ryukus in April. While joining up with the MISSOURI, she ran aground and had to be towed off. Then she was at Buckner Bay and was in Ulithi when the war ended.)
Then they took me off at Tokyo Bay to stand MP duty in Yokosuka. I didn't get to get on the MISSOURI when the peace was signed because they only took the higher grades.
One time we were escorting the USS MISSOURI *(see above for details)*. We had five Jap plane silhouettes and they had one. One of their officers asked how we had shot down five. I asked him how he had shot down one! Later a guy told me I had been talking to "Bull" Halsey himself.
Another time I was on a mail run. It was foggy, and so was I- kinda daydreaming about my brother on the USS MEADE (DD-602). I remember thinking about wouldn't it be funny

if he came in. Sure enough, later on he did *(talk about deja vu)*. We got together for the day. That was my brother, William C. "Bo." I also saw my stepmother's nephew on an aircraft carrier, the USS LISCOME BAY. I asked if there was anyone from Picayune on board and was told to wait while they went to get a Cuevas. Before they could get back, the LISCOME came under attack and cut our lines. I never did see him, and she was torpedoed about an hour later *(USS LISCOME BAY was sunk 23 November '43 20 miles SW of Butaritori Island. They had been preparing for a dawn launching when a Jap sub fired a torpedo into the engine room at 0510hrs. At 0533hrs the ship listed to starboard and went down with 54 officers and 591 enlisted. 272 were saved.)*.

In Korea I was on the "Jolly Roger'" the USS JOHN R. CRAIG (DD-885) from June '50 to June '51. We did picket duty off the coast for battlewagons and carriers.

Bob earned the A-P Medal, Korean Medal, Victory Medal, and nine battle stars. His brother, Van Arnold Casanova, was on the same ship in the Korean War. Yessir, Casanovas all over the place during mid-century.

SMITH

The Smith brothers from Crossroads turned in a good performance during this war. In a total of about 13 years on or near the front lines, not one of the boys received so much as a scratch. Lavelle C. was an anti-aircraft gunner with the Army in the Philippines, and fought through the rest of the war. Oliver E. was in the pipe department, Army. He started in England in 1941, walked all the way through North Africa, Sicily, and Italy, and ended the war in France. Clyde was in the Navy. He was at Saipan, Iwo Jima, and Okinawa as a bosun's mate. Roy was also in the Navy, and we hear all this from him:

> I got there just in time to reinforce Saipan on the USS LOWNDES. Then we landed on Iwo Jima. I was on Boat 6 carrying the 4th Marines ashore at Yellow Beach. It was my 19th birthday (19 February '45). Oh, yes, we had a lot of fireworks!
>
> At the battle of Iwo Jima we were part of the first group at the base of Mt. Suribachi. I was carrying troops and supplies back and forth for seven days. I was supposed to be a signalman, but our boat driver lost his nerve, and I had to do the driving. I had been around boats all my life. We pulled in for a coffee break once, and the Japs poured down on us from Suribachi. This was after the flag raising. We thought the island was secure. That was quite a birthday!
>
> Then we went back to Encento Sartos to pick up the 2nd Marines for the invasion at Okinawa (1 April). We lost 12 out of 25 ships there just off the air strip. We were the feint. One plane dove at us, but missed. I was hanging over the side and didn't get to shoot at him. I could see the whites of his eyes.
>
> We went back to Saipan (18 April).

Eleven of us were relieved and told we could go home. I had to work my way home as a cook on a cargo ship! There was no available transportation. I had gotten to San Francisco when the war ended. It was funny. I was supposed to go to an aircraft carrier, but I got sick in boot camp. Since my class had already gone, I was assigned as a signalman on small boats. I still don't know how I got to be a signalman.

Roy didn't see anybody he knew. He found out when he got home that his brother, Clyde, was on Saipan, Iwo, and Okinawa at the same time he was. Roy earned the A-P Medal with 3 battle stars. Of that, he says:

I didn't pay a whole lot of attention. As long as we were fighting, I was okay. It was the sitting around and waiting I didn't like. On this war *(Gulf)* I think we got out too quick. We should have gone on, got Hussein, and whipped him good.

Prentis James, Navy, was on four different submarines. On one, he met Emile Williams of Picayune. On another, he was with a pack mining a strait; the idea was for the subs to lay mines, and the planes to bomb same. One of the planes got shot down, and Prentis' pack picked up the future president, George Bush.

Speaking of subs, we are presented with William Shirley Stovall, Jr. (deceased). Street in Picayune named after his family. What did Shirley

133

Stovall do, you ask? Good question. He earned two Navy Crosses for his work in WWII. This makes him the highest decorated person in Pearl River County; not most, highest. From several sources we are able to get a glimpse of this man's work (Ray Seal, Norman Stockstill, *Silent Victory* by Clay Blair, Jr.).

Shirley's first command was an exchange boat, the USS GUDGEON. He was to go to Freemantle in the sub by way of Truk. The command duty was considered foolish because Shirley had been to codebreaking school (*This is probably where he earned the two Navy Crosses. There is no way he could have overcome the backstabbing campaign perpetrated upon him by his executive officer and earned anything. Stay tuned.*). Stovall was credited with 4 ships sunk for 35,000 tons on this patrol. He also survived a vicious depth charge attack. Stovall was shaken by "the depth charges and heavy responsibility of command" in his own words and requested to be relieved in 1942. Stovall's commander said he had cracked up.

Stovall took over GUDGEON again and attacked four separate convoys. His commander credited him with three sinks for a total of seven, worth 57,000 tons. His exec went over the commander and discredited all but one. Then Halsey praised the exec (*sound familiar?*) and ommitted Stovall. Remember, Shirley has already earned two Navy Crosses.

After five patrols Stovall and the GUDGEON were ordered to the Philippines to land a party of guerillas on Nagros Island. Then Stovall and his exec argued about whether to enter Lingayen Gulf.

They were heavily attacked by a subchaser and only escaped because a storm covered them. They had to perform some major at-sea repairs. Stovall then received orders to evacuate a party of guerillas off Timor. They had all kinds of diseases, but Shirley evacuated them all safely. After this patrol his exec put him on report for not being aggressive enough *(To a man with two Navy Crosses. Is this man playing with all his bubbles intact, or is he just an Academy graduate? Whiskey Tango Foxtrot!)*

We pick up Shirley one more time in 1944 as skipper of the USS DARTER. He patrolled off Eniwetok, Ponape, and Truk and sunk nothing. Then he went on patrol and missed all his targets there.

(We can assign credibility to the executive officer, Dornin, according to the American Naval Fighting Ships dictionary one more time. Shirley's patrols were highlighted by: first (GUDGEON's second) scored two kills on two unknown marus on 26 and 27 March, drydocked in record time; second, made the Battle of Midway as part of the submarine screen; third, sank NANIWA MARU in a night submerged attack on 3 August and an aggressive attack on a four-ship convoy on 17 August; fourth, sunk 8,783 ton CHOKU MARU on 21 October and carried out a daring attack on a seven-ship convoy 11 November and; five, carried out the two guerilla actions 4 January and 10 February '43. While skipper of the DARTER Shirley was blamed for missing shots by Blair, his exec on that boat. In fact, DARTER reconned Eniwetok 12 January '44, scored a torpedo hit on a large ship and received a severe depth charge attack 13 January,

and stood by on the carrier air strikes of Truk in February. My job is not to editorialize -well, not too much - so you decide what kind of submariner Shirley Stovall was for yourself.)

Once Shirley Stovall came to Picayune High School during the war. He was a LCDR at that time, but had already skippered a sub *(Ray Seal)*. He said that, if they sunk two ships, they tied a broom to their flag on entering port to show they had made a clean sweep. Shirley had done that.

Shirley Stovall, he's been dead for years. He used to be my neighbor about 150 feet away. *(This was given us by Lorena Thigpen, who reminded me she was 95 years old.)*.

Arlie Lott, 27th Infantry, served on Saipan, Guam, Okinawa, and Iwo Jima. Arlie described it as follows:

I didn't get into any of the action on Saipan. I came up on General Buckner just after he got killed. We got 21 Japs out of holes, and I saw the jumps at Suicide Cliffs *(Many Japanese committed suicide by jumping into the ocean rather than surrender. Many of these were civilians.)*. I have a doctor friend at the Gulfport VA now. He was with us on Saipan, but we didn't get together until after we got home. I also ran into George Spiers from McNeil.

On Guam we were hunting Japs out of caves. I was only there for a few days. We were supposed to take captives if we felt like it; but we were young, so we didn't take many.

136

One time we had a cave full we couldn't get out. We got the idea to tie a rope to a 55 gallon drum full of high octane fuel. Then we swung it back and forth into the cave until it went deep enough. When one of the guys shot it with a tracer round, that brought 'em out!

The war was most necessary if ever there was one. I only hope they finish this one in a hurry *(I called Arlie at 1900hrs 16 January 1991, about one hour after we found out we were at war again in Operation Desert Storm with Iraq.)*.

Clyde Welch was with the Army; the 749th Field Artillery, to be exact. Clyde was with the only group of 8" howitzers in the Pacific. His war went like this:

I went into Okinawa after the Marines and Army had secured a beachhead. While we were waiting to go in, we got pretty worried about the Jap suicide planes. They were hitting all around us; we were in such a large convoy.

Easter Sunday 1945. I was the gunner in my battery. We loaded 200 pound projectiles with 50 pounds of powder and a fuse. I pulled the cord that fired the first artillery round on Okinawa. It was a shame, but with my gun's ten mile range, I blew up a brewery in Naha. It was a direct hit!

I was there when the war ended. Because of the seniority rotation system, I had to stay over for a while. My group was sent to Pusan, Korea. We actually carried Japs back

to Sasebo, Japan, on LSTs. Can you
believe that? They lost, so we
carried them home, gave them a dip
for critters, and gave them some new
clothes. That felt strange.
Clyde got home in April '46 after all the
parades and hoopla were over. All he remembers about glory and medals is that he
"survived to come home." *Amen*.

Turner J. Deshotel was in the 1874th
Aviation Engineers in WWII and the 981st
Army Engineering Construction Battalion
for Korea. Mr. Deshotel remembers:
I was on British and Dutch New
Guinea, Leyte, Mindoro and Mindanao,
and on the way to Japan when the war
ended. I was one of the lucky ones
and saw very little action. On
Mindoro we built runways for the
"Jolly Rogers," B-24s or 25s. On
Leyte we built short, quick runways
for P-38s to drop in, fuel up, and
get out. One night Jap paratroopers
dropped in on us, and the sky was
lit up all night.
Other people I knew? It was funny.
Coming home through the replacement
depots, I saw thousands of people,
none of whom I knew.
The war now (Desert Storm)? I'm for
it. If we don't get him over there
he'll be over here.
Turner was there in 1944 and 45.

FLYNT
The Flynt family seems to have been
rather active for several generations.
Brothers Samuel Aurelius, Elmo D., James
W. "Jimmy," and Robert Fay were all the
the war. Jimmy was in the Navy, and the

138

rest were in the Army. Elmo started in Hawaii and went through the Pacific on such islands as Palmyra, Christmas, and Okinawa. Jimmy was in the Air Force in Korea too. Aurelius' son, Jimmy, was in the Army in Vietnam. Elmo's son, Greg, was also in Vietnam with the Special Forces.

KUCHLER/ESCUDE

From Alice Kuchler we get a family tie over many generations of veterans. Her grandfathers fought in The War Between the States. One, a Captain Von Stubbe, had something wrong with his legs and served as a surgeon for the Glorious Cause. Her husband, Norman, was in the Seabees in the Pacific. he built gun emplacements in Panama *(no doubt for Paul Lagarde's use)*, helped rebuild Hawaii, and built installations on Guam from '43 through '45. Alice's son, Lonnie Escude, spent five and a half years as an Air Force microwave electronic specialist. Her son, Jeff Escude, was a linguist with the Marine Corps. Through all that, Alice has a story:

> I have been corresponding with some Russians. I wrote a letter to PRAVDA in Moscow about freedom not being free when the *(Berlin)* wall came down. I got about 85 letters back. Then we sent another card to our friend congratulating them. We were at a reunion, so we had everyone sign the card and put their addresses on it. Now the Russians want more letters on personal US soldier war experiences.

Alice herself of the first two female MPs appointed in the Army at Newport News.

She also helped set up the port of embarkation. Oh, yes, her first husband was a veteran, too. Quite a story.

STOCKSTILL

There was a passel of Stockstills on hand for the draft, all in the Army. Ira L. went in just after the war. Allen and Alvin L. were in Germany. Arvin Adolph and Arthur E. were in the Pacific. Arthur tells us:

> I started in New Guinea and stayed for 22 months as an airborne engineer between '43 and '45. We parachuted in after the island was taken and built air strips. One time I got to see Bob Hope and a USO show on New Guinea.

Arthur thinks this war with Iraq worked out well *(interviewed 7 March 91)* because it was well planned. He says the bombing helped out a lot.

Arvin Adolph Stockstill, 129th Infantry, Company A, took part in the North Solomons invasion and the Luzon campaign. He received the Purple Heart with two oak leaf clusters, Bronze Star, and the Philippine Liberation Ribbon with bronze star.

A.W. "Goofy" Stockstill was in the V-4 Division, Naval Intelligence, in Admiral Nimitz's office at Pearl Harbor. Goofy is full of stories like this:

> I reenlisted with four other guys from Picayune. Three of them had graduated from Mississippi State and I never finished high school. Well, I got into the Naval Intelligence, and none of them could. One got turned down for military duty and went on to play pro football. That's

the truth.

The Americans broke the Japanese code very early in the war. We learned "Maru" meant ship, so the Japs may as well have been sending their messages in English. We kept files on every bit of intelligence. When subs, planes, or anyone came in, we could tell them things like the last reported position of an enemy ship, etc. As an example, we found out Admiral Yamato was taking a private plane somewhere, made a phone call, and, BLAM, no more Yamato.

I saw rush films of the Battle of Tarawa. We had many bombs dropped there to soften them up for a landing, and sent the Marines in. Just about the time they got to the beach, the tide turned. We landed on a reef and had to disembark too early. Then it really turned because all the Japanese in the whole world came out of pillboxes and started pouring lead into us. They slaughtered the Marines. About three days later reinforcements arrived to a beach full of bloated Marine bodies. That must have done something because, when the new Marines got there, they kicked the holy hell out of the Japs. They killed all but three, and cut the clothes off them before interrogation. That was gruesome. The news never got hold of that film.

I got to see all kinds of people, being in Pearl Harbor. At one time or another, Jack Boone, Norman Kendricks, Bill Dyle, and Fred "Red"

Cochran came through. I had gone
over on a ship wih Red two weeks
after he won a boxing championship.
The Army drafted everyone then. I
saw him two years later on his way
back to defend that title. Joe Lewis
was another story. He defended his
title while in the Army and donated
all of his winnings to the
Government. Then he ended up broke,
and the Government wanting more
money from him.
I got to come home after being away
for two years because I had a
serious ulcer. I was informed that
my brother, Norman, was MIA. Because
I was a good gambler, I had won and
saved a lot of money for those days.
One time my Chief got taken in a
game, so I loaned him $20. That got
me my pass home. On the way I had to
go to the hospital in San Diego. A
guy I got to know rather well was
travelling with me. One day he took
this sack out of his seabag. When I
asked hiom what it was, he showed
me. It was a dried Jap's skull he
was taking home!
We'll meet Goofy's brother, Norman,
later.

Speaking of Tarawa, Frank Donath was
with the Marines, 2nd Division. Frank
started out in New Zealand:
I went to New Zealand for training
and staging. Then our unit got sent
to Guadalcanal. I fought my way
across that island about 80 miles,
including Bloody Ridge for about
four months or so (6 August 1942 to
9 February 1943). I got hit in the

eye with a piece of shrapnel, so I went back to the hospital tent. The airport beside us was bombed right after I got there, so I went back to the front line where it was quieter! Guadalcanal was nasty because the Japs kept trying to retake it with everything they had *(The number 7 HORNET was sunk here.)*.I also got foot rot, malaria, and yellow jaundice here. When we first got to Guadalcanal a monkey got under one of the guys mosquito net one night. We all started shooting at the noise. Since we were so green, we were a little nervous. No, we didn't hit the guy-or the monkey! We had to fight with Springfield '03s. Talk about old equipment.

After that we got sent to New Zealand to stage our invasion of Tarawa (21 November 1943). That was a rough one *(the bloodiest battle in WWII)*. I got shot in a tail cheek. My buddy just put sulfur on it, and I kept on fighting. We were on the island of Betio with "Howlin Mad" Smith. We got dumped and had to swim and wade to shore. I was with a group that took a pillbox. We had to use flamethrowers. The walls were 15 feet thick. On this island we were issued M-1s. I fought all the way through the Gilberts for about two months. *(Because of no maps, the coral fringing reef of Tarawa was not known about. The tide went out during the assault and left the landing craft high and dry and the 2nd Marines stranded in the lagoon. About a third of them were killed*

*during the first three days until
reinforcements came.)*
Then our unit got sent to Hawaii for
deployment home to train our replacements. We kept being told we
would be sent home, but, of course,
that never happened. We were next
sent to Saipan (15 June 1944) on the
first wave with "Howlin' Mad" again.
Even though I was a machine gunner,
we were issued carbines for this
island. I fought there for 19
days. We had to take Mount Tapotchau
and go to the end of the island. We
had a <u>banzai</u> attack one time. They
came one night, all drunk on sake.
One Jap was even dragging his gun by
the barrel! I piled up so many dead
Japs with my machine gun that I had
to move the gun so I could see them
coming. This time I got hit really
bad (right shoulder) and that ended
my war. *(The 2nd and 4th Marines
suffered 13,000 casualties, including 3000 killed.)*
I worked my way back through various
hospitals. My mother thought I was
MIA. The only person I ever saw that
I knew was a doctor friend of mine.
I looked up from the stretcher, and
there he was. He got in touch with
my mother. He also got the doctor
who was tending me to do a good job.
I really had no complaints. We
weren't ready for a war in the
Pacific. We were not very well
equipped, but the leaders did a good
job with what they had. The bad part
was the lack of ships. They'd take
you in to an island, drop you off,
and leave. It was sink or swim for

Marines landing at Saipan (Frank Donath).

*Some of our Marines didn't go
too far up the beach on Tarawa
(Frank Donath).*

*Landing craft on Guadalcanal
(Frank Donath).*

Recipe for Jap flambe: (a) drop one smoke bomb in hole inhabited by one or more Japs while being backed up by a flame thrower, (b) when fresh Jap rises, flame him. Presto, Jap flambe! (Frank Donath).

What happens when you mess with
the Uncle

Buster Strahan's paratrooper.

Japs at recreational sumo
wrestling on Guadalcanal before
the US Marines showed up. This
was developed from a roll of
film Frank Donath took from a
dead Jap.

Nose art in the Pacific on two
of the longer-lived planes (Paul
Nichols)

Paul Nichols in his more
youthful days. He'd rather have
been aloft.

150

Q.C. Smith and his PT boat, the
188. Q.C. is on the right.

Battlewagon USS ALABAMA

152

us.

Frank received one Purple Heart and the
A-P Medal with three battle stars. I
asked him how he got the pictures we're
using in this book, and he said:

We weren't supposed to have cameras,
but we all did. During lulls in the
fighting, we'd take a few pictures
of the happenings; each one with a
camera would. We also picked up film
off the dead Japs. Then we gave them
all to the medic X-ray technicians.
They developed them and made copies
for all of us. No, I didn't shoot a
gun with one hand and the camera in
the other! *(Oh, 50 tanks just
surrendered to the Egyptians. Good
[we're talking 0900hrs 17 January
1991. More Operation Desert Storm.
The older veterans seem to be
enjoying this good old ass
whipping!])*.

James L. Carbonette was with the
Marines from 1940 to 1946. He remembers:

I was with the 10th Marines, 1st
Battalion, VF-142. We staged on New
Caledonia and went to Guadalcanal to
relieve the assault troops. I stayed
there 11 or 12 months. So many of us
got diseases, we had to go to the
New Hebrides and back to San Diego
to regroup. I still get malaria
attacks.
Then I landed on Okinawa on Easter
Sunday morning. I was in on the
first and last offensives. After
that I flew up to Japan for the
occupation.

Jim went in with Leo Thigpen, Jr. and
Henry Campbell. He saw Rayford Thigpen on

Okinawa.

"It was scary as hell."

BAKER

David W. Baker was a machine gun-
ner/ electrician with the 206th Antiaircraft Batallion. He says:

I left in December 1943 for Hawaii.
Then I went to Eniwetok, Saipan,
Tinian, and Iwo Jima. We had a few
air raids, but no action to speak
of. I kept the generators running to
turn the 40 mm ack-ack guns- kind of
like power steering on a car. We did
shoot down one Jap plane in an air
raid.

David received the A-P Medal with two
battle stars. He saw Cornelius Wise from
Henleyfield over there because Wise was
with another battery in the same outfit.
David's son, Daniel, was in the Guard for
six years. His great-grandfather, Bullock
Wise from Covington County, was in The
War Between the States.

Vernon Catha, 6th Army Division
company clerk, made the Pacific theater.
Vernon says he was always "near the
action:

I was on a WWI boat for about 63
days, the USS REPUBLIC, going to
Guadalcanal (sailed 31 March 1944).
We got a message about some sort of
outbreak, so we went to Milne Bay,
New Guinea (got there 12 June). Then
we went to Hollandia and Toem. We
got to see three air raids one
night.

Ernest "Bud" Lovell was in the 10th
Battalion Concor from 1944-46. His main

154

action was in the Philippines something like the following:

> I started out going to Guam. Then they sent us on a landing craft to the northen part of Luzon. We fought our way toward Clark Field and reestablished Fort Stossenberg. Then we went down to Manila, where 2100 Filipino Scouts joined us. They were mostly the Americans left over from Bataan and Corregidor who had been fighting as guerillas *(like Morris Megehee)*. We then became a construction battalion at war's end. I enjoyed the Filipino people and saw a baseball stadium with Ruth, Gehrig, and others' names on it.

Bud was a Sergeant-Major, and earned the A-P Medal and Philippine Liberation Medal.

NAPIER

John H. Napier III was in the Marines in the A-P in '45 and '46, but he wants to tell us about some of the earlier veterans in the Napier family:

> I would like to note that my father, the late Dr. John H. Napier, Jr. served as a sergeant, US Army, in WWI; that three of my great grand-fathers and one great-great grand-father served in the Confederate States Army; that my great-great-great grandfather, John Staples Napier, served in the 24th Infantry in the War of 1812; that his father, Ashford Napier, served as an officer in the American Revolution; and that his grandfather, Robert Napier, Sr. served in Virginia in the Colonial Wars *(We're talking about a heavy*

155

dose of patriotism and family pride hereand, rightly so.).

In June 1945 at the USMC replacement center on Guam, I met Paul Balaski of Picayune and that December in Sasebo, Japan, was with Jack Nix, who had been my father's football coach at Picayune High School in 1943-44. These were two amazing coincidences when one considers that 13 million Americans served in WWII. In that summer of 1945, on Guam, I saw a USO show featuring Hollywood personalities and "hoofers" Donald O'Conner and Peggy Ryan. Earlier, in 1942 and 1943, I twice met Bob Hope and got his autograph.

John had a long, illustrious career, and we'll pick him up again in Vietnam.

Several gallant veterans died during these campaigns: Leroy Sampson died from a wound in the abdomen he received on Leyte (16 December '44). Gene Clifton Ladner was killed in action at Okinawa (6 April '45) aboard the destroyer, USS BUSH. *(The BUSH was operating as a radar picket ship at Okinawa. At 1515hrs a Jap suicide plane hit the starboard side, causing a bomb or torpedo to explode. A rescue ship coming to assist was sunk. At 1725hrs a second suicide plane hit the port side and nearly severed the ship. At 1745hrs the coup-de-grace was delivered by yet another kamikaze plane. The ship's ammunition caught fire and exploded. Heavy swells caved her in, and she folded and sank.)*

The amphibious forces had plenty of air support in their endeavors, and that

156

air support had its attendant support. Pearl River County was again represented. Delos Burks, Army Air Corps of the "Snafu Snatchers" Air-Sea Rescue Organization of the 13th Jungle Air Force, worked in close support of bomber and fighter strikes. His plane, a B-17, was named "Ready Teddy." Delos's tour included 35 combat missions, totalling 357 hours, in such places as Netherlands East Indies, Admiralty Islands, Tarawa, New Guinea, Philippines, and Okinawa. On one occasion his plane brought back 25 airmen, and, on another, the "Teddy" was badly damaged and lost on the invasion of Balikpapin, Borneo. Delos' plane carried a motor boat underneath with enough rations on board for ten people for thirty days. His group saved over 700 downed pilots. Delos earned the Distinguished Presidential Unit Citation, the Air Medal with three oak leaf clusters, A-P Theater Ribbon with three battle stars, the Philippine Liberation Ribbon with one star, and the National Defense Ribbon *(from Clarion Ledger and Picayune Item)*. For more on Delos, he is under the section on the fighting Burks brothers.

Robert L. McDaniel was in the 4th Marine Air Wing in the Pacific. You've heard how great the F4-U Corsairs were. Robert's work was one of the reasons; he was a scout:

We went up in the lighter planes. There were two or three of us per 20 Corsairs. Our duty was to scout out strike areas and report back. I started out in Fiji in '43, went to the Marshalls for Kwajelein and Eniwetok, got to Saipan, and lost

157

all my outfit except for two or three planes at Iwo Jima. I went back to Guam for reassignment, but my tour and the war ended there.
Zekes put me in the water three times. Twice my pilots were killed. One time I spent the night in the water. I had on a Mae West for flotation, shark repellant *(which later proved to be ineffective)*, and a flare gun. I was plenty scared. I fired my flare gun the next day when somebody I recognized, a friendly plane or ship, got in my area, and a pontoon plane picked me up.

Robert's decorations have been lost over the years, but he is proudest of having won two Presidential Unit Citations.

Emmett Smith was involved in politicking for his son when I caught up with him. Emmett's story goes like this:
I was with the 13th Army Air Corps, 5th Bomb Group, on B-24s from '43 to '45. I flew as a nose gunner from New Guinea to the Philippines and back on 50 missions. We flew mostly against the marshalling yards in Formosa and all up and down the coast of China and never got hit. My plane was called the "Southern Comfort." Yes, we had some of that, too.
We had an old, converted C-47. We called it the Bomber Baron's Airline and used it to bring in necessary supplies, such as beer. We'd stop at the end of the runway and kick out all we needed before we delivered the rest to the Quartermaster.
We had "Pisscall Charlie" over

there. He must have been on every island. Pisscall Charlie would pull fake air raid alarms at night to disturb us and try to get on our nerves. He was like Kilroy in that respect. He was everywhere. Kilroy was, too. He had gotten everywhere I went before I got there.

I was in the outfit with Shorty Barnes. He was 22 when he went down and became a KIA. Shorty's on the monument. I ran into Roy Newsome and Bill Archer. Roy built most of the schools around here. Bill, I forget where I saw him, Bill customized a Jeep. He had tear drop gas tanks on the front and a Pearl River County tag on the back. He was a line mechanic.

Our war was allright. This latest one (Iraq) wasn't a war. We proved our weapons, but we didn't get finished *(interviewed 27 October 1991)*. We also put the Japs on top of the world. They already own two-thirds of the United States. It's just not right, I tell you.

Emmett earned the A-P Campaign Medal with 5 battle stars, the Philippine Liberation Medal with bronze star, and an Air Medal with 4 oak leaf clusters among others.

Paul Nichols was a pilot with the 43rd Bomb Group, 65th Bomb Squadron of the 5th Air Force. Paul flew a lot of planes on a lot of missions:

My initial training was in a biplane, a Steerman PT-13. As I progressed, I wanted to fly B-26s because I had helped build them before I went in the Air Force *(Even though the Air Force was not officially formed until 1947, the WWII pilots called it that anyhow.).* Senator Truman did away with the B-26s, and the Army made the A-20 into the B-26. I ended up in a B-24. The itinerary for our flight overseas was from San Francisco to Oahu to Canton Island to New Caledonia to Australia to New Guinea at 160 mph at 10,000 feet in our brand new B-24.

I joined the "Lucky Dice" Squadron. The 4 and 3 of the 43rd make 7 and the 6 and 5 of the 65th make 11. These numbers were shown with dice on our tail sections. We flew out of Nadzab against the north area of New Guinea at first. My first mission was on 1 July '44. Ten men took off for a target five and a half hours away, Noemfoor Island. The Japs had large forces there. My first excitement was getting into the proper position for takeoff. We were carrying 18 300-pound bombs. I wondered if we'd ever get off the ground! Once we got off the ground, it seemed simple enough. All you had to do was follow the leader and open our bomb bay when he did. Then we spotted our target. At the same time, we spotted another Group flying towards us from the opposite direction, about 500 feet over us. I was not worried about the flak ahead of us, I was more worried about them dropping their bombs on us! That experience was our first combat goof. However, they dropped their bombs and missed us. On the way home we found a cloud cover over the mountains of our valley. There were no landmarks for quite a while, and we didn't have enough fuel to go anywhere else. Our only hope was that we were over the valley before we flew into a mountain wall. Remember, we didn't have any radar or navaids back then. Eventually we saw our river and followed it home. Man, we thought we were invincible after that!

Next we went to a new base on Owi Island from 26 June '44 to 24 November *(Fortunately, Paul was able to get all this information from his logbook.)*. I flew 23 missions out of there against ammo dumps, air strips, oil refineries, towns. Some were 16 hour missions, and the average was about 11. We carried fuel tanks in our bomb bays. We had about three days between missions. Because our crew was the same all the time, we became known as an extremely good crew. We led the second element on 20 August for the first time. We led the Squadron on 28 October for the first time. On 10 October we destroyed the Jap oil fields at Balikapapan on Borneo. They no longer had fuel to fly their planes *(I asked Paul why the Japanese did not invent an alternative to fossil fuels during the war since they did not have any. He said they were not smart enough until we gave them the technology. Interesting. We beat them so they could now beat us.)*. That was one of the toughest missions we flew. We

161

got over 100 holes in our airplane.
I lost my navigator. He was sitting
about six feet away from me, holding
open the bomb bay doors. An
explosive shell came through his
back pack and got him. There were
over 50 interceptors up there. They
were even using pontoon seaplanes. I
could see the face of one of the
pilots he was so close. We had the
whole 5th Air Force up there that
day. The Japs couldn't do anything
after that. They had little or no
fuel. On another mission out of Owi,
we made the first daylight raid on
the Philippines. There was a lot of
ack-ack and Zeroes around that day.
The pilot of the plane right behind
us got killed that day.
We moved to Leyte after that. There
was no wood on Leyte, so we had to
carry that and sometimes squadron
personnel from Owi to Leyte. We then
would fill up with fuel and bombs,
and go on up into the mountains. On
many of our flights from Owi to
Leyte we flew over a large contingent of US Navy ships, about 800 to
1000 of them in the Leyte Gulf. They
even shot at us! The engineering
guys had to do a lot of work so we
could fly out of our new base, so we
essentially took leave from November
to February '45. We went down to
Sydney, Australia, for two weeks, We
called that the "Battle of Sydney"
for obvious reasons. I was 22 and a
pilot. Our base was called Tacolo-
ban. My next door neighbor when I
lived in Ponderosa was an infantryman in those mountains then. His

name was Buster Everett (deceased). We flew ten relatively short missions against the likes of Hong Kong, Samah, and Formosa until March of '45. Then we moved to Clark Field above Manila. I'm glad they closed Clark and Subic Bay, by the way. We don't need all those bases over there.

My first mission was March 18th, and my last was April 15th, 1945. In between I flew six more for a total of 43 missions. The last mission was ten hours to Formosa. My logbook says "We missed the target, but I don't give a damn. I'm through." We had bad weather that mission. Anyhow, I got enough points and came home. My only accident was a nose wheel lock-down failure. We had sparks coming up through the cockpit you wouldn't believe. We got the heck out as soon as we could.

Paul Nichols. Pilot of B-24s par excellent.

British and Indian troops started up to Japan through Burma. Merrill's Marauders were with them. American troops were sent to Burma as part of the task force to remove the Japs and open an overland route from India to China. As though the fighting weren't bad enough, there was also typhus, malaria, and dysentery to contend with. These boys were all volunteers led by Frank Merrill under "Vinegar" Joe Stillwell. Dr. Ray F. Mitchell spent 23 months there *(Thanks for the background material)*. Wallace Dossett was also there as a heavy machine gunner. He earned the Asian Theater

Ribbon with two battle stars.

Ernie Hotard (deceased) flew the
"Hump" in the China-Burma-India Theater.
He used to sit in a hotel bar in India
and give a couple of civvies a hard time
every night after a hard day of flying.
Then he went on a mission in his B-17 and
got shot down over China. He carried his
musette bag wrong when he parachuted.
When he hit ground, he not only broke his
wrist but also cracked several neck
vertebrae. He had to fight his way out
with some Chinese guerillas. On the way
he helped put out a hospital fire, and he
broke his wrist again. When he came back
to Florida to be repaired, he was walking
down the street with a friend of his who
wanted to go to a John Wayne movie. On
the way a man stopped him and said
"Aren't you the guy who kept busting my
chops in India?" Ernie said he looked
almost familiar. Then he asked the same
about his companion. Ernie said he looked
a little more familiar. They turned out
to be John Ford *(director of the movie he
was going to)* and Ward Bond, a character
actor *(courtesy of Ernie's wife, Elnor)*.

*Air attacks were launched from the
Aleutian Islands. While we did not have
an Air Force per se, we did have planes-
many of them. In fact, many of them in
the Pacific.*
Emmett Smith was a nose gunner in a B-24
Liberator from 1943 to the end of the war
with the 394th Squadron of the 5th
Bombardment Group in the 13th Air Force.
His plane, "Southern Comfort," flew 50
combat missions. Leslie Albritton was in
Company A, 11th Battalion, 55th Regiment

as a longshoreman helping with supplies for the effort. Rodney W. Clukey, 11th AAF, joined the "I bombed Japan" club in 1943 following a successful raid of the Kurile Islands. He received the A-P Ribbon with the Aleutian Island battle star.

CARR

Vern and Roy Lowry Carr were in WWII. Their father, H.L. Carr, was in WWI. He was on a boat going over when the war ended, so they turned around and came home. This proved to be auspicious for the Carr family fortunes of war. Vern says:

> I was in the Air Corps. I was trained as a radio operator, then a gunner on a B-24. Somewhere in my tours of the U.S. between Miami, Sioux Falls, the Rio Grande, and Colorado I became a pilot of a P-47. I was on my way to Europe when that war ended. After a furlough, I came back for the Pacific war. About that time they dropped the big bomb, so I didn't get out of the States.
> I went in with "Minnow" Simmons and my cousin, Ruffin Lowry. All three of us signed up together, went in together, and were supposed to stay together. Sure enough, after basic training, we were sent to the four winds.
> My brother, Roy, was also in the Air Corps/Air Force for over 30 years. He went to the Aleutians early and flew P-40s against the Japs. He even knocked one down! Roy was in during Korea too, but not as a fighter. He had tours in Saudi, England, and

165

Germany- all over.
Vern thought the experience was interesting. At first he wasn't very fired up
over this war *(interviewed 2000hrs 13
February 1991)* with Iraq, but now he
thinks we're going the right way.

Edward Parker was already involved
when the war broke out. We've met his
brother, Bill, on the ARIZONA. Ed:
I was in in '39 before the war even
started in the Pacific. I was in the
Navy Aviation Engineers *(like the
Seabees)* up on Metlakatla Island,
about twenty miles out of Ketchikan.
It taken a year to build that runway, and we finished in 1942. I was
working for Gibby Holden *(Dobie's
father)*. One time a man from
Picayune landed on that strip. I saw
four or five pilots going to chow
and asked them if any were from
home. Lowry Carr had landed *(see
above)*.
I left there and went to Omnak, a
place in the Aleutians about 80
miles west of Dutch Harbor. We
finished there in late '44. I picked
up a "Life" magazine one day and saw
my brother *(article on Pearl
Harbor)*. That was the first I heard
about it.
Then we came back to the US to refit
for the invasion of Okinawa. I
helped build Kedina Air Base. The
last job I had was to build a 1000
man hospital. They dropped the
atomic bomb while I was there.
Ed put in 20 years with the Navy around
this war and Korea. He earned most of the
"normal medals for that area." Ed told me

166

what he could about his brother, and I put him at the start because he was our only representative on the ARIZONA.

C.J. "Cliff" Carbonette was in an over-30 group, the 5th Special Naval Construction Battalion. Now, keep in mind these guys were not mere lads. They were seasoned dockworkers before they were ever drafted. Cliff tells us:

We hold a reunion every year and still have our colors. We refuse to retire them even though the museum at Port Huaneme has repeatedly asked for the flag.

I never saw any war action other than what we created amongst ourselves. We worked on Attu, Adak, Kiska, and Dutch Harbor in the Navy's northernmost supply depots, loading and unloading ships. We thought we were going to be attacked on Dutch Harbor and dug in. We stayed there for three days. The attack was a sham.

One time I came home on leave. A friend had found a black goat, and he gave him to me as a pet. I sent the goat to Port Huaneme and tried to get him on board my ship from Bremerton back to the Aleutians. I sneaked him up the gangway under my peacoat, but got caught. I had to ask the Captain's permission, and he gave it even though the goat left a trail at his sailing party. We kept the goat in our barracks for a while until another group stole him. Of course, we organized a rescue party and got him back. The medics wanted us to get rid of him for health

167

reasons, but the wild dogs got him first.

Admiral "Black Jack" Reeves. We actually unloaded a cow for the Admiral. He was the only person up there who had fresh milk. One thing he didn't have was beer. We stole it. He'd have it special delivered, but we knew it was coming from the ship's manifest. Since it was always guarded by Marines, we loaded it on trucks way in the back so it would bounce out. Our trailing Jeep would pick it up and go hide it in the snow *(probably the only advantage to being in the Aleutians)*. We had some great parties! One day the Admiral sent a regiment of Marines on a search party...a whole regiment. Unfortunately, party HQ was in my tent of six. The first thing they discovered was a knothole in the floor, and, lo and behold, hundreds of beer bottle caps. Even worse, some idiot in our tent had just brought in two bottles wrapped in his poncho When it wasn't snowing, it was raining. The Admiral gave him 15 days bread and water. Us, we kept on stealing his beer!

The final drive on Japan was led by massive bombing. In the words of Donald Hale, who was a pilot at that time:

While stationed on Tinian Island in the Pacific in World War II, I served as a B-29 pilot. Most of our bombing missions were carried out at night; however, on this day, we made a daylight raid on a propeller factory at Osaka, Japan. Forming up approximately fifty miles from Osaka, we started our bomb run. The only fighters we saw were two Jakes, and they did not try to attack but were calling our speed and altitude back to the ground so that they could set their guns to fire exploding shells at our altitude.

Suddenly the sky was filled with puffs of black smoke where the flak shells were exploding. We could not deviate from our course and, as we got into the heavy flak, a B-29 off our wing got a direct hit and broke in two. Our tail gunner reported that he saw only one parachute as the B-29 plunged into Osaka Bay. We received 12 hits, but nothing vital was damaged; however, on our way back to Tinian, we had a fire erupt in our number two engine, it appeared we would have to bail out or ditch in the ocean. As fate would have it, we were nearing Iwo Jima, a tiny island which the Marines had recently captured from the Japs at a very high cost of lives. We made an emergency landing, and no one was injured. As our crew waited for a spare plane to fly back to Tinian, I spent most of my time looking at Mt. Surabachi where the Marines raised the American flag after capturing Iwo Jima. I wish they all knew how many B-29 crews they might have saved. Thank God for the Marines.

Delos Burks also was in on the softening up process by flying combat missions on August 1, 2, 3, and 5. On 6-9 August 1945 Fat Man and Little Boy were dropped on Hiroshima and Nagasaki. Delos flew one

last mission on the 9th just after Nagasaki. Japan surrendered 14 August 1945.

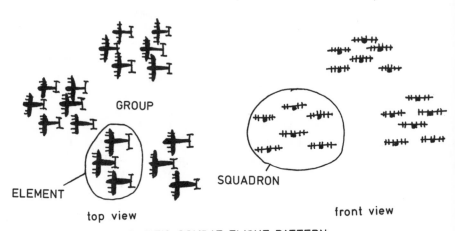

GROUP

ELEMENT

top view

SQUADRON

front view

PACIFIC COMBAT FLIGHT PATTERN

World War II (Africa and Italy)

Meanwhile, the Army got cracking on the other side of the world in November 1942 with the North African campaign. They drove the Germans out (May '43) and invaded and occupied Sicily (July-August '43). Rome was liberated next (June-August '44) after beachheads at Anzio and Naples. Battles in the North Appenines and Po Valley followed.

RING-DANG-DOO

When I was barely sweet sixteen,
The cutest thing you ever seen,
I was young and pretty, too,
I had what I called my Ring-dang-doo.

Oh, ring-dang-doo, what is that,
Round and soft like a pussy cat,
Round or square and slimy, too,
It's what you call my ring-dang-doo.

A pilot called one night at ten,
He slipped a pillow neath my head.
Taught me how to pitch some woo.
And how to use my ring-dang-doo.

REPEAT CHORUS

My mother said you've been a bad girl,
You've gone and lost your maiden curl.
So pack your socks and Kotex, too,
And take along your ring-dang-doo.

REPEAT CHORUS

So I set out to become a whore
And hung a sign on the old barn door.

From sweet sixteen to sixty two,
The pilots paid for my ring-dang-doo.
                    -Anonymous

I have to mention Dewey Palmer at the start. He started as a truck driver in the 106th Medical Regiment, and drove from Algiers all the way to Berlin with stops on the scenic tour at French Morocco, Tunisia, Sicily, Foggia, Rome, Arno, Southern France, Rhineland, and Central Europe. Dewey was with the 53rd QM TRK BN at Sicily. He got a commendation for extraordinary heroism on or about 1500hrs 11 July '43 near Gela. The transport ship ROBERT ROWAN caught fire from an enemy bomb. Dewey was cruising about in a DUKW waiting for a load from a nearby ship. When the ROWAN's crew started abandoning ship because an explosion was imminent, Dewey pulled up beside it and carried a capacity load to safety. Dewey received the European-African-Middle Eastern Theater of Operations Campaign (EAMETO) Medal with 8 battle stars and a bronze arrowhead. The EAMETO itself is probably obscured!

Hugh K. Wood also followed the same route for over three years. That should qualify him as a tourist agent! Richard Hastings was with the 88th Infantry Division, 2nd Battalion, 35th Infantry Regiment from Africa through southern Italy, where he was wounded at Cassino. Landris Thomas Lee, Sr. was with the 5th Army, 175th Combat Engineers from Tunisia through the Po Valley into France. William Otis Seal was in North Africa and Italy. Franklin Lumpkin, Jr. served in the ETO for 15 months with the 165th

172

Combat Engineers. Walter L. Penton served 22 months in Europe with the 339th Infantry. He earned a Purple Heart and, 45 years later, a Bronze Star. Warren Tynes was wounded in North Africa.

Pete DeMarsh led an interesting career starting with the 9th Air Corps in 1942 in North Africa:

I flew P-40s. In Africa there were several significant events. We were in Algiers in Moslem country *(We have been made familiar with Moslem law in this day and age.)*. Well, the Moslems could really interpret their bible *(Koran)* to suit them. There were all kinds of bars and whorehouses in Algiers. A Moslem could have four permanant wives and as many "temporary" ones as he might require. Our theme song then was "Lili Marlene," which the British borrowed from the Germans and brought with them from WWI. Algiers was a lot of fun.

After North Africa I went to Sicily and then to England with the 8th Air Corps. We became the 8th just before the invasion because they had lost so many men by '43. We went in as ground support and escort duty. The Germans had lost a lot of pilots by then, so we didn't have a great need for escorts.

Pete's war ended with an Air Medal and the EAMETO with 3 battle stars. He went back to college, and we'll pick him up in Korea.

SMITH

Connis Smith started in North Africa

with the 36th Infantry, the Texas National Guard. Talk about heavy duty! He has a tale; in fact, a Texas sized one:

I went to Oran, North Africa, on 1 April 1942. We were training in amphibious ops. On 9 September 1943 I was sent on the initial invasion of Salerno. We went ashore in Higgins crafts *(those boats that got shot to pieces and hung up on the reef at Tarawa)* at Pasteum. We got our butts kicked but held the beachhead for 12 days. Our intelligence information was a little off by sending us in against 4 to 1 odds! Next, I was committed at Cassino (15 October 1942-28 March 1943). After that we reorganized and went to Anzio.

We made the breakthrough and went on through Rome to just south of Pisa. Then we went back to Salerno for regrouping before being sent to Cannes, France. We met very little resistance, so we went on up the Rhone Valley to Vosges Forest. I got to Tendon and ran into a big shell. This shell hit a tree behind me, and that finished me for a while. I got sent back to Naples to the hospital, where I spent four months. While there I went to a Red Cross club. We had to sign in. Later I found out the next guy in was Bill and John Moody's brother. He came out looking for me, but no luck.

I went back to the front in Italy and made two more beachheads with the 34th Division. Then the war ended. I was lightly wounded at Cassino (3 January 1944) and wounded again (3 February 1944). On 26 September I ran into that big one. My opinion is that we had to stop Hitler. He was another Napoleon. He also used inhumane treatment of people. We were aware of what he was doing to the Jews in 1943. Saddam is Hitler all over *(interviewed 0900hrs 18 January 1991)*. Anyone who would use gas on his own people and give us unprovoked attacks on Tel Aviv and Haifa can have no regard for human life. We are doing the right thing.

Connis earned for all that heavy duty *(30 months over there without seeing "the first soul" he knew)* the Combat Infantryman Badge, Purple Heart with two oak leaf clusters *(wounded three times)*, five campaign stars, and three bronze arrowheads. This man has to walk with a port list! Connis' father, James M., was in WWI *(see writeup in that section)*. His brother, James D., was a driver in an Army artillery unit in the ETO. Another brother, Van B., was an Army quartermaster in Korea. His son, Waylon R., was in Vietnam *(see writeup in that section)*.

Hooker Quick was in the 67th Quartermaster Company. These guys supplied everyone with fresh food, and Hooker recalls his effort:

We worked with everyone. We had the first refrigeration trucks in the military. We took the trucks in on LSTs and drove them right up on the beaches. I went across North Africa to the boot of Italy. Then I went up to Florence, over to Marseilles, and up to Metz, where I was when the war

ended. I was over there 35 months
and survived strafings and bombing
raids. I bumped into Blaine Ewing,
Roy Stockstill, and a few others
from home. I think we did a good
job, and we're doing one now *(2115
hrs 16 January 1991-D plus 3 hours
15 minutes)*.

WOODWARD

Poor old Louis E. Woodard. He went
to North Africa with the First Armored
Division. Louis' story of 2 February '42
goes like this:

I was a gunner on a halftrack in
Company G. I had my helmet strapped
on just before we went into battle.
That was unfortunate because a concussion picked me up and knocked me
back about eight feet. It hurt my
neck, knocked my teeth loose, and I
was bleeding from my mouth and nose.
They sent me back to treat me, but I
only stayed about three hours. I
told them I wanted to go back for
the attack. We went up into Fed Pass
with Montgomery. Well, we took about
12 tanks and us into that blind
pass. There were cliffs on both
sides with holes in them, high up.
Sure enough, the Germans fired their
.88 morters and knocked us and the
back tank out. We couldn't go back.
I fired two and a half boxes of
shells through my water-cooled
machine gun. The water was boiling
...you could hear it. Then it
stopped and I got out and found
Robinson, one of the men on our
tank. Some of us got killed in the
first blast, and some got killed

trying to escape. We saw a hole and ran to jump in. I jumped astride a German in my hole! He was just as scared as I was and jumped out and left it to me. I stayed there for a while because they had me pinned down in a four machine-gun crossfire. Finally, Robinson called for me to get out. He had seen a column of men coming down a steep bluff and thought they were French. I took one look at the helmets and knew otherwise, but by then it was too late. The Germans took everything we had, even our rifle stocks. They loaded us up, and one German asked me "Hey, what are you doing over here?" One took my helmet off and said "New York, New York?" Then the German, who could speak English pretty well, said: "For you the war is over." They took us to Tunisia and put us in a barn. The next morning they put me on a plane to Naples. To my remembrance, I stayed there about a week and a half. A priest came up and saw me. He wrote my Daddy that I was doing allright, which I wasn't. The next part of my journey I went to Germany in a boxcar where everyone had to stand up. They would take us out for one hour and run us around in circles with our hands behind our necks. There was no air in the boxcars, only a small hole. they took us to Stalag 17B in Moosburg, then to several camps til we got to Hammerstein on the Polish border. There were about 10,000 of us there. They asked for volunteers to go work

on a farm, so about 25 of us said
yes. We stayed in an old dairy barn
and lived on the Irish potatoes we
dug. We got three a day.
I had two escape attempts. The first
time we kept digging up the brick-
bats on our floor. We dug a hole
that came out on the cliff that
formed one side of our camp. Me and
another guy made it out one night.
We stuck to the timber. That morning
the guy I was with wanted to get on
the road. I told him not to, but he
did it anyway. After we passed a
lady, the Germans caught us again
with their dogs. They took me to a
Russian camp and put me in a pen
where I had to stand up all the
time. They fed me one Irish potato a
day. Eventually, they took me to
another place. I sat down and talked
with a German who had been educated
over here. I told him I wanted to go
to Switzerland. He said he'd give me
a map, a compass, and a sack of
Irish potatoes, and I still couldn't
get to Germany. I became pretty
downhearted. The second attempt I
got caught before I got anywhere.
I saw some German atrocities. Before
I say this, I want you to know the
German soldiers were just like us.
They didn't like Hitler either. They
would tell us, but they couldn't say
it around another German. They never
knew who was SS. At Stalag 17B we
had one barracks full of Jews or
Russians, I don't know which. They
killed every one of them and had us
bury the bodies. The Germans tried
to get the people out of the bar-

racks. When they wouldn't come out, the Germans sent their attack dogs in. The people tore them apart and threw them back out a piece at a time. This infuriated the Germans, who threw a chemical into the building and gassed them. We had to bury them in burlap bags. If a bag wiggled, the Germans finished killing it before we buried it. Another time we had an outdoor latrine that you slid a box under. Every morning a detail took the box out, dumped it, and cleaned it. The Germans told a guy to do it. He said no, that he had done it the day before. They told him again. Same. The Germans left, and the guy sat down. When the Germans came back, one of them shot the guy through the back and killed him. You had to go along with them after that.

The Germans got us one morning and marched us to another camp for a few days. They were cutting trees behind them so that they fell like this (jackstrawed) to hinder the Russians. One German came up to me and told me Hitler had ordered him to kill all the Allied prisoners, "but I'm a Pollock," he said. "I'm going to open the gate for you, and the Americans are four miles from here." I ran up to a black man marching beside a tank and said "Man, you look good!" The Germans were taking off all their weapons and throwing them in a ditch. They were putting on civilian clothes as fast as they could.

I weighed 170 when they caught me. I

weighed 87 pounds then. When you're in a place like that, you don't eat any fats. You have no blood pressure problems. Sometimes we got a little meat. We had no tobacco. Towards the end we started getting Red Cross packages. I guess the German officers were taking them before that. Anyhow, the German guards didn't think the US had anything because of the propaganda. Once we started, it was good. We made hot water by stripping two wires, twisting them on a stick, and laying it across a bucket of water. It would boil. I put a lump of sugar in mine one day and gave it to a guard with a cigarette. He even sat down his gun to enjoy that!

That was Louis Woodward. Liberated in May of 45 after 39 months in captivity. What a man! Now he has to be put on a diet. I tell you, there's no justice at all! Some of the Woodwards are Woodards, but they're all the same. Louis' brothers, James and Jake, were in the Army. James was in the Army Engineers in Italy during WWII. Jake was in the Army in Korea. Louis' uncle-in-law, James Ottis Hayes, was in the Pacific during WWII with the Army. Louis' brothers-in-law were there. Jerry Judon Sellers was in the Navy and fought with MacArthur in the Pacific. Clarence Edward Sellers was in the Navy in WWII and then joined the Marines. James Baisel Sellers was in the Navy from 1954 to 1974. James had two sons in the military. James Vector Woodard was in the Air Force. Jerry was a Green Beret in Vietnam. Jake had two veteran kids. Jake Junior was in the Army in 'Nam. Sylvia

Joyce Woodward served one tour in the Army and is now in the Navy. Louis' daughter, Zora Lane Woodward, served in the Air Force during the Vietnam era. Now Louis' grandson, Richard Arthur Heath, 2nd, is in the Navy *(Louis got some help from his wife, Zora, on some of this data.)*. "I'm 73 now. Some things I forget." *(Louis really had some feelings about his war, and I hope I have accurately portrayed them. He was the first Pearl River County POW.).*

***** McCORMICK *****

The County is blessed with another WWII 5-Star family, the McCormicks. Brothers Thomas "T.J.", Joseph E., Jesse Boyd, and William W. were all in the Army, and John H. was in the Navy. These are the sons of James Elliot and Margaret Leona McCormick. This is T.J.'s story:

I first went over to Belfast, then Inverness, then back to Belfast *(sounds like a tour of the Lake Country)*. I landed in Algiers in 1942 with Eastern Task Force and fought across North Africa into Tunisia. While we were marching, it even snowed on us one time! The desert certainly has extreme temperatures. We met the Germans sneaking back through Kasserine Pass and had a brisk fight with them. I won a Silver Star at El Guettar by capturing many Italians. Patton pinned it on me himself. *(I had to do some coaxing here. This was the first time tanks were successfully beaten by infantry.)* We were crouched in holes. Many of us were armed with rifle-grenades. When the

181

tanks rolled over us, we just stood up and shot their treads. Once the tank's tracks are displaced, they are easy picking. No problems.

(The American held Kasserine Pass was a direct path to a vital Allied communication and supply base. We had been on the retreat and were badly demoralized. Rommel and Arnim wanted to charge through. After stiff fighting, the "Desert Fox" made it. Then he made an uncharacteristic move by becoming cautious just before he reached his final goal.

When the British 8th Army came up his rear, he had to give up everything he had won in the last week's fighting. After losing to the British, Rommel went back to Germany, and the rest is history. Patton came in to take over the Americans and fired them up with sayings like: "...we're going to cut out their living guts, and use them to grease the treads of our tanks." We started advancing and got to El Guettar before running into minefields and barbed wire. The Germans overran the dug-in Americans, but we fought back and won.)

Then, in July, I went to Sicily. We landed in LSTs and went up through Troina. We ran into a lot of skirmishes, but no real resistence. *(Sicily was ours by mid-August.)*

After that I got a furlough and came home (17 December 1943). Short lived though. On 13 February I went back to join the 9th Infantry Division, 39th Infantry, Company I. We had a

fearsome fight at Omaha Beach, but
very little damage was done
according to the high command
(Eisenhower). Personally, I saw some
dreadful things. I was on the 5th or
6th wave, and things on the beach
were pretty hectic. There were a lot
of sick men. We had a lot of noise
before us and behind us, so this got
us disoriented. We went on to
establish a beachhead despite everything. Then we went on to the Battle
of the Bulge, Rhineland, and my war
ended at Magdeburg on the Elbe River
(19 April 1945). We were supposed to
stop before Berlin to let the
Russians get there first. We all
wanted to go on, but we also needed
a rest. Boy, was that a mistake!
T.J. earned, aside from the Silver Star,
the EAMETO Medal with at least 5 battle
stars. T.J.'s other great contribution to
the US war effort is his two sons, Henry
and Howell *(see Vietnam War section)*.
Brother John Henry had a son, Johnny
McCormick, in Vietnam as did brother
Jesse, a son named Arthur. T.J.'s wife
was a Megehee, and, if you don't think
that opens up another story, think again.
Her brother, Henry Ira Megehee, was
killed in action at St. Lo after a successful invasion of Normandy. Her other
brother, Woodrow Megehee, was in WWII and
Korea.

Glenn Frierson served in beautiful,
sunny North Africa in the 2nd Armored
Division. Then he went north *(hot weather
must have reminded him of home too much)*.
We'll pick him up later. Marty Faust and
Horatio Frierson were there in the Navy.

Claude "Dump" Culpepper of the 44th Bomb Group was a bombardier with "Killer" Kane on the Ploesti oil field raid and won the Distinguished Service Cross. William F. Woessner, Company B, 362nd Infantry, 91st Division, was at Rome-Arno, the Po Valley, and the Appenines. He was wounded 13 December '44. His decorations include the Purple Heart and the EAMETO Medal. Hubert Roland Spiers was a tail gunner and chef (!) at Rome.

W.Z. Chavers, 7th Infantry, 3rd Division, went from Casablanca to Cassino, where he was injured. In that time he earned the Silver Star, Bronze Star, and a Combat Infantryman Badge. He says modestly :

> I don't really care to comment. I will say that I got a medal from Montgomery or Eisenhower. I don't remember which. I never got a Good Conduct Medal and no Purple Heart, even though I got wounded. One of my COs told me one time that what really counts is getting home in one piece, and that's what I did.
> It was rough, just like what's going on now. Saddam is an analog to Hitler. We should have already hit him *(interviewed 1330hrs 17 January 1991)*.

BROWN

Dallas Brown was a Navy file clerk in North Africa from April '44 to April '45:

> I took care of records for the flag officer, a Commodore. It was an experience. We went in right after the Army and Marines invaded and set

up a naval air station. We had PBYs,
PB4Ys, SNJs, and a blimp squadron.
The blimps were to patrol the coast
looking for submarines. They were
not very successful. We also had a
French squadron stationed there with
us. I was not finished high school
when I joined, so you can imagine
the time I had filing their records!
I never lost even a letter though.
*Dallas' father, William Henry Brown,
    was in the Army in WWI:* Pop
survived the "death march" from
France to Belgium to Luxembourg to
Germany. He was shell shocked and
gassed. He saw a lot of fighting in
the trenches, snow, rain, and sleet.
It was pretty bad. He had a stroke
right after he got home.

Frank Dawsey started the war as a
replacement in the 45th Division in
Algeria, and proceeded like this:
After we got there, the Army sent us
up to Naples. After that battle I
caught pneumonia and got frostbitten
feet. I was in the hospital tent
with the walking wounded at Anzio.
We didn't have any arms. The Germans
surrounded us, and I was captured 23
February '44. I was sent to Rome for
two weeks, then on to Moosburg to
Stalag 7A. I had to hike about 60
days across Germany to Russia. They
had us digging foxholes until the
Russians got so close they had to
move us out. We were doing all this
hiking in the cold with only one
blanket for warmth. We slept in
barns. We were near Hannover, near
Salvader I think, when we were

liberated. It was right after FDR died in April 1945.

We had "TGF" letters six inches high on our clothes, a German dogtag, and a US dogtag. If we got caught without any of these, we would be shot as a spy. We were just a bunch of dogfaces. We didn't know what to do if we did get away.

My first cousin, Herman, was on that hike. He was a Ranger when he got captured (see Herman Dawsey). Herbert Lowe from Caesar was also on the march with me. I met Bill Ruffin in LeHarve. He got captured at Kasserine Pass (North Africa).

Frank weighed 165 pounds when they caught him. He weighed less that 100 when he came home.

C.L. Seal was in the Army 36th Division. His story follows:

We entered into the fracas at Salerno, made Anzio, Rome, and Southern France. I was a muleskinner, carrying arms and food to special forces in the mountains, and I brought dead men down *(talk about "muleskinner blues")*. After bypassing Monte Cassino, I fought through Anzio and entered Rome on a mule. I had been 16 of my 18 overseas months in combat, so I got a furlough. When I returned to Metz, France, I was assigned to the 56th Field Artillery. That is where I finished the war.

He earned the EAMETO Medal with 5 battle stars and thought the whole experience was worthwhile.

Herman Dawsey went in at the Anzio battle in Italy with the Army's 3rd Ranger Batallion, Darby's Rangers. He got captured and eventually had to hike almost to Russia. Herman was liberated at the end of the war *(courtesy his wife.)*

***** BURKS *****

The bypass around Monte Cassino and the trip to Rome are another story in themselves. We listen to Houston "Goshie" Burks:

Highway 6 ran from Naples to Rome, so we started out. I was with the 7th Army in field artillery. The Germans had really dug in on top of the mountain. There was a monastery up there and a lot of antennas, so we settled in to make short work of them. We even pulled up 8 inch howitzers. After our air strikes the Huns would just crawl back out of their holes and set their machine guns to firing. Finally, we realized we could take Highway 7 up to Rome, so we set up fake guns under the camouflauge and withdrew at night. We lost a lot of lives at Cassino. Then we ran into the Huns at Anzio. We could have overrun them, but for some reason we stopped. Bad mistake. We could have spent the night in Rome. They brought in reinforcements, many reinforcements, and cleaned house. Clarence Frierson was there as a paratrooper. Sonny Lane of Darby's Rangers was killed there.

From that victory Goshie rode into Rome on 4 June, went across the Arno, fought in Southern France, Nuremburg, and Salzburg, Austria, where he was when the

187

war ended. The Germans were fighting a rearguard action the whole way. For his action he received the EAMETO Medal with 4 battle stars and a Unit Citation.

Let's get Goshie and Delos together with the rest of the Burks family. William Harvey and Alice Virginia Mitchell Burks moved from Henleyfield to Pine Grove to raise a family. The Burks had plenty of background for the war effort. William Harvey's father, Joseph, was in the War Between the States. Joseph's father, Daniel, was that 7-year-old drummer boy at the Battle of New Orleans. We have veterans everywhere here. William's number one son, Harold A., was in WWI and died of service connected disabilities. Willie A. "Bill" was in WWII in North Africa and Italy. He too, died of service connected disabilities. Daniel W. was a B-17 engineer/gunner in Africa and Italy. The remaining three Burks boys all retired from the service, so the family has dedicated about 100 man years of service to the country just in this century.

Goshie's outfit was commanded by Pat Wilson, who became Adjutant General of Mississippi from 1948-1968. Goshie was also in the Korean War. Delos was a teacher/coach when the war broke out. He was required to oversee the registering of young men for the draft. Delos registered himself, too, and the rest is history. Delos stayed in the Reserves until he became the legal staff officer for the Mississippi Air National Guard. He is now a General, and has earned the Mississippi Magnolia Medal. George T., another Air Corps soldier, was in Africa and Italy with the "Hat-in-the-Ring"

Squadron, Rickenbacker's 94th Fighter Group. He started the war right by crossing the pond on the QUEEN ELIZABETH to join the first pursuit group of P-38s. George was a member of the ground crew as a communication specialist:

> In November 1942 my group went to North Africa, Sardinia, and Foggia in Italy until 31 July 1944. I was bombed lots of times. My group lost many planes, and I spent countless hours trying to keep them in the air. One time there was a bombing raid on us in Bizerte. My brother, Daniel, was there. We were sitting on the edge of a foxhole watching it. Another time, in Italy, I had to take about six men and a truck and go replace some DF wire. We'd ride a while and splice a while and ride a while. We never thought about mines. We did see blown out trucks and tanks. We also saw plenty of dead Germans and Italians, but we didn't touch them. We were afraid of booby traps. I used to watch B-26s coming in, shooting off flares. They hit the runway sometimes. They sometimes blew up. We could hear the pilots screaming, but we couldn't do a thing.

This family was "in to win, no matter what it took."

Johnnie Glen Stockstill, a technician in Truck Company 287th Quartermaster Battalion, made Naples-Foggia, Rome-Arno, the North Appenines, and the Po Valley campaigns. Burmah Smith, Army, and Reese Smith, Coast Guard, met in Naples for the only time during the war.

Johnnie Burks was a replacement in Italy for the 141st Infantry, 36th Division. He marched through southern France to the Black Forest. We pick him up on patrol:

I went out on patrol. I was 19 years old and a BAR *(Browning Automatic Rifle)* man. I got cut off from my outfit and had to spend seven days in a foxhole getting shelled by the Germans. No food either. Later I went on a night patrol becase they said you couldn't do night and day back to back. We got in a mine field, but got out okay. The next morning they told me I had to go out again because I was the only BAR man available. We left at 6 A.M. and caught a German right away. During the fighting my platoon got separated and ran into a big mass of Germans. They poured so much lead into us, we had to give up or be killed. It was nearly dark. We had to lay between their foxholes that night. The next day I carried my buddy 12 miles in a poncho stretcher (26 Oct '44). Then we marched to Strasbourg and spent ten days in boxcars getting to our prison. There were about 300 of us. The Germans took all our clothes. That's what they wore for disguises in the Battle of the Bulge. I got a suit from the Red Cross and wore it the rest of the time I was a POW. On 30 April 1945 Patton's Army liberated me. I had spent my 20th birthday in prison camp and lost 30 pounds. We had a monthly shower to delouse us.

There were no lights. We could not
go out at night for fear the dogs
would get us. When we were going to
try to escape, a guard told us to
sit tight. The war was almost over.
We had some ups and downs. They'd
threaten to kill us, but never did.
We had very little food. Potatoes
for supper, grits soup for lunch if
on a work detail, and no breakfast
ever.
When I got home, I hadn't received
mail for 11 months. I found out my
brother, Charles E., had died on 9
May '45, nine days after being
wounded on Okinawa. He was a Medic.

After we solidified our hold on
Italy, we were able to establish air
bases and use them to launch strikes
against the "fatherland." Al Wylie was
with the 783rd Bomb Squadron, 465th Bomb
Group of the 15th Army Air Corps as a
B-24 Liberator tail gunner. He made 40
missions without a scratch. Al recalls:
On 13 February 1945 we were sent to
hit a marshalling yard from 26,500
feet. Our number three engine was
running away, so we had to feather
it. Over the target we took a direct
hit on number two. We were in an 85
degree bank and went into a flat
spin. Somebody was looking out for
us because we pulled out at 12,000
feet. By now, number one had a small
oil leak, and number four had a
large one. I had a 5 or 6 inch hole
in my turret about 10 inches from my
head. No escort fighters were
available, so we limped home in the
clouds after jettisoning out arms

191

and ammunition.

Apparently we had been reported as MIA. As we approached Pantanella it was dark. We shot our flares and landed safely. We tried to get some food, and the mess hall sergeant tossed us a gallon of cherries *(not exactly what these guys needed after such an Excedrin headache day)*. We went back to the hall and shot the lock off the door of the food locker. We liberated a loaf of Spam and an entire box of vittles. We hid the food and had plenty to eat for the next few days. Of course, we got caught. Under the circumstances, nothing was done about it *(Al says he never saw any of Hooker Quick's fresh food)*.

Our next mission was Regensburg, Germany (16 February '45), which was home for the ME-262 German jet aircraft that had been hassling us. We bombed their airfields and factories every other day, using frag bombs. This was a max effort. Something happened to our plane on this day, and we had to abort the mission. I got "volunteered" to fly with a rookie crew! As we approached the I.P., I came up to the waist gun and found all the gunners lying down, sound asleep. I had a friend, Al Honey on Blue R. I saw White J drop a load of frag bombs on Blue R and saw it literally explode in the air with my friend on board. Now I was really mad. Then the green pilot cut power too high on the landing, and we bounced 3000 feet down the runway *(This is starting to sound*

783rd Bomb Squadron insignia.

QUID FIT

"SLEEP TIGHT TONIGHT
YOUR AIR FORCE IS AWAKE,"

*Al Wylie with nose cone art
typical of many WWII planes.*

"Blue R" on the way down with Al
Honey (Al Wylie).

Bye-bye to some town in Germany.
this is an actual bombardiers
photo taken at the time. Note
the bomb cluster in the upper
right corner (Al Wylie).

Al Wylie at the House of the
Vetii in Pompei.

like a Wile E. Coyote story!). Yes, there's more. While I was laboring in the wild blue yonder, a pal took my Aerial *(British MP motorcycle)* for a ride, caught it on fire, and covered it up with dirt. Ruined the damn thing! *(Al Honey was standing on the catwalk with another guy trying to loosen a load of frag bombs that had been jury-rigged in the bomb bay. Al had hooked his parachute to the D ring. There was a great explosion that blew him free of the airplane. He had enough presence of mind to open his parachute at 5000 feet, landed in a tree all broken up, and became a POW because of this mistake.)*

Al tells a couple of stories about the famous 302nd, a P-51 squadron of black pilots commanded by Colin Powell, father of the present Chairman of the Joint Chiefs of Staff. The tails of their planes were painted a black and yellow checkerboard:

Towards the end of the war we were flying some tactical missions at about 17,000 feet. We were around Lake Balaton, Germany. All of a sudden a P-51 on our right peeled off *(escort service)*. The ME-109s were downstairs flying in support of their ground troops. We could see them. At any rate, a few minutes went by and the P-51 hit the liaison button and said: "Come on down, you black sumbitches, I got 34 of 'em cornered!" We all had a laugh at that.

Another time our P-38 was being chased by an ME 109, and the ME -109

197

was being chased by one of our 302nd P-51s. The P-38 couldn't loose the ME-109, and the ME-109 knew that if he shot the P-38, the P-51 would blow him away. So they were screaming all over the heavens when the P-51 pilot hit his liaison button and said: "Look to Lockheed for leadership!" We all had another good laugh and don't know what happened to the three of them.

Al's record shows that he participated in the battles of the North Appenines, Po Valley, Rhineland, and the Balkans *(this is where they were escorted by the 302nd because the flights were so long over enemy territory)*. Al earned the Air Medal with one oak leaf cluster and the EAMETO with 4 battle stars. His brother, David G., drew the airplane pictures shown here while he was in the service.

Norman Stockstill was with the 15th Army Air Corps, 2nd Bomb Group. This was Billy Mitchell's outfit. These groups normally have 28 B-17s. The group got two Presidential Unit Citations for three horrendous missions in a row. Norman was the bombardier. They went against Steyr, Austria, after a ball bearing factory (24 Feb '44) and lost 14 B-17s, then Regensburg, Germany (25 Feb), where they lost 9 more, and finally Steyr again (26 Feb) where they lost another 12 *(Doesn't add up, does it? Reinforcements every night!)*. The German Air Force was using new tactics and weapons, including aerial rockets, aerial FLAK cannons, and phosphorus aerial bombs. The Americans were attacked by no less than 110 German fighters. We pick Norman up:

I made six missions. On the first Steyr raid we lost a waist gunner and a radio operator. On my fourth mission we lost a co-pilot. On the sixth mission I got shot down. We were headed for Turin. On 29 March '44 we were supposed to make a run on the marshalling yards. We turned at the IP and started for the target. The bomb bay doors accidentally opened, and four bombs fell out. Then we lined up our run in heavy FLAK. We took a direct hit in the middle of the plane. I was rocked back three or four feet pretty hard, but didn't hurt anything. When I discovered we were still on course, I got back to my bomb sights and, miraculously, dropped my payload on target. We then tried to stay in formation for our return trip, but couldn't keep up. Two of our engines were out. Ten German fighters came in and finished us off. We had to bail out over Northern Italy.

One of our crew members fell into the hands of the Italian partisans, and, eventually, got back with the unit. The rest of us were captured near Cairo. Two of the guys were wounded. We were moved steadily north, and we were given no food for four or five days. We were interrogated at Verona, then taken through Munich, Berlin, and on to Stalag Luft 1 in Varth, Germany on the Baltic. We were held 14 months until we were rescued by the Russians on 2 May '45. I was always hungry and lost from 192 to 126 pounds. I was

only given four or five spoons of
dehydrated vegetables once a day for
two months. We dug 86 tunnels trying
to get out, but they were all
discovered.

Norman has been most helpful in the
compilation of this living history. He is
a buff, plus an old time native. Not only
that, but he also is blessed with the
"gift of glib" associated with his
brother, Goofy.

Bigelow Frisby, Navy, was in the Med
on the USS SWERVE, a minesweeper. *After a
port call at Gibraltar, the SWERVE
bounced around all over the Med during
1944, making Naples, Palermo (20 May),
Bizerte, Naples again, and Anzio (5
June). She was under enemy air attacks
during that time, but was not damaged.
SWERVE was sweeping mines off Anzio (9
July) when she struck a mine on her port
quarter at 1300hrs. At 1307hrs the order
was given to abandon ship. Fifteen
minutes after hitting the mine, SWERVE's
bow was in the air and her stern was on
the bottom. One hour later she had deep
sixed. The SWERVE had a short life. So
did Bigelow Frisby. He was one of the two
sailors killed in action that day.*

Among the reasons we were over there
was to help some of the oppressed peoples
of Eastern Europe. One of them, Julia
Kubat, now lives in Poplarville. She has
many trophies for training dogs. She
makes her own thread and weaves. Julia is
a pleasant lady to visit. Julia is also
an ex-underground member of the Polish
Army and an ex-POW. Julia's story:

The Germans came in and occupied the

country in 1939. They confiscated
our radios and newspapers...every-
thing. I had to go underground just
to finish high school. The Germans
allowed vocational schools, so I
went to nursing school in 1942. The
school was run by nuns, and they
were also protecting a lot of Jewish
children. Toward 1944 the Germans
starting losing the war and the
English convinced us to start
fighting the Germans. They said they
would arm and protect us. We hurried
with the school, and I finished and
passed my final nursing exams. We
even had Germans on our examination
boards. When they brought out our
diplomas, they were in Polish. The
Germans made them reprint them with
German on the top and Polish on the
bottom. The insurrection broke out
before I got it; however, I just
went back to Poland for a visit,
looked up the records, and got my
diploma. It's all in Polish!
(A note on the Jewish situation)
They were taking Jews and sending
them to Treblenka. Some of my
friends were caught. We knew what
was happening. I saw many times many
trucks of Jews being taken away. The
holocaust was real. The Jews didn't
have any food in the ghetto in 1943
and had an uprising. The Germans
just burned them alive. I saw the
flames, but we couldn't help them.
They would have done the same to us.
Sometimes they would put the Jews in
big trenches...to the east of us...
pour gas on them, and set them on
fire. We knew our rationed soap was

made out of Jews. It was brown. We thought they took the Jew's grease when they were burning them to make the soap.

We were hungry all the time...no work...frozen potatoes. Country people would smuggle food in under their coats. If they were caught, the Germans would shoot them. I had to go to school across the river in Warsaw. The Germans would stop our streetcars to check labor cards. If you didn't have a labor card, they would take you to their camps. My good friend was put in a Gestapo house as a servant. We were derailing trains if we knew they were coming in. From time to time we would kill a German in the street. We soon stopped because they would round up 100 of us...indiscriminately round us up. They'd print the names and post them on bulletin boards around the city to draw a crowd. Then they would put the people up against a wall and kill all of them.

In 1944 the time was ripe for an insurrection. The English told us they would arm us and back us up. We prepared underground hospitals. Mine was an orphanage. We sent the children out into the countryside. There was a lot of enthusiasm. We tore up the sidewalks and made barricades. The Germans were on one side of the street, and we were on the other. There was shooting from window to window. The Germans were bombing and bombing and bombing us. They even bombed the "old town," buildings from the 14th and 15th centuries. I think my mother got killed there. I don't know what happened to my father. People were coming to my hospital through the sewers. I treated hundreds of wounded soldiers. They got infected coming through the sewer. Some even got maggots in their sores. The Germans poisoned some wine and left it in one of the buildings. The Polish underground found it; they were doctors, I think. They were tired, so they stopped and drank some of the wine. They died. After about six weeks to two months we had no more food...no more provisions. We were eating horses. The Germans intercepted most of the English supplies. The Russians just stood by and watched. Finally, we had to surrender in October 1944.

The Germans said all the men had to go to prison camps. They said the women could go or stay in Poland. I had nothing left, and I was a patriot. I went. I thought I could help at camp. They let us take a little food, blankets... silverware if you had any, and loaded us on boxcars like cattle. I remember seeing the red berries of the mountain ash and wondering if I would ever see them again.

The Germans put us in a camp in a field between Dresden and Leipzig. It had towers on the corners and was surrounded by barbed wire. They gave one barracks to the nurses. There were Russians, Italians, and us in camp, but we had no contact between

us. I was there nine months. Our
food ration was picked over by the
kitchen people and the service
people. We had one slice of bread,
one tablespoon of sugar, one tablespoon of margarine, and flavored
water. All the rutabagas and corned
beef were gone.
We saw a lot of bombing between the
two cities. One day in May 1945, we
looked up and the towers were empty.
The guards had run away to the west
because the Russians were
approaching from the east. The
Germans were dropping stuff on the
road. Our boys were picking it up,
and we started to eat good! The boys
picked up some bicycles so we could
leave, but the Russians confiscated
them. The boys went out and picked
up some more that were not in such
good shape. I had to learn how to
ride. I could, but you had to push
me to get me started! We also had to
take care of the Russians. They were
in the last stages of tuberculosis.
I was afraid of getting it. Several
would die every day.
We decided we had to run away. We
came to the Grimaud River in May.
Americans were on the other side.
The Russians didn't want us to go.
One night we got on a raft after
standing silently in line, and the
Germans pulled us to the other side.
They didn't know we were Polish! We
went to the Americans. They fed and
kept us. They took us away and put
me to work in a hospital. We went to
Italy, and then to England in 1946.
I spent five years working there in

Berlin
Germany
Cherbourg
Normandy
Muese - Argonne
Rhineland
Ardennes
Bulge
France
Po Valley
Arno
Appenines
Rome
Naples
Italy
Sicily
Morocco   Algeria   Tunis
North Africa

U.S.S. HENRICO

J. WILLIAMS, CAPTAIN
COMMANDING

C. BEAVER, LT. CDR.
EXEC. OFFICER

26 NOVEMBER '43 — COMMISSIONED (HOBOKEN, N.J.)
6 JUNE '44 — NORMANDY INVASION
15 AUGUST '44 — SOUTHERN FRANCE INVASION
26 MARCH '45 — KERAMA-RHETTO (OKINAWA) INVASION
2 APRIL '45 — JAP KAMIKAZE CRASHED SUPERSTRUCTURE

If these guys are really in the Navy, they SHOULD be on the ship-of-the-desert. James Broom is on the right.

Unloading supplies from an LST on a North African beach (Hooker Quick).

A Maginot Line pillbox (Harlon Frierson).

Harlon Frierson shooting at an ME-262.a, the first jet plane. That's not the paratrooper shaking, it't the machine gun giving him a free ride!

Richardson

208

a Polish hospital. They wouldn't recognize our diplomas and told us we had to go to school for five more years if we wanted to work in their hospitals. In 1951 I came to America.
Julia Kubat. We're lucky to have a citizen like her in this County.

World War II (Northern Europe)

Another Allied front started from England. D-Day, 6 June 1944, was the Normandy invasion at Utah and Omaha beaches. Paris was liberated (Aug '44), the Battle of the Bulge was fought in December, and a steady advance brought Berlin to its knees in May '45. The war in Europe was essentially over, although some of our hierarchy thought we should keep on going to Moscow. In retrospect, it sure would have saved a lot of trouble in the next section. Our old friend Glenn Frierson is back on the scene earning a Belgian Croix de Guerre and a Bronze Star in Normandy, and continuing on to Northern France, Ardennes, Rhineland, and Central Europe. Tercy Smith, 611th Ordnance Battalion, was at Rhineland and Central Europe. Reuben William Carroll was there. John W. Hawthorne, 342nd Engineers, was involved in the battles at Normandy, Northern France, Ardennes, and the Rhineland. He received the EAMETO Medal. Benjamin J. Breland was a cannon-eer with Battery C, 969th Field Artillery Battalion at Normandy and Rhineland where he earned the EAMETO Medal and a

Distinguished Unit Badge. Ben was wounded
in the Battle of the Bulge. C.J. McGin-
nis, 4th Infantry Division, was in the
the D-Day invasion at Utah Beach, St. Lo,
and Bastogne. "Mac" asked for active duty
after having been an instructor for a
while. After his European tour his unit
was about to be shipped to Japan when the
war ended. Mac won a Bronze Star and the
EAMETO Medal *(data courtesy his wife,
Marge)*. Here is another rough duty.
Clinton McQueen served June 1941 through
April 1944 with General Patton. Robert S.
Bowman, Sr. began his military career in
France with the Army engineers. We'll
pick him up later.

Granville Pearson was there for the
Normandy invasion. In fact, Granville was
a day early. Let him tell it:

We shipped out to Scotland on a
British liner with 12,000 men on
board. On the way we got strafed.
Turns out it was an American plane.
Fortunately, no harm was done. Then
I was in Liverpool for a few weeks
and met another man from Picayune,
Guy Wheat. Anyhow, we armor plated
our LSTs. Eisenhower sent us over to
Utah Beach on 5 June. I was a
helmsman on one of the five LSTs
that made it all the way to Normandy. Because of bad weather the attack had been scrubbed. We returned
to Portsmouth and did it all again
the next day. That was something
else, having to get psyched up twice
for the same thing *(sounds like he
was a veteran before he was a veteran)*. I carried three tanks and an
anti-aircraft gun on my LST and was

210

in the second wave to hit the beach.
After the equipment was offloaded,
we went back out a little. We picked
up some survivors from a mined boat,
and stayed in the area a week. It
was like a giant-sized July 4th
fireworks display. After about a
week we got to go ashore. It was a
disaster area: cut barbed wire all
over the place, fried Krauts in the
bunkers, destroyed equipment. One
bunker had six or seven cooked Germans in it. It was a mess. Being in
the Navy was a great experience,
especially the travel. The most
exasperating part was not being able
to get a beer in California after I
got home. Imagine that. Taking part
in one of the biggest fights ever
and can't even get a beer. Not 21!

SMITH
Billy Smith (deceased) was a medic
attached to the 121st Infantry, 8th
Division Army. He recalled:
I went in at Omaha Beach, where I
was wounded, and recuperated until
August. Then I went to La Haye-du-
Puits. We took and lost that place
three times and lost a lot of good
men. Then we had smooth sailing to
Reims and back to Denain, where we
had to take out a pocket of German
resistance. From there we went to
Brest, where we stayed for a good
while getting rid of submarine pens
and pillboxes. After that we went to
the Crozon peninsula across the bay
to knock out some artillery that had
been firing back on us. About that
time the breakthrough started, and

we liberated Paris. We went on to
Belgium, Holland, Luxembourg, and to
Schwerin, Germany where the war
ended. I crossed the bridge at
Remagen and met a Fleming from
Picayune at Cologne. We were all
waiting to cross the river. I got
the Purple Heart and the EAMETO
Medal with 5 or 6 battle stars.
This war going on now *(interviewed
1430hrs 18 January 1991)* is a push-
button war. There are some mighty
good men in it, and they're moving
right along. That feller was setting
himself up for a dictator. Fanatic,
just like Hitler. For my war I found
out what they use the Army for, and
I don't want any more.
My grandfather was William "Junkie"
Smith. My brothers were both veterans. David R. was in the Navy in
WWII on the ENTERPRISE and the
ESSEX. Kenneth O. had a tour in
Germany after the war.

MITCHELL

Let's see how far we can get into
the Albert Mitchell family tree. Albert
himself was not in the military, but he
sure sired a passel who were. First, we
have great-uncle Calvin in The War Between the States. Then we skip a generation *(Albert's)* and get to his sons:
Forest W., Wiley Preston, Toxie H., Sam
T., Robert Earl, Lester, and Eulas.
Forrest was in the Air Corps *(later Air
Force)* from 1949 until 1967. Wiley
Preston was in the Army 1942-43. Toxie
we'll get to. Sam T. was in the Navy as
part of the gun crew on the merchant ship
SS STERLING MORTON. He won the A-P

212

Theater Medal. Robert Earl was in the Korean War with the 138th. Lester was in the National Guard. Eulas served in the Army. Toxie Mitchell is a good representative to this generation:

> I went over in June '44 with the "Workhorse of the Western Front," Roosevelt's SS Troops of the 30th Infantry Division. Just in our battalion we had James Nelson from Poplarville. He was a BAR man. I saw him get killed. We had Charles Hartfield from Picayune and a King boy from Carriere. One of those freaked out in England and didn't make the trip. It was common for this to happen. Calvin Triplett was in another batallion in our Division. I was in a heavy morter crew.
> We went to Normandy and took the 1st Division's place. We were only there a few days. We could hear fire, so we tried to flank the Germans. We crossed the Vi River and got hit by "screamin' mimis." Welcome to the war! There was all kinds of artillery. We put up a line of morters on a hill to open fire on them when a German OP spotted us. They zeroed in and knocked out a couple of our guns and a few men. Then we got into some hedgerows into some really rough going. These were a series of five to six foot high mounds checkerboarding the area. *(The significance is that the brush and trees surrounding these plots was so thick you couldn't penetrate them, only shoot through. Tanks couldn't get through until they devised a plow.)* If you made 1000 yards a day, you

were doing good. *(This is weird. I'm turning down the radio on one war so I can write about another one. Are we always at war? 1 February 1991).* Then we brought in our tanks. I remember we got bogged down one day. A German tank, a captain, and 20 riflemen got into the hedgerow. Our Major thought they had launched a major offensive, so he ordered us to retreat. Of course, we ran into a Colonel who sent us back in. We knocked the tank out, set the woods on fire, and burned the Germans' uniforms. I took a silk map out of the captain's pocket. After some discussion we sent it back to HQ. It turned out to be their withdrawal plan! I still have that map.

We kept on going through that hedgerow. "Bedcheck Charlie," a German spotter plane, kept tabs on our movement every night. We were afraid we didn't have any support. One night (24 July 44) there was a large ACK-ACK discharge at "Bedcheck." We found out quick we had plenty of support! On 25 July we had a bomb attack. Somebody shot a phosphorus shell across the line between us and the Germans to show them where to bomb. Only problem is, the wind was blowing in our direction, and the line ended up over US! Our own bombs fell within 30 yards of me, blew out a lot of our heavy infantry division, and killed General McNeer. That was the nearest I ever came to a bomb. While I was in the hedgerows, I was scared. Shells were falling all over the place in my block, so I crawled over to the next one- in a trench it was. There was a guy sitting up, cradling his rifle, on the other end. I said "Getting pretty hot around here, isn't it?" No answer. "How long you been here?" No answer. I moved down to him and started to ask again. When I looked up, I saw he had been shot right through the forehead. I had been talking to a dead man!

We went on to St. Lo. Again we put up our line of morters. The Germans hated these heavy morters. They picked up our position by the sun glinting off our elevator screw. We were in a hole. A German shell fell behind us. Then one fell in front of us. You know the rest. We heard it coming like a freight train and got the hell out of there. It didn't hurt us, but it did knock out two of our morters.

I reckon I walked all the way across France. I carried my pack plus that 40 pound morter barrel across my shoulders. Another guy carried the bipod, and a third carried the base plate. At least his back was covered. Several stories come to mind about this hike. One night me and another man were lying under a blanket. It was cold in those pup tents. Anyhow, we were awaken by machine-gun fire. Good thing we were laying low, because a bullet split that blanket! I still have it. I can't believe it didn't hit us. Another time, we were out of our holes taking a stroll for a breath of fresh air. Shells were screaming

all around. It was just three of us.
We stopped to talk to a guy sitting
under a tree writing a letter. Well,
here comes this shell. I ran for the
sergeant's hole, and he ran to mine.
I'm still here. The sergeant took a
load of shrapnel in the chest *(Some
people might start getting jittery
or superstitious by now.)*.
Toxie made Ardennes, Northern France,
Rhineland, and Central Europe. His war
ended at Magdeburg *(see T.J. McCormick)*.
Toxie earned the EAMETO Medal with 5
battle stars, the Bronze Star, and the
Combat Infantryman's Badge. Toxie was
also in the Army for Korea. He was
stationed at Fort Benning GA. He says "if
you thought Korea was tough, you should
have lived in Phenix City AL at that time
like I did!"

The next generation of Mitchells
includes Forrest's son, Arthur, in the
Air Force with NORAD. Wiley Preston's
son, Michael "Mickey" Preston, served in
the Army in Germany during the Vietnam
era and is now in the Guard. Toxie's two
sons served. Leland Albert was a communications specialist in Vietnam and earned
the National Defense Service Medal, Army
Commendation Medal, Vietnam Campaign
Medal, and the Vietnam Service Medal.
Kenneth is in the 890th.

FRIERSON
Harlon Frierson hit Omaha Beach with
the 79th Infantry Division, 312th Field
Artillery as a recon and forward
observer. Harlon's tour brought him in
contact with half the country:
After Normandy we went to St.
Mere-Eglise and hooked up with the

30th and 4th Infantry Divisions after a paratrooper drop *(The 79th arrived D+8, 14 June 1944. They all hooked up 16 June after the paratroopers secured a bridge over the Douve River at St. Sauveur.)*. Then we went to Cherbourg with Patton's tanks (18 June; *The battle was 22 June for pillboxes and bunkers.*) and south to St. Lo for the breakthrough. *(The 79th went to La Haye-du-Puits on 3 July. It was only able to advance one kilometer a day into steady German fire and the bocage, the hedgerows.)* This was supposed to have been the fastest one on record. Then we went on to Strasbourg. On the campaign of Northern France my job was to find out where to put the guns, spot where the shells were hitting, and zero in on where they should be hitting.

We established our OP *(observation points)* on hilltops and in church steeples. In fact, we once knocked out a German OP in a church steeple at 15,000 yards with one shot. Now, that was some shot! Somewhere on this trip across France we took, lost, and retook La Haye-du-Puits six times. We had hell on that one. We also had six major river crossings including the one to Paris. We couldn't go in because we smelled too bad. We had to go three weeks once without a shower, but we usually had one once a week *(I can just see them calling a timeout to the ragheads; better yet, a TV timeout, on the Desert Shield Operation. That*

217

*way the players can spiff up for the
cameras!).*
Then we went on to the main crossing
of the Rhine River on rafts with
outboard motors because there was no
bridge yet. I made Cologne and
Dusseldorf and ended the war at
Schweinfurt on the Main River. I
came home in November 1945.
I saw Clyde Wheat of the 101st
Airborne right after the Battle of
the Bulge. War IS hell, buddy, and
very confusing. You only know what's
happening right where you are. The
one now *(interviewed 1900hrs 5
February 1991)*, we're starting to
get behind. We've got a madman on
our hands, and we have to stop him
or he'll be over here.

Harlon earned the EAMETO Medal with 4
battle stars. He has many family ties to
our veterans. His father, Henry "Jack"
Frierson, was in WWI. In his generation
are cousins Glenn, in the 2nd Armored
Division with Patton in North Africa *(see
above)*, and W.C. in the Air Corps. He was
shot down and spent two years as a POW.
Harlon's son, Eric Holland Frierson, is
in the Air Force. He served in Korean
Occupation Forces and is now an ROTC
instructor in school.

Clinton Smith *(of the Henleyfield
Smiths)* was with the 102nd Signal Corpss,
102nd Infantry Division:
I landed at Cherbourg in 43 and went
north up through Belgium and Holland
to Germany. We stopped at the Elbe
River. I was in the Battle of the
Bulge, but I don't know where. We
started in Holland, went into Ger-

many, went back to Holland or Belgium, and back to Germany.

I was a mess sergeant, but sometimes it got pretty uncomfortable back where we were. They threw a lot at us, some strafing too. We had some close calls. All we had to "prepare" was C and K Rations. We had a German Jew in our Company. He hated the Germans. Every time we would take one, he would personally question the German about the whereabouts of the local wine supply. He'd get ahold of them and get rough until they told him. We had some pretty good champagne!

I never saw the first person I knew.

Vernell Cowart was with the 4026th Troop Transport after serving with the tank destroyers. He was in the ETO in 1944-45:

I went in at Normandy on the Omaha beachhead. Then I went to St. Lo, Paris, up through the Seigfreid Line, and over into Germany. I wish ours had been as quick as this one with Iraq *(interviewed 8 March' 91)*, but I really don't think this one is finished. I think they should have stayed on him *(Saddam)* until they got him. We got him on his knees, but we should have stretched him out completely.

Vernell earned the EAMETO Medal with 5 battle stars.

J.T. Fleming was with the 1st Army, 1st Division-the "Big Red One." He was attached to Patton's group as a machine gunner in a Jeep. He remembers it this

219

way:

> I was at the Battle of the Bulge
> (went over 1944-1945) in Belgium.
> Then I was one of the first to cross
> the Rhine on a pontoon bridge at
> Remagen. The real bridge was being
> saved for the heavy artillery, so we
> crossed at 0200hrs, I remember that.
> Then I was on the campaign for the
> Rhineland (wounded), Central Ger-
> many, and Czechoslovakia. I was
> there when the war ended.

J.T. earned the Purple Heart and the ETO
Medal with 3 or 4 battle stars. His son,
Steve, is in our National Guard unit.

George Spiers was in the 100th
Infantry Division, 3rd Battalion, 399th
Infantry from 1942-45:

> I went in at Marseilles by LST and
> had to fight the whole way up
> through France. We went through the
> Maginot *(old French)* and Seigfried
> *(old German)* lines. They were loaded
> with pillboxes. Then we joined up
> with Ole Blood-and-Guts *(Patton)* for
> the Battle of the Bulge. We were
> going to be relieved by a new
> company, but the Germans demolished
> them and we had to keep on fighting.
> After that, bombers softened up the
> Holbern bridge. I remember Mannheim
> was on one side of the bridge. All
> of us who fought in that one belong
> to the "Son of a Bitch" Club in New
> York now. Anyhow, we went north
> toward Berlin and the war ended. It
> was rough going.

George won the EAMETO Medal with battle
stars *(He can't remember how many: "You
should have called 30 years ago.")*, two

220

or three Bronze Stars, and a Unit Citation. George also ran into Lavelle Penton, Bodie Jarrell, and talked to Otis Lee about 30 minutes before he was captured in the Battle of the Bulge.

Melvin Dale Wentworth saw it all. He made the Normandy beachhead in 1944 with the Armored Division, 121 Calvary Recon Squadron. He fought through the Rhineland, Central Europe, Bastogne, and Luxembourg on the Red Ball Highway. On 18 January 1945 his family was notified that he was MIA. In fact, he had been wounded, captured, and sent to POW camp, Oflag 13B, in Hammelburg, Germany. Dale escaped, and word came home on 28 April 1945 that he was hospitalized in England until he could travel. For his bravery and sheer guts in the face of the enemy Dale Wentworth earned the Purple Heart, the EAMETO Medal, and the WWII Victory Medal.

Lewis J. Krail, 2nd Battalion, 137th Infantry, 35th Infantry Division was assigned at various times to Generals Omar Bradley, George Patton, and Simpson. His Division helped relieve American forces at Bastogne. Working under enemy observation while subject to intense fire that disrupted Battalion communications (Jul-Sep '44), Lewis worked long hours in an "outstandingly meritorious manner" to repair lines and assure continuous maintenance of communications in the vicinity of the Moselle and Meurthe Rivers. For that he received a Bronze Star. Lewis was also in Luxembourg, Holland, and crossed the Rhine into Germany. At Recklinghausen, Germany (Apr 45) Lewis stepped on a mine. For that he earned a Purple Heart

221

and a trip home.

From Erwin Smith we receive a first-hand account of the Battle of the Bulge. Smitty was with Patton at the start, but ended up in the 9th Army after being assigned to Field Marshall Montgomery. He got to Cherbourg after the fact, but helped win hard ground in Belgium, Holland, and Germany. He picks up his story Linnich, Germany:

We moved out through a frozen beet field and ran into a German machine-gun crossfire. With only 12 of the 42 men in our platoon left including a green Lieutenant, we decided to advance to the rear and beat feet back to Linnich. A mortar shot killed the two guys in front of me. We got to town and took shelter in the first house. Nobody was there, but we heard a radio going-found it in the basement. It was connected to Hun HQ. We fought to a Mexican standoff, so the Germans had one side of the road and we had the other.

I was called to our HQ, and went on a banked road. I saw two heads in a foxhole, so I slipped up on it. Nobody home! Anyhow, we put two guys on guard duty and went out on patrol, hopefully to intercept an American battalion coming for rein-forcements. We figured the Huns would try to retake Linnich in the morning. I went out on the road. There was six to ten of snow on the ground. I yelled at a guy in the foxhole, but no answer even though several heads popped up. We went out about 5 to 600 yards and met eight guys approaching. Fortunately, they were ours, one of whom was a battalion assistant commander. We took him back by a different way. After a runin with a guard and delivering the deliverer to HQ, I went to lay down. I was immediately awaken to go back to HQ, fetch the assistant, and return him to his command through all these Germans. The next morning the attack started. I happened to go by the same foxhole. Remembering the previous night, I lobbed a grenade into the hole; and, sure enough, out popped a host of Huns. Since they were all carrying bags that looked to harbor bombs, I killed them all except one. The captured one revealed that the bags were shaving kits! I went down in the foxhole, and there was a tunnel. It ended up in the same house where we had found the radio.

We took the town, and it had a Ford agency. We tried to get cars out of the showroom to drive, but there were too many bricks on them. Then we "appropriated" a piano for our boogie-woogie player and had a street party. We looted the banks for what we thought was worthless money. In fact, we burned it to heat our K rations. Little did we know all that money would be worth something after the war. We went on to keep Linnich and took Bracklen, where the Germans were dug in with over a hundred pillboxes. Our position during the Battle of the Bulge was to hold the 9th Army front. Then

we took off for the Rhine. There was
a dammed river we had to cross. We
figured the Germans would blow the
dam just about the time we got to
the middle of the river, so we
called for a bomb strike on a dam on
the river. Man, you should have seen
the water flow! The P-38's were most
succesful, we crossed, the Germans
attacked, and I was wounded. For all
this action I received the Purple
Heart (still have a piece of an 88
in my leg), Bronze Star, and Expert
Combat Infantryman's Badge.

As an asidem, I went back there last
year for a 45th reunion. While I was
walking down the street an old man
rode up on a bicycle and started to
chat. It was his house that I had
found the radio and later hand
grenaded. He thanked the Americans
profusely for winning the war and
said he could not imagine what would
have happened if Hitler had won.

Calvin Triplett, Army 30th Infantry
Division, was home on leave for D-Day. He
got back in time for the fights at
Belgium, Holland, in penetrating the
Ziegfield Line, and back to the Battle of
the Bulge. He then got frozen feet and
was transferred to the Air Corps. Let
Calvin tell it:

The Germans had the town, but we
pushed them out. We found ham,
beans, Christmas presents, everything. I even found a wooden shoe
(sabot) with "Stockstill, Picayune,
Mississippi" written in it. We had
taken a chateau the day before.
There were 27 live Belgian civilians

224

in it. When we got back, we saw blood coming out the front door. The Germans had killed all 27 of them. Then the Germans came back in US uniforms and started capturing all kinds of people. I was wounded on the first day back (took one in the hip pocket).

Later we captured Alsdorf, Germany. When we went out on night patrol, I took the lead (better night eyes). We started getting fired on from a haystack, so we turned and ran. I made a ditch, and my partner hid behind a dead German soldier. When we returned their fire, they all surrendered. Most of the Germans were tired of the war by then. Even the "dead" soldier gave himself up! My buddy went white on that one. Then we went back to town and entered the first house we could. Germans started firing up at us through the floor, so I dropped a couple of grenades into the basement. When the enemy (SS troops this time) started coming out, one tried to run even though we were only about ten feet away with loaded guns. BOOM. Another came out with his arm hanging only by the back muscle. I loaned him a knife to finish cutting it off. Tough.

For Calvin's actions he earned a Purple Heart with oak leaf cluster, EAMETO Ribbon with 4 battle stars, Combat Infantryman Badge, and a Distinguished citation. Calvin's wife had to tell me this part. Imagine, a bashful ex-football coach!

Paul Raymond Kirkland, Army, was captured in the Battle of the Bulge and remained a POW for the remainder of the war.

MICHOT

Allen Michot. Army. "Acorn Division," the 87th Division of the 3rd Army. In 1944 Allen went to England; LeHarve, France; and up to Belgium for the Battle of the Bulge. Allen continues:

We pulled back off the front line for Thanksgiving of 44. Then we went back in and were on the move for Christmas. I hit the Battle of the Bulge in January 1945 as part of a light-weapons company. I was a bazooka man. Once we saw some brick buildings with 50 to 100 women locked up in them. I don't know how long they had been there, but we set them free. They were sure in bad shape. Because I could speak French, our company commander always sent me out to find a place for us to sleep for a few days. Most of the towns were deserted. I shot at plenty of tanks, but they were mostly out of range. I saw a lot of my buddies get knocked out. One night in early January we was on outpost duty. I was carrying the bazooka and two rounds. My helper was carrying another three rounds. We got to a place that had already been taken. I fired the bazooka too close to my target- like down a cellar- and a big fireball came back on us. It knocked out my gun, but I had a .45 left. Our outpost was a few miles out from the company, and we were

226

expecting reinforcements on our
right. That night communications
went out, and we took cover in a
brick building. Early daylight,
instead of reinforcements on our
right, we got Germans on our left
with a halftrack. I couldn't even
fire a shot. What could an M-1 do
against a tank? Couldn't outrun 'em,
couldn't communicate. We had to
decide, so we gave up. With a
halftrack within 200 yards of us, we
didn't know which way to run.
They disarmed us, took our
overcoats, and took us back
someplace. I didn't see nothing,
didn't know nothing. For a while
they kept us in pigeon holes in a
rack off the floor. We were close to
the front line, about 3 to 400
prisoners in our building. We had
one buddy killed because he wouldn't
come out of that building. They said
they'd do the same thing to us. They
put us to work on a railroad track,
breaking sidetrack into sections and
bringing it to the trunk line. US
airplanes began strafing us, so the
Germans moved us back a few days.
Then they had us moving sections of
quonset huts and unloading onto
stacks in the woods in the night.
They would call us out three or four
times taunting us. Later we knew
when someone was missing from the
work detail. We could hear- POW,
POW, POW- back where we had been.
That lasted two weeks. All the time
we were moving we had a loaf of
bread for three days and a hunk of
meat. They took us to a concentra-

tion camp that held 10,000 prisoners of all nationalities...I think it was at Badorf, Germany. We didn't do nothing there. At night, we'd pull our clothes down and pop lice. In the morning, we got a cup of coffee. We came back at noon for a cup of rotten Irish potato soup. We could sit there and watch the fire from the big guns getting closer. I said "Well, boys, we're getting closer and closer to home now."
In April, I think about the 10th, we got liberated. We'd sleep on straw mattresses and had no showers or clothes changes since we got captured. The US guys took the guys in the worst shape first. I got to go in a big field tent and shower. I mean, hot water. You could stay as long as you wanted. I got a clean towel, got sprayed down for lice, and went down a line to get fitted for new clothes. Then we got some good food.

Allen Michot was lucky when he came back to Picayune. He had a wife and a three month old child he had left behind, and they were waiting for him. Allen's older brother, Marshall, was a medic in the ETO. Younger brother, Uray, was in the Aleutians in the Seabees. Baby brother, Sanford, was in the Army in Korea.

Eldred Graham was a replacement. He joined the 35th Infantry Division, 134th Regiment, Company B at St. Lo (Jul '44). His outfit pushed on to Nancy, France, and a couple of miles across the Moselle River. Let Eldred tell it:
We attacked a little town, took it,

and the Germans made a counter attack. I took a rifle bullet that smashed my thigh. Everyone ran off and left me. The Germans picked me up and carried me back for first aid. They splinted my leg, put me in a boxcar with a bunch of wounded Germans, and took me to Strasbourg. From there I was sent in a hospital train to Nuremburg and put in a prison hospital. On 27 September a repatriation board met and set me free. The last of January 1945 I made a switch in Switzerland and came home. The Germans treated me just like their soldiers, and I even received Red Cross parcels.

Eldred received the ex-POW Medal, Purple Heart, Combat Infantryman Badge, and two battle stars.

Houston J. Stewart was a tank destroyer commander. In fact, he was the First Sergeant of the first tank destroyer group organized. He had to stay home and train others in the fine art, so he got in after Normandy. We catch up with him in Belgium:

Tank destroyers were like tanks, only they had 90 mm guns, were faster and more maneuverable. I made Belgium, Holland, then the Bulge. We were on the south side fighting defensively. The company was patrolling a town, Nancy, France, defending Patton's headquarters. We were living in a luxury hotel leading the life of Riley. I got a call from HQ- seems they always called meto report to the Colonel. He sent us out on a snowy night to

229

try to get through to the Germans. We got to a burnt-out bridge, and I had to get all this equipment turned around on a narrow road to go back. The round trip was 95 miles, yet the Colonel cussed me out when we got back. He threatened to bust me, so I told him to go ahead. Something happened to the Colonel that night, and I never got busted. The Germans had dug in right beside us, and I'll never understand how, what with all our intelligence people running around. Things were pretty hectic for a while. Anyhow, we beat them and advanced to the Elbe River.

I entered the service in October '40 and got out in October '46. There was an awful lot of murder. I saw them loading bodies on 6x6 trucks like cordwood. I hope the next two or three generations don't have to bail out France again. France always quits. It seems all their men want to do is just get a bottle of wine and find a woman. We let them guard the rear. I finally got disabled in a freak accident and came home. I was supposed to go to Japan. I went to a movie and saw an announcement about Japan quitting the war. You never saw such a happy man. War IS hell!

WHITFIELD

The Whitfield descendents of Daulton and Susan gave many years of service to the "good old USA." That family history has been presented to me by Claude Whitfield, one of the many sons to have served:

I was in the Marines at first and was among the last to leave occupied Haiti in 1933. I'll bet you didn't know we used to occupy Haiti. Anyhow, I had a break in service and then went back in the Army. I was in the Philippines in 1945 and, later, was part of the occupying forces of Austria and Italy. In fact, I was in Austria during the Korean War. I went to OCS, and the Army put me in the Quartermaster Corps, attached to the Signal Corps.

You ought to see the rest of the family history. I'm working on one, and I think we have at least as much service as the Burks family. I have 24 years myself and retired in 1957 *(Mr. Whitfield has got to be in his 80s at this time.)*.

Claude has/had five brothers that figure into the "veteran quotient." Brothers Morgan and Jessie served in WWI. Morgan was in the Medical Corps in France. He became seriously ill during the great flu epidemic and was bed-ridden for 34 years. Jessie was on a submarine chaser and a battleship with the Navy. Jessie also had two sons-in-law with many years service. Jessie's sons, Charles Ray and Francis E., also served in the Navy. Morgan's son, Jackie, and three of his sons-in-law were in the service at the same time. H.S. Calhoun was one of them. He was in the Medical Corps in WWII attached to the Air Corps. Brother Fred was a Post Office employee when WWII broke out, so he and two of his sons, Daryle and Edgar, joined up. Fred worked out of the APO in New York. Then he landed in Casablanca and set up an APO. After that he did the same

231

in Oman, Tunisia. Fred had a post office named after him somewhere in Africa.
Daryle was in the 82nd Airborne in Sicily, Italy, France, Belgium, Holland, and Germany. He was wounded three times.
Edgar was in France, Germany, and Austria. I was able to track him down, and he told me:

> I was in the 42nd Infantry as an intelligence scout. I went over in '44-'45 to Europe. My job was as a forward observer with two or three other guys from our company. If we got back, we told the mortars and artillery where to fire. When the war ended, I became part of the occupying forces and came home in '46.

Fred had another son, Gary Wayne, who served with the 138th in Korea *(see that section Gary's story)*. Still in Claude's generation, brother Fritz was not in the service; however, he had four sons and two sons-in-law who were. Tommy was in the Army Air Corps from 1945-47. He was sent to Europe attached to the Signal Corps. Leroy was in the Pacific from 1942-45 with an Army transportation unit. L.D. was in the Navy, and Don was in the National Guard during the 70s. These guys were a busy family.

Russ Brown served with the 1135th Engineers Combat Group under XII Corps, 3rd Army. Russ participated in campaigns in Northern France, Ardennes, Rhineland, and Central Europe. When asked about it, he said simply :

> I went in from '43 to '45. Combat engineers were bridge and road builders. Our group built Bailey and

pontoon bridges. We moved with the artillery behind the infantry.
Russ earned the EAMETO Medal with 4 battle stars.

Willie A. Baucum, 248th Engineers, was killed in action at Sarre Union, France (3 January 1944).

***** DICKERSON *****

Vernon Dickerson was in Europe from 1943-45 in the 171st Airborne Division. He went in on foot to Bastogne and parachuted into Germany at Westel. Vernon was in a mortar platoon that "got shot at a lot. It was pretty cold in Bastogne, I remember. I earned the EAMETO Medal with 2 battle stars." In making the Dickersons a five-star family we present his brothers. Carroll and Arthur were also airborne and in the ETO. They saw each other in France. Wallace was in the Navy, but retired out of the Air Force. Young'un, Archie, was in the Air Force.

I think we're doing a good job now *(interviewed 1900hrs 27 February 1991)*. I admire Schwartkopf. I don't believe we'll be the ones to get Saddam. I think someone else will.

WORTHY

Sid Worthy was a medic with the 55th General Hospital. He started in England in a 500-bed facility, then went to France on D-Day. He was over there from 1943-46. His brother, Frank G., was in the Korean War in the Air Force. Another brother, Dewitt "Boots," was in the Coast Guard. The father, Evander D. "Ed", was in the Army in WWI.

Navy personnels include Hollis D. Stockstill, who sailed all the way around the world on the USS FRANCIS E. WARREN and never fired a shot, and Benson E. Maxwell on the USS BRISTOL. And, we all should remember Jesse Wells from WWI. He got drafted for this one, too *(They must have really needed warm bodies to draft someone in his 50's.)*. Well, here comes his son, J.L.:

> I was in the Navy on a hospital ship in WWII. We hauled out loads of displaced persons in both oceans. I was a fireman, water tender, and oiler. Then I was in Korea and Vietnam with MSTS *(more later)*.

These guys all had to get around somehow, hopefully other than Shank's mare. Sad Sack couldn't live on sore dogs forever. Who better than Holly T. Smith to drive? A halftrack driver with the 5th Armored Division, Holly participated in the drive to Berlin. After being at Normandy, Northern France, Ardennes, and Rhineland, his outfit made the run from the Rhine to the Elbe River in 13 days, 260 miles through enemy territory. They did nothing but fight and push- no eating, no sleeping- to 45 miles from Berlin. No list of medals was offered, but we're sure there must have been one or two.

Ernest Albin Robinson was injured by bomb shrapnel and captured in Germany in 1945 while he was driving his lieutenant in a jeep. The Germans discussed killing them both, but decided to keep Robinson as a driver. They executed the lieutenant behind a barn.

234

Eugene Dawsey was in the 175th Infantry, 29th Division at Normandy and St. Lo. Ted Goleman served in England, France, and Germany. J.Q. Frierson won the European Campaign Medal with six battle stars. James Crosby received a Bronze Star in Belgium by helping save a supply train from German airplanes. He also was in Northern France, Rhineland, and Central Europe and earned the EAMETO and American Defense Service Medals. Eastman J. Moody survived in the European Theater from 1942 to 1945, only to die from a coronary two days out at sea on the way home.

Did we mention flyboys and airplanes before? That was just a start. Pearl River County had many flyboys. Since they were so mobile, they mixed fronts. These guys have a story of their own. James C. Spiers was with the 82nd Airborne glider troops. James was at Sicily, Naples, Foggia, and Normandy. Starting with the Med Campaign and working his way north, Don Harris joined as a paratrooper. He was a light machine-gunner serving in Europe with the 505th Parachute Infantry Regiment of the 82nd Airborne Division. Don was in five major combat engagements: Rome-Arno, Southern France, Ardennes, Rhineland, and Central Europe. For them he earned the Combat Infantryman's Badge, Purple Heart, Belgian Croix de Guerre, and Bronze Arrowhead. C.W. "Chuck" Hoyt, Jr. flew 35 missions over Nazi Germany from Foggia as command pilot on a B-17. His 21st mission was on his 21st birthday *(talk about BLOWING out the candle!)*. He also was involved in testing the first hydrogen bomb at Eniwetok. Chuck earned the Distinguished Flying Cross, the Air Medal with three oak leaf clusters, and the Distinguished Unit Citation. *(To put these flights in their proper perspective, a short note is warranted. In the 1943 raids over Europe 53 of 178 planes were lost at Ploesti, 60 more in the raids over Schweinfurt and Regensburg, and 65 of 291 at the bombing run on Schweinfurt. This was surely hazardous duty.)*

Chester Lawless...a real hard luck story. Fortunately, he seems to have overcome all obstacles to the game of life. Here is Chester's brush with the flying fickle finger of fate:

I was with the 8th Air Force, flying out of England. I went over in June of '43. On 30 July I flew into Germany on my first mission and dropped bombs. Ack-ack hit us on the return trip. I was in the ball turret when the ack-ack exploded between the two guns I was shooting. Shrapnel went into my right leg. Oil from the number three engine also covered the turret, so I couldn't see. Somehow I got to the waist gun to try to help. I got hit a second time there by shrapnel in the back...Messersmits and FW-190 fighters came in as we fell out of formation and hit us again. The next thing I remember is the radio operator coming back and lifting out the other gunner to bail out. We all finally got out over Holland.

A nice lady helped me when I got on the ground. I couldn't even get up,

236

much less run to hide. A Red Cross guy patched me up some, and the Germans came and got me. Later on, they brought the pilot in, and he got me a doctor. We hadn't started bombing Germany yet, so they actually treated us like human beings. Then they put me on a school bus and took me to Amsterdam. I don't remember much of that. A German doctor operated on me, and I stayed there a month. The Germans had captured our whole crew by then and brought them all to where I was. Then they sent me to Frankfurt for interrogation. Remember, they hadn't been bombed yet, so they weren't hostile at this stage. Later they got nasty. I got sent to another camp that was run by Germans but had English doctors who had been captured at Dunkirk. They operated on me again.

I moved to southern Germany, Lithuania until the Russians came, to Stalag Luft 4, and finally Stalag Luft 6 around Rostock on the Baltic Sea. The Russians came again, so we went to Stalag Luft 1 at Boris. I found out that later Norman Stockstill was there, too. The Russians liberated me in early May 1945.

By and large, we were treated OK to fair. We unloaded coal when it came in, unloaded potatoes, and served food at the hospital for something to do. Our guards were older men. The Germans had conned them into visiting the old country and drafted them into the army. One guard actually owned a restuarant in

Chicago! Another's son was flying Spitfires out of England. We tried to escape a lot, but we kept getting recaptured. We were lucky. When we were liberated, me and another guy picked up a rubber wheeled wagon and two horses and just started riding down the road. A Russian soldier on a bicycle playing a concertina rode by and told us the war was over.

Chester said his pilot told him he was sorry that he had to fly the "Purple Heart corner" on his first flight. That spot is the lowest aircraft in the formation.

****RICHARDSON****

James Collins Richardson started a legacy with his family and the military that spans much of this century. The large picture is the refernce. Bottom row center is James the elder. He was a chaplain in WWI with the 140th Field Artillery in France and Germany. After being the pastor in Poplarville for 11 years, James was in WWII as a chaplain again, this time in the Pacific Theater. First son, James F. (upper left), was in the Coast Artillery during WWII. He was in the Caribbean Theater. Second son, Bland Z. (lower right), was in the Army Air Corps in the European Theater. He was also in the Korean War. Third son, Jack Collins Richardson (upper right), was in the European Theater with the 1st Army, Lightening Division. Jack was killed in action and buried at Margraten, Holland. Fourth son, John w. (lower left), was in the European Theater with the Army Air Corps. Bland had a son, Jack C., who was in the Army in Vietnam. Bland had a son-in-law, John E. Greames. He was in the Air Force in Vietnam. *(This information was freely and proudly presented by Bland Z. Richardson. He says that the main point is that his family has always done its part. Hear, hear.)*

Charles Emmitt Walker flew 20 bombing missions against the Germans with the 466th Bomb Group, 8th Air Corps:

I was stationed in northeast England as a B-24 pilot. I flew missions against Berlin, Stuttgart, Magdeburg, mostly against railroads and aircraft and materiel plants in 1944 and 45. I flew ten missions just in the Battle of the Bulge and even bombed the bridge at Remagen *(for which several of our guys were thankful, I'm sure)*. The Bulge battle was the worst mission I ever went on because we were flying low, and tanks were even shooting up at us. We lost very few planes. We lost a lot more crazy ground crew than of us. They lived right next to the plane and did a tremendous job of keeping us in the air. We flew a different plane every mission, so there was very little nose art. Oh yes, the "Memphis Belle" was a pretty accurate movie. They must have had good advisors.

Charles received the Air Medal with 4 oak leaf clusters.

Hal Province went to England toward the end of the Battle of the Bulge as a replacement for the 8th Air Force:

I was a toggeleer on a B-17 with the 34th Bomb Group, 391st Squadron. We were on the way over when we spent New Year's Eve of '45 in Wales. I was reporting to a good group. They had flown 133 missions without getting hit by fighters.

My first mission started with the usual long pinochle game, followed by two hours of sleep. It was in March 1945. We were supposed to hit Ruhland, but it was socked in. We went to Dresden and dropped our load *(These were the bombs Julia Kubat saw from her prison camp. I hope these two people meet each other.).* Anyhow, this was their 134th mission and my first. Sure enough, we got hit by ME-109s. They didn't have much fuel, so they just came right down our bomb stream...One pass... Just like a dog running up against a parade. There was a dogfight at 6 o'clock. We got hit all over the plane...It sounded like hail. I was riding as a nose gunner until bomb time and got to fire at one of them before I had to go to work. We were in the air 11 hours. Our lead plane lost an engine, so we dawdled along at 125 mph all the way back to give them help.

I flew 19 combat missions. We flew one down to Rouen to knock out some naval guns. The next to last mission was to Czechoslovakia, trying to keep ahead of Patton. But, the last mission was the most interesting, April '45. *(That's 19 missions in less that two months, folks. This guy must have grown his own wings!)* We flew 150 feet over Holland and dropped food. General Beedle Smith had negotiated with the German general. I can't remember his name. Beetle told him that we were going to fly corridors to deliver food to the oppressed people. The German said: "That leaves me cold." Beedle said: "You're damn right. We're going to hang you as a war criminal." Sure enough, nobody fired on us. We lowered our flaps and wheels and slowed down to drop. I could see the Germans standing guard. The Dutch were under quarantine. I know we helped them a lot. On the 40th anniversary the Dutch government flew us over there from New York and took us to all the drop sites. It really made me feel good.

Hal earned the ETO ribbon with 3 battle stars and the Air Medal with 2 oak leaf clusters.

David Schaller was in the 385th Bomb Group, 548th Squadron, 8th Air Force. David was in England and France from October '44 to September '45:

I was a radio operator on a B-17 stationed at Great Ashfield at first. I flew my first combat mission in November '44 against ball bearing factories at Merseburg, Germany. Since the German fighters were all wiped out by then, we had freedom of the skies except for flak. We flew between 12 and 36,000 feet. The factory? We got it. We went after some warehouses in Munich where we dropped some 100 pound GPs. We also dropped some 200 to 500 pound clusters of incendiary bombs. We'd put 100 in a cluster, put in a charge, and bind them together. They would blow up just before they hit the ground. We did this on a Sunday morning, just after the Germans got out of church. I was also in on bombing raids over marshalling yards in Berlin.

I made 31 missions before the war ended. At the end we were dropping K-rations to the French populace to keep them from starving. A funny thing happened on one mission. The pilot and engineer were asleep, the co-pilot was reading, and I was listening to the radio. We were on automatic pilot. Directly, a slag pile appeared before us, and we had to make a screaming ascent. Just missed it!

Another time was not so funny. I had to bail out. It was on the 2nd of January, 1945, during the Battle of the Bulge. You know, the Bulge was where the Germans were trying to penetrate our lines to get to our supplies in Antwerp. Anyhow, we were over France. An engine started vibrating. We didn't know which would go first- the engine or the wing. Both were only held on by four bolts. I tried to get to the equalizers to feather the engine, but couldn't. The co-pilot said for us to wait a few minutes to see if we could stall it out. We had a load of bombs.

When we started parachuting out, I had to go back and get my gloves. I think I was the last one out. We all made it. We were dropping through the clouds and had no sensation of falling at about 125 mph. We were supposed to wait until we could hear dogs barking or chickens clucking before we opened the chutes to keep the Germans from spotting us. I had a 24 foot chute with a hole in the center to prevent swaying. I opened mine- still have the ripcord- and tried to guide it. That was a mistake because it half folded up on me. I saw the plane hit the ground. Then I saw a town, which I fortunately drifted over and missed the buildings. Unfortunately, I hit a mill pond. It was an iced-over beet mill pond; and, man, did it stink! Just like a hog pen. I broke the ice. Then I broke some more ice with my captors/rescuers. After this Frenchman tried to spit in my face, I made him understand "Schaller" was now an American name. They carried me into town for some Irish potatoes and French bread. That was all they had, but it was good. Of course, the cognac helped. It was good stuff- 6 star.

Then our MPs picked me up. We stopped by a bistro and had some more cognac. We went to a B-26 base. I had never been so cold in my life. I had to stay in an eight-man pup tent. We had one lump of coal for warmth. It was cold. It was so foggy during the Bulge. It cleared up Christmas, and that's why we were all in the air. We had over 2000 bombers and fighters up there.

David said he was with Moses Attaya over in England, and that was a good thing. Moses didn't drink, so David got his own

243

daily allowance of one shot of cognac and then he got Moses'. That helped with the cold. After the fighting stopped, David became part of a C47 crew flying as-needed missions carrying mail, exPOWs, tires, whatever. David's brother, Henry, was a baker in the Pacific during WWII. His real vocation was as a welder, but that didn't seem to matter. His half-brother, Roy May, was in France in WWI. David said he also saw Clyde Stewart in England the day before Clyde was being sent home. David earned the Air Medal with 4 oak leaf clusters and the EAMETO Medal. David added:

> We did have one more story. Our waist gunner, a Pollock, had already flown 35 missions in the Africa campaign. Our leaders wanted to get him a DSC *(Distinguished Service Cross)*. They cooked up the idea for me to pass out from the lack of oxygen. The Pollock came up and revived me, and they put him in for the medal. They figured anyone who had flown 65 combat missions deserved something.

***** WHEAT *****

It's now time to introduce the fighting Wheats. We've already met grandfather W.G. in The War Between the States. Mr. and Mrs. Griffin Wheat had five sons who fought in WWII at the same time. Delton was in the Air Corps. He was trained to be a B-17 bombardier, but wound up as a skipper. On his second mission over occupied France, his plane was shot down by six German fighters, although his mission was accomplished through a flak layer. His B-17 was limping toward Britain when the crew had to bail out over Dieppe, France. Delton was rescued by a woman and her son. They nursed him back to health in the midst of all the Germans occupying the area. Delton was trying to get through to the French underground in Paris when he was captured in 1943. He underwent constant interrogations and was on his way to the firing squad when he was knocked out after trying to escape.

Delton dropped from 206 t0 135 pounds in the two years of his captivity. In Paris the food was almost non-existent, and his cell was infested with fleas. He was then moved during these two years to several German stalags, where he was liberated from Moosberg on 29 April '45, over two and one-half years after his capture. Among his celebrities were (1) looking up to see General Patton's pearl handled revolvers in the stalag, (2) eating with Ike on the way home, and (3) training with Jimmy Stewart in Idaho *(this info from the Daily News)*.

Delton's brother, Crawley, was typical of the young men of the time, as he was initiated in North Africa, took a tour of Italy, and was involved in action at Anzio. Vernon served with the infantry in the Mediterranean Theater and saw action in Italy. In fact, Vernon and Crawley met in Rome during the conquest. Magnus was with an engineering unit in Belgium. His unit was overrun by a panzer division, and he spent eight days in a foxhole playing dead to avoid capture. The last of these courageous boys, Dentson, made it in time to occupy Japan, as he enlisted in November 1944.

PEARSON

Three sons of Mr. and Mrs. Dallas Pearson covered this war. One, Lemual A., was a B-24 pilot with the 8th Air Corps. For his career against the Huns, he earned the Distinguished Flying Cross, the Air Medal with five oak leaf clusters, and several battle stars. Lem was recalled for duty during the Korean War with the Headquarters Squadron, 315th Air Division. Brothers D.L. Junior and Malcome H. were in the Pacific Theater with the Navy. D.L. was a gunners mate, and Malcome spent 18 months over there as an aviation mechanic.

Moses Attaya, 8th Air Corps, was an aerial gunner on a B-17. He was David Schaller's friend, as noted earlier. Moses made eight combat missions while earning the Air Medal with three combat stars. Wilfred Westbrook was there four years. J.P. Rester, co-pilot of a B-24 in the 455 Bomb Group, was awarded the EAMETO Medal with four battle stars and the Air Medal with one oak leaf cluster. Shirley Goleman served with the 766th Chemical Depot Company, Aviation, in England and France. He was awarded the Meritorious Service after his arrival in Normandy. Morgan D. Pringle, 261st Infantry Regiment, 65th Division, was killed crossing the Rhine.

Ted LaMunyon was in the Army's 9th Air Corps as a flight engineer on a "cut wing" B-26:

> I liked them *(the planes)*. I flew on the plane with the commanding general sometimes. The B-26s were used for almost everything, even

246

hauling. I went over in '43 and started by flying out of England. Next, when we were stationed in Luxembourg, we pulled something very unusual. The weather had just broken, and the Battle of Bastogne was about to start. The Germand were coming close. I was on the plane that took four generals at one time on the same plane to Liege, Belgium. I mean, Vandenburg, Doolittle, and two others. That's never supposed to happen!

We came in at Weisbaden toward the end. Somebody had found some high-potency wine in a cellar. They had filled up jerry cans and taken them back to the group. By the time we got there, everyone else was already drunk. Being the only sober one, I took another guy to go back for resupplies. They had run out in two hours. When I got there, the cellar was being guarded by MPs. We sneaked around back and crawled in a window. There were a lot of GIs still there. Wine was over an inch deep in the cellar! Also, the day we arrived at Wiesbaden I was assigned to a flight to Berlin before I was even assigned a barracks.

Ted enjoyed the job and the people he worked with. He was there for about 10 years, and they were always good to him. Ted received his basic training at Keesler of all places. Ted says that "anyone who spends time with the military will be improved by it." We'll see Ted again after the war.

Let's talk about a large dose of

patriotism done in a big way. The entire Industrial High School 1940-41 basketball team enlisted, including the coach! They were John "Red" Taylor, Julius Seal, Charles Sherrer, Laverne Stuart, Ralph Nations, Clyde Stewart, Marvin Moody, Lawrence Nix, J.C. Smith, Edward E. Smith, and Delos Burks (coach). There were Navy and Air Corps pilots, navigators and other bomb crew members, Army tank commanders, and Naval personnel.

Lastly, but certainly not least, somebody had to keep all these knights in shining armor patched together. Meet Herma Philippi Smith of the 110th Station Hospital in Great Britain from April 1942 until the end. We're sure she handled more bandages and blood than a zombie convention.

And, of course, all good stories have a boy-meets-girl part. So do we. It seems as though Verna Roche was in the Nurse's Corp's 64th General Hospital in North Africa and Italy. In fact, she earned the EAMETO Campaign Ribbon with two battle stars. Samual Whan Doan was an air observation pilot for the 178th Field Artillery group of the 5th Army in North Africa and Italy. Doan got shot down behind enemy lines while on a reconnaissance mission. He was awarded a Purple Heart and a Bronze Star Medal for exercising a high degree of courage, daring, and ingenuity in escaping and making his way back while wounded. You guessed it. He and Verna met in the hospital, were married in Florence, and lived a long, happy life together. They must have, they still have six daughters living around here!

We are given a local newspaper *(from 15 April 1944)* listing employees who had recently come home from the war. Included was: Louis T. Jackson of the 461st Q.M. Laundry Company; L. Arnold Stockstill of the H/S Company, 163rd Engineers Battalion in England; Claudia Stockstill of Headquarters Company, 34th Construction Battalion from "Island X" somewhere in the Pacific as a mess cook; and Albert McCallum in McCloskey hospital. We are also given the hint of another 5-star family, that of W.A. "Ole Settler" Breedlove. His sons are Lamar, Clifford, Leslie (in the 954th Signal Company), Toxie (just back from the South Pacific), and Robert (England).

The most famous American during the war was, oddly enough, not from Pearl River County. You ask why he's here. It's Kilroy. Kilroy was an actual person somewhere who inspected tanks before they went overseas, stamping "Kilroy" on them if acceptable. The idea spread so much that the GIs would write or draw "Kilroy was here" on everything. Our hat is off to the donor of the Kilroy Washere brick. The person shows true genius!

The second most famous to later generations has become "Rosie the Riveter." We are fortunate enough to have a representative of that esteemed group in our midst, one "Grandma" Tha David:

> I welded on ships, four or five of them. On airplane carriers at the Willamette Shipyard in Portland.

249

Eisenhower christened one of them. I can't remember which though. I welded down all the tables and chairs on them. We *(Grandma's sister and two sisters-in-law)* worked there from 1941 until the war ended in 45. I sewed tarps the first year and then went to welding school. I graduated in three days. We had hundreds of women working on the ships.
Once I had to get on a Russian ship to make repairs. They had a big ole hog on there. Every time I would get up on the scaffolding to start welding, that hog would come around. He made me nervous *(You wouldn't think farmlife would scare Grandma. She has a great garden now.)*. One of the other girls would have to stand there with a broom to run him off while I welded!

Bond Drives were a popular way to raise funds for the war effort. Rationing became popular-if not necessary- as well. One of the ditties during that time among the warriors went something like this:
"Don't back the attack
by laying a WAC
or riding the breast of a WAVE.
But lay in the sand
and do it by hand
and buy bonds with the money you save."

-Anonymous

World War II was the war that glorified the business. It was also a war that showed that some peacetime officers belong to the ranks of politicians in the

time of war, because several were shunted
out of the way for more competent men
whose lips may not have been so puckered.
The military is not the only place where
this phenomenon occurs, but it is more
costly in lives. It has been said that we
won this war because we made fewer errors
than did the Axis. So be it.

Interregnum (Cold War)

Police action was been the name of the game during the Cold War. Pearl River County troops have been representative of the population in all branches of the services everywhere there was a need. We have been the watchdogs in Europe, the Far East, Central America, seemingly the whole world, at great cost to Americaboth in manpower and money. It seems to have been a great investment because it apparently has worked. As this is being written the Communist empire is crumbling. There is talk of cutting our troops in all foreign places and, in fact, finally starting to dismantle the mighty war machine that emerged from WWII.

It is hard to restrain a fighting animal on a leash, and humans are not much different. That is what Cold War fighting was all about. Given an objective, an American has always taken it. When told "do this, but don't do that," the tables turn, the mighty fighting machine gets rusty, and demoralization sets in. Regretably, sometimes the President of the US thinks he is bigger than his constituency or his military advisors. Since the "Great Wars" this has happened several times at a great cost of human life with no return to us. The President has to go to Congress to get a war declared, and this has not been done since WWII, thereby fulfilling Eisenhower's prophesy of the military-industrial complex.

At the end of WWII the US had a worldwide committment to peace and non-

252

communism. Ralph Pierce was in the 5th Fleet, Navy, helping to do that very thing:

> I was on the IOWA, VICKSBURG, APPALACHIAN, BAYFIELD, and SIERRA in the Pacific theater between Hawaii and Guam in 1946 and 47. I was a cryptographer on message traffic.

The evolution of arms and armament has been a fact of life since time immemorial. Its deleterious effects on the welfare of all have been repeatedly felt by those who did not have the biggest stick. In 1947 if war weren't enough on land and sea, it took to the air with a vengence in the form of our Air Force. This arm of the service became increasingly important during the Cold War.

In 1948 Russia sponsored the Berlin blockade, so we countered with the Berlin airlift. Pearl River County had several young men help in that cause. Ted Lamunyon, who made 136 flights, recalls:

> We flew anything you would expect in normal trade in to them on C-54s. We worked at least 12 on and 12 off, seven days a week. Your name went on a board, and when it came up, it was your turn to go. We never had the same crew all the time.

The Republic of China fell in 1949. We had been "assisting" there since WWII, theoretically preventing the spread of Communism. This was true in Korea. A Communist outbreak occurred when the South Koreans were overrun and pushed back to the vicinity of Pusan.

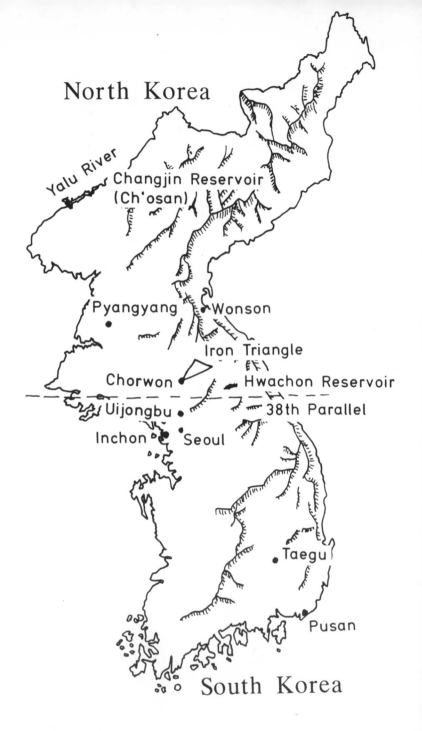

North Korea

Yalu River

Changjin Reservoir
(Ch'osan)

Pyangyang • • Wonson

Iron Triangle

Chorwon • Hwachon Reservoir

Uijongbu • 38th Parallel

Inchon • • Seoul

Taegu

Pusan

South Korea

Korea

PORKCHOP HILL-YALU RIVER- PUSAN- INCHON-
SEOUL-38th PARALLEL-CH'OSAN RESERVOIR-
M-1-MacARTHUR-SABRE JETS-SYNGMAN RHEE.
*The concensus of our veterans seems to be
that they were ready for Korea, and that
an aura of patriotism still rang true
from WWII. Our Pearl River Countians were
sent to Korea to stop the spread of the
Communists and to push them back to the
north. We were well represented from
1950-1953. While these men were making a
good account of themselves, General Mac-
Arthur recognized the need to go all the
way to China. Unfortunately, President
Truman did not agree and fired MacArthur.
The conflict never ended, and we still
have men stationed in Korea.*

Paul Merrill provides a running
commentary on early Korea. Paul was with
the 25th Division, 27th Regimental Combat
Team, 8th Field Artillery as part of the
occupational forces in Japan when we
catch up to him:
I was sent to Pusan from Japan on
July 7th, 1950, in a converted Japanese wooden boat. We were to try to
hook up with the 24th Division,
which had been there for a few days.
They were shot up pretty bad, and my
first introduction to war was find-
ing a dead MP in a Jeep on the side
of the road. MPs are rear echelon
people, so this got me sort of nervous. At first we had ROK *(Republic
of South Korea)* support. They had
really old guns. Later, we got a
battalion of Brits from Thailand,

followed by two brigades of Canadians. The main reason we were able to establish the Pusan perimeter was because the Air Force helped by strafing and bombing runs. I was a forward observer and was wounded in the leg at this time while running all over the place. In about October we headed north. I'm living out of a Jeep. No tent. No hot food. My clothes eventually rotted off my body, so I found some more.

We were holding a hill for 11 days, living in a foxhole, when the gooks came. They sent in Russian tanks. Ours were much smaller, so we sent them off to fight another day. I called in artillery, and a shell hit one of their tanks. As fate would have it, a passing Brit plane had a rocket left and delivered the payload. It looked like a tincan exploding with the lid going straight up. Anyhow, we lost the hill and had to split up and regroup elsewhere. Then we tried to recapture General Ding of the 24th (*They had all been captured at the start, including Clarence Penton, Jr.*) from Taejon but didn't succeed.

Our supplies, arms, everything was not up to standards, and reinforcements were being trained right on the line. We finally secured a line about 25 miles from Pusan (*If you look at a map, you'll see you can't go south. These guys were hanging onto a cliff by their fingernails, so to speak!*). In September we secured Taegu Air Base after a couple of tries. By now we had lost about half of our people. We took Seoul, did some mop-up work, and joined the Marines who had landed at Inchon. We jointly pushed up through the North Korean capital across the 38th Parallel on to the Yalu River. Then we got word that 11,000 Chinese had gotten in behind us, so we pulled back in December. Leadership between units (crosstalk) was lacking, so this was done in a haphazard fashion. We found out the Marines were still on the frozen Ch'osun Reservoir. We sent tanks, but they all got wiped out in a valley by old howitzers that had been dug in somehow. We lost a lot of equipment at this time. I was driving all over the place in my Jeep with my green lieutenant and an interpreter. We came up to the out-skirts of Seoul, saw a hut, and called out. Somebody came out -they all wore the outfit of the day, not uniforms- walked up to us, and killed the interpreter by shooting him in the neck. Me and the lieuten-ant jumped out, ran to the other side, and kept the jeep between us and them. We walked 27 miles that night, and the next night we made it to Seoul. We discovered we only had 80 to 90 UN forces in Seoul at that time, where I found only 11 from my regular outfit. We also had two tanks, one of which was parked under a culvert, much the same as on the Ozona road. I was trying to tell the tanks where to fire and getting in touch with any airplanes in range. I also got our howitzers to quit

shelling us. Seven more of us were
killed in this action. At that time
I took a piece of shrapnel in the
right shoulder that penetrated to my
lung. They put me in a Jeep and hid
me behind the tank for a while.
Eventually, 16 of the 80 to 90
troops were all that made it through
3 Jan 1951.

For Paul's work in Korea, he earned a
Silver Star, Korean Service Medal with 3
battle stars, Presidential Unit Citation,
and a Purple Heart with oak leaf cluster.
Paul says the Air Force kept them from
being annihilated in Korea. He also says
he has no regrets because he got to finish high school while he was recovering
at Walter Reed Hospital. Paul used the
G.I. Bill to graduate from the River. His
son, Greg, was in the Navy from 1977-82.

Rod Martin was with the 31st
Infantry, 7th Division:

I went in 1949. I spent eight months
on patrol around Inchon and Pusan. I
got hit three times, all at the same
time. I woke up in a hospital, went
back to the outfit, and got sent
home.
We were fighting more Chinese than
gooks. They sent droves in on us. We
didn't have the right weapons.
I believe that if you didn't have
America to defend everybody else,
we'd all be hurting.

Rod earned a Purple Heart for his action.

Clarence Penton, Jr., was in the
24th Division, 19th Regiment, HQ Company,
sent over in July 1950. Let this man
talk:

258

We were pulling out of our position (11 Aug). I stopped to get a switchboard and some telephone equipment. I got cut off and had to fight my way back to my unit. I was wounded, and was sent back to Japan to recover. For that action I received a Bronze Star with "V" for Valor and a Purple Heart with oak leaf cluster. My first wound came in the defense of the Pusan perimeter. I came back 27 September and was captured 1 January 1951 *(what a rotten New Year's present)*. I spent 33 months and 17 days as a POW. I escaped a couple of times and was recaptured. Depending on how the peace talks were going, we were treated accordingly. They tried to brainwash us by torture. I was almost starved to death, as I dropped from 140 to 86 pounds. I was MIA for the first 14 months, so I never heard from home or received a Red Cross package. I do feel that we should have been there to keep Communism from spreading throughout SE Asia.

Our honor roll for the Korean War includes Air Force pilot William T. Powell, who also spent four years in WWII; infantryman Gordon Hughes Dailey, Marine Cecil O. Sand, and Houston "Goshie" Burks. Goshie tells us that: "On Hangman Hill the Chinese would try to take it every night. They took everything our boys could throw at them, and kept coming back for more. As an advisor, I suggested arming the defenders with shotguns. Once was enough!" Goshie, by the way, picked up another battle star in Korea. James W. Flynt was in the Navy in WWII and the Air Force in Korea; Joseph Moore, Navy and Army. Frank Evans pulled both duties in the Navy. Turner J. Deshotel was in the 981st Army Engineering Construction Batallion. Samual A. Whitfield was in the South Pacific and Korea in the Army and Air Force.

Leo B. Wood had a real love for the sea: Order of Shellback, Golden Dragon, Magellan Award, and all. He had just come in from fishing when I caught up with him. We can now all be privy to just how he earned those and many other awards. Leo says:

> I was in the Merchant Marine in WWII. The first ship was the SS BEN T. OSBORN from September '44 to January '45. We took a load of planes, fuel, and parts up to Calcutta for Christmas, I remember. I sailed all the way around the world on that one. Then I went to the SS STONY POINT until January 46. We also sailed around the world on the one. We always ran alone carrying Navy Special (a fuel). Once we got strafed by a Jap bomber near Truk. We had five injured, but no serious damage. I also saw some air raids at Ulithi. I got out after that war and went into the Navy Reserves.

Leo earned the American/Atlantic and American/Pacific combat ribbons for the Merchant Marines. What happened next adds to the story and explains why he is in the Korean Chapter:

> I was in the Navy Reserve and

volunteered for active duty in 1950. After I got in, I was extended for a year by Truman, so I didn't get out until '52. I was on LSTs for the Korean War- the 803 and the 1148. I was sailing from Pusan to Kojedo Island making prisoner transfers at first. One time the Chinks tunneled under the prison and captured an Army general. We had to negotiate to get him back.

While on the 1148, we had a Marine helicopter on board. It was used to take fresh ice, clean laundry, and so on to Admiral Joy at the Peace Camp at Seoul. From there I went to the AKA-54, the USS ALGOL, for the rest of the tour until I got out again.

(The LST-803 saw extensive service in the Korean War and was awarded 5 battle stars overall.) I earned one of those for an amphibious exercise we carried out hauling the California 40th National Guard. We were the only LST to make a landing on Sendai, unload, and get off safely.

(The LST -1148 also saw extensive service in the Korean War, earning one battle star and a Meritorious Unit Commendation. The ALGOL went to Korea with reinforcements and supplies for the Marines and stayed. She took part in the Wonsan landing in October and the Chinnampo evacuation in December.)

Not that Leo had enough by now, he stayed in the Reserves until:

I got called back in one more time for the Berlin Crisis in 60. I reported aboard the USS VAMMEN, a destroyer escort. We were using it mainly as weekend warriors until our Reserve unit was sent to the WESTPAC. We went on patrol off Vietnam as a show of strength for six months. Once we escorted the POINT DEFIANCE, the NAVARRO, and the VALLEY FORGE when they took a bunch of Marines up to Bangkok *(40 Naval Reserve Training ships were reactivated during this time. The escort duty to Bangkok came on 13 May '62, when she was with the 3rd Batallion, 9th Marines. They went into Thailand to help the friendly regime deter Communist efforts to cross the Mekong River. She also participated in "Exercise Powerdive" before returning home.)*

Leo earned many war medals and battle stars over a varied career. He says he had a sleeve-full of hachures before he hung it up. I believe him!

We met Pete DeMarsh in WWII. Ha had gone to college. Well, along came the war, and Pete was grabbed up again:

I was just about to finish college when I was reactivated for Korea. The school started piling on extra homework and tests just so I could graduate before I went back in. In 1950 I went to Ellington Field and trained as a navigator on a B-25. Then I flew navigation students until 1951. I got sent to Korea to fly C-51s *(Mustangs)* in support of the 8th Army. I was stationed at K-1 Field. It was a nasty war- I won't give all the details. It wasn't popular. All the reserves were called back up, but none wanted to be. We thought we had just fought the war to end all wars. I thought it wasn't being fought in the way it should be *(shades of Vietnam)*. The supplies and logistics were different from WWII. We did have tremendous esprit de corps among the troops, though.

Pete said he was given the option to get out of the service because of longevity, and he took it. He was only in Korea for a few months. One of his better tales is about cooling beer *(Yes, Lewis, you old guys did a good job of passing on your knowledge of "high tech" refrigeration techniques.)*. Pete just threw the ammo away from his wing guns and replaced it with beer before taking off *(Veddy interesting, but without practicality in a dogfight!)*. Pete DeMarsh.

Billy Batson Pardue was in the 3rd Army, Co. C, 31st Infantry. Hilton Elwin Stinson, Air Force, was among the first to be sent over to Korea to evacuate civilians. Hershel J. Overton was in the 14th Engineers Combat Battalion. Roger R. Simmons, 11th Airborne Division paratrooper, says cold weather and no supplies caused most of the casualties in his Division. Roger earned a Bronze Star, Korean Combat Medal, and a Korean Presidential Citation. Billie W. Lee was in the 7th Division, 31st Military Police. Bobby Joe Burge was in Korea with the 3rd Medical Battalion, 3rd Marine Division, FMF.

Arnold Matthews was with the 1st Marines at Inchon (15 September 1950).

263

The Marines had to blow their way ashore,
helped by Corsair strafing, then they
joined the 7th Army and fought their way
to and through Seoul:

> We fought our way through barri-
> cades, from house to house, through
> machine gun fire, snipers, and
> cannons...whatever. It was really
> rough taking Seoul. When it was
> finally over (28 September), I
> stayed in Seoul to guard the
> prisoners for a while before the 1st
> went on up to the Ch'osan Reservoir
> for the winter. We brought all our
> men and wounded and equipment out of
> Ch'osan. I came out on a stretcher.
> I got three battle stars for Korea:
> Inchon, Seoul, and Ch'osan.

Arnold earned a Bronze Star at Seoul and
a Purple Heart at Ch'osan. We'll catch
up to him again in Vietnam.

*(The attack at Inchon, Operation
Chromite, is one of the US military's all
time bright spots for boldness of con-
cept, competence of planning, and skill
in execution. MacArthur pulled off the
"impossible and insane." It also brought
the Chinese Communists into the war. The
fight and retreat at Ch'osan are an
American epic. From 27 November to 9
December 1950, three Chinese Divisions
tried to overwhelm two Marine Regiments.
The temperature was always below 0
degrees F, sometimes as low as -25. Most
of the BARs and carbines would not work
at that temperature.*

*The Chinese attacked at night from the
front in a narrow file formation only to
spread out when they got into hand
grenade range. At two in the morning, a
Marine fired a hut to light the area, and*

*the Marines made a good account of
themselves. But, the Chinese kept coming.
I have even heard of Russians being up
there, too. This was one of the bloodiest
battles of the war. The American general
had an airstrip built to evacuate the
wounded. Then the Marines pulled back
with their equipment and more of the
wounded in an orderly fashion. It has not
been called a retreat because they were
constantly fighting and taking the high
ground and bridges to cover their trail.
The !st even had to get out on the ice to
fight. One assumes that this is the
reason for "frozen Chosin." They crawled,
clawed, and crept their way out until it
was over on 11 December 1950. Between 15
September and 11 December Arnold was in
three major battles.)*

Burt Pearson. You all remember him
from WWII- Ranger, escaped POW, the whole
nine yards. He began his Korean War
early:
In '49 I was in Japan for the war
crimes trials. We hung 21 command-
ants for various atrocities committed against prisoners. In '50 I was
at the "Big 8" stockade pulling
guard duty in Japan when the action
broke out. I got sent into the 7th
Rangers again, this time with the
7th Infantry Division to do recon
work. I went in at Inchon, then to
Yongdungp'o, then Seoul. I went to
Ch'unch'on. After that there was a
big tank battle with the 7th and
the Marines at Ch'orwon Reservoir.
On Halloween 1950 I got shot up in a
fire fight at Uijongbu. I got hit by
a mortar shell and woke up 14 days

265

later at Walter Reed Hospital. I was in the Korean War one month *(These Rangers surely did move around a lot! This was about the time of the total Chinese committment all over the country. This shock would not have happened if our leaders would have listened to the incoming intelligence.).*
Burt doesn't talk too much about certain things, but, in one month, he earned another Silver Star and a Distinguished Service Cross. Neither his body nor his uniform could ever pass a metal detector test at the airport. He totalled one DSC, two Silver Stars, two Bronze Stars, a couple of Purple Hearts, and escaped from the Japs to extract his ounce of revenge in the two wars.

Walt Powers was with the 2nd Division, Army, from 1949 to 1952 as a 1666, medical technician. He recalls for us that he "just did as I was told." He continues:

I went in at Inchon after the Ch'orwon battle- up to the Upper and Lower Alligator Jaws (hills). I was a front-line medic who carried a gun. Somebody forgot to tell the Koreans and Chinese about the Geneva Convention. We wore the Red-Cross armbands anyhow, but they made excellent targets.

Sabre jets were big in Korea. We'd sit in a foxhole and guess which pilots were single and which were married. When they came in for napalm strafing runs, the married ones always flew higher.

266

Ford Evans was in the medical unit of the 5th Anti-aircraft Battalion. Ford was on his way to Alaska when he was diverted in 1950:

I was a dental technician who got sent to Japan to a small hospital and then to a big one in Osaka. We had an 1800 bed facility and 4100 patients. I was in that hospital 28 months during the Korean War, except when we went to Korea to pick up casualties. I put enough sutures in to sew from here to Jackson!
I wouldn't take anything for the experience. It was a good one. We got to see Grandpa Jones. We also saw Joe Louis fight an exhibition. Of course, none of us could stay in the ring with him. This war? *(interviewed 1800 hrs 5 February '91)* If someone is going to do you dirt and you know it, you don't give him a date you're going to do it back. You just jump on him.

Ford says he was the only one in his unit to come back alive. He feels that because he was an only son, he stopped in Japan instead of going to the front line in Korea. Whatever, these guys were all integral parts of the effort.

AMACKER

Sollie Amacker and his three sons made their presence felt. Sollie was in WWI with the Army. One son, Cleveland:

I made two trips to Korea. The first one was the bad one. I was there in the 2nd Infantry Division, 23rd Infantry Regiment from October 1950 to October 1951. I was also there

267

from December 1954 to December 1955
with the 7th Infantry Division, 31st
Infantry Regiment.
Son Raymond was in the Army. The last
son, Hershel, was also in the Army. Even
though he belongs in another era, I
include him with his family:

I was in Vietnam in 70-71 with the
"Big Red One," the 84th Engineers. I
went in as a cook at DaNang and
ended up in a rear echelon air
engineer batallion. I was resupply-
ing forward observer NDPs with food
and ammunition. My biggest thrill
was winning an Air Medal.

WHAT PRICE GLORY

I knew him first in childhood
When only just a boy.
He'd top the fence and watch the trains
And chant with childish joy.

His days were full and happy
The simple things were good;
Fishing in the little creek,
Hiking in the wood.

Blue eyes calm, serene;
Worry - far away,
Take life as it comes,
Live it day by day.

Came the day when Uncle Sam
Needed him to fight,
Only in his teens,
Against the German might.

What he thought and saw,
No one ever knew.
Bombs falling all around,
Death to comrades, too.

Later on again,
A police patrol
Fought in South Korea,
Casualties untold.

Where went all the carefree days,
Joy of wood and stream;
Men must kill each other
End of summer's dream.

Somewhere in those cruel years,
Blue eyes lost their glow.
Behind them was the sight of death,
The courage brave men know.

I'd like to see those blue eyes smile,
To take away the pain
Of youth and manhood spent in war,
And let him live again.

He didn't win a medal,
Bronze Star or Purple Heart,
His only scar - those sad blue eyes,
His only claim - his part.

> *-written by Mary Yvonne*
> *Carroll about her*
> *brother, Darrell Luther*
> *Mitchell*

THE 138th

Joining the regular Army in Korea was the 138th Engineer Co. of the National Guard. This company built bridges, two long and many short, in support of this police effort. One of the longer ones was built with American tanks behind the engineers and the Chinese Communists on the other side of the river *(Is this a bridge over troubled waters or what?)*. We are told that was a nerve-

wracking experience! Taking part were:
David W. Gillis, Billy Buckley, Horrace
Dossett, Olan Rayburn, Roland Baxter,
Thomas Pearson, Jr., Hascal Stockstill,
Herman Bennett, Pinkney Broom, Alex
"Buster" Fisher, Joseph Lenoir, Toxie
Mitchell, Vaughn Brayson, Douglas Burge,
Houston Burks, Brandon Creel, John
Dupont, William Fleming, Robert Kelly,
Robert Jordan, Jimboye Lumpkin, Norman
McCaskell, Samuel McClinton, Bobby McRee,
Neville Pearson, Cyril Piazza, Danial
Price, William "Buncie" Sheffield, Jr.,
William Simmons, Allen Stockstill,
Theodore Stockstill, Lonnie Strain,
Charles Thomas, Louis Varnado, John
Walker, James Watkins, G.D. Williamson,
James Winstead, Hugh Adcox, Ollie
Alsobrooks, Jr., Hershel Beal, James
Becker, Dewey Booty, Edward Bridges,
Bernard Burge, Clinton Carter, Benjamin
Crosby, Glyn Dubuisson, Curtis Ekes,
Douglas Holcomb, Lewis Holloway, Donald
Hughes, Joe Jennings, Bruce Jones,
William Jones, Willie Jordan, E.J.
Landry, William Penton, T.J. Powell,
William Preston, Robert Ritchie, Lester
Seal, Joe Seals, Thomas Seals, Donald
Shamber, Jerry Shaffield, Varon Spiers,
James Stewart, Leo Stockstill, Billy
Tate, Herbert Thompson, Francis Lee,
Garland Lee, Jack Lee, Bobby Lenoir,
Billy E. McCaskell, James A. Martin,
Brookler A. Mitchell, Jr., Lonnie E.
Morris, Lepole R. O'Quin, Cecil D. Patch,
Forrest C. Pearson, Robert A. Pearson,
Jr., Jewel Penton, Jr., R.J. Penton,
Charles G. Warren, Walter L. Watkins,
Jack S. Wilkinson, William R. Ballard,
Clayton J. Bond, Guy T. Burge, Thomas O.
Cook, James D. Dillard, Laverne L.

Garriga, James Johnson, Jr., Larvie D.
Kennedy, Leslie L. Kirkland, Elroy Lee,
Elwin D. Lee, Ezell G. Lee, Garland O.
Lee, Grayson W. Lee, Virgil. R. Lee, Jack
W. Lloyd, Gifford R. Megehee, Charles A.
Mitchell, James A. Penton, Alvie E.
Stockstill, Curtis R. Walters, Marvin H.
Watkins, Lewis W. Kennedy, Jr., Smith W.
Kennedy, Wilmer J. Lott, Benjamin S.
Randie, Earl Rester, J.D. Stewart, James
Z. Russell, Lloyd D. Varnado, Rayburn H.
Bates, William T. Booth, Curtis L.
Carter, Monroe F. Crell, William F.
Creel, Julian D. Davis, George A. Harvey,
William C. Jarrell, Herbert H. Jones, Roy
L. Kennedy, Herbert R. Knight, Willie D.
Mason, Hilbert G. Miller, Charles F.
Mitchell, Eulas O. Mitchell (Korean
Service Medal with two battle stars),
Jackie B. Mitchell, Jay H. Mitchell,
Robert E. Mitchell, Gwendell L. Pearson,
Daris Pigott, Darriell Pigott, Haskell
Smith, Elvin E. Walters, Charles E.
Wells, Gary W. Whitfield, William C.
Wilbanks, and David H. Williams. Hank
Stockstill, who was left over from the
Pacific Theatre in WWII, and Samual
McClinton, who had been in the Navy in
WWII, were also there.

Ezell Lee signed waivers as a 16
year old to join. Ezell has several
stories:

We unloaded in Pusan and travelled
three days and nights through dust
and snow and ice. We were going to
bridge the Han River. Four of us
were selected to help the 24th
Infantry across the river. That was
our introduction to combat. The rest
of the group came up later and
bridged that river. After we built

that bridge, we helped maintain
roads. I came home when I was 18.
The Han River bridge broke loose in
a high water stand even after eleven
hours of trying to save it. Four
members of the crew caught up with
it a few miles downriver and secured
it. Two days later they had
dismantled the bridge and rebuilt it
at the original site *(now, that's
determination)*.

G.L. Pearson adds his stories to our
collection. He remembers:

As you probably know by now, our
tour of duty wasn't real exciting.
There were probably more human
interest type stories than war
stories...were fortunate not being
involved in the "shootin" part and
not the "police action."

On one occasion our barracks was
penalized because, at the morning
inspection, the officer found an
empty beer can which had been
overlooked by the barracks orderly-
me. Nothing was said about the error
until midnight that night. The entire barracks was called out in full
gear, backpacks, rifles, etc., to
march to a mountain about a mile
away. It was snowing and cold as
could be. We were required to dig a
full-sized grave and bury that
fateful beer can. As I recall, my
next assignment was latrine duty!

When we first arrived in Korea, we
were to set up camp, but only for a
short time. We moved out at night to
go build a pontoon bridge over the
Han River at Seoul. We had to drive
with blackout lights, which was

272

A reminder of the beautiful
winter weather in Korea (Buster
Fisher).

This is really the ground
trembling because of "Long Tom.

Floyd Croney doing his thing

The 138th builds a bridge over
troubled water (Buster Fisher).

Buster Fisher

Floyd's "thing"

hazardous. One of our cranes was damaged along the way. We arrived at night and were told to sack out wherever we could find a place. I found a place beside a place that had been bombed out. Next morning, we all awoke to find that we were surrounded by dead Koreans all along both banks of the river. Right next to me, on the other side of the piece of bridge I slept by, was a dead Korean. I was too tired that night to bother him, and he had seemed quite comfortable, too. That was quite a feeling knowing how close to death I had been. My first thought was that he could have been alive, and I would have never known it until daylight!

After our unit was broken up in preparation for return to the States, Jackie Mitchell and I were assigned to a post on the upper Han River, north of Seoul. We were outfitted with a radio to report river stages back to headquarters. We lived in an abandoned bunker. We had a large three-quarter ton truck on top of us to supply power to the radio. We also had a .50-cal machine gun for our protection.

One night we were sure we could hear some boats coming across the river as the sound of waves lapping up on the side of a boat came through very clear. We decided we must protect our area, but we were a good way from the river and couldn't see well enough to shoot the .50-cal gun. We elected to go down nearer the water and use our burp guns. We fired away

277

for quite some time. When we
stopped, we could still hear some
sounds. Uncertain of the situation,
we decided to retreat to our bunker
and wait for daylight. The next
morning there was not a sign of the
enemy, only the waves lapping on
shore. Disappointed and relieved, we
chalked it up to experience.

Kenneth Howard Rapp led an illustrious career. He did two years in the Navy.
Then he joined the Air Force and
graduated as a pilot 29 March 1950, just
in time for Korea. He went over and flew
100 missions in an F86 Sabre jet, shot
down a MIG, and got shot down himself
several times. He finished his first tour
in 1952 and was sent to California. On a
furlough he got married. Then he went
back to California as a test pilot. His
practice flights coincided with the
Navy's. Unfortunateky, so did his flight
path. He and a Navy jet collided in
mid-air, and Kenneth Howard Rapp was
killed between tours, just ten days after
he got married *(courtesy of his sister,
Edith McDonald)*.

Oscar Bradley Eckhoff volunteered
for the draft in August 1945, when he
turned 18. He was given the choice of
Army or Navy, and took the Navy. He
stayed in 8 months and 26 days and
mustered out with the GI Bill. Oscar:
In October 1950 they took me back
into the Army because I had not
completed enough time. This time, I
went to Aberdeen Proving Grounds for
ordnance training, and then to Korea
in the Spring of '51 with the 328th

Ordnance Batallion.
I remember being scared on the way up to our station about 200 yards from the 38th parallel. We were in the back of a truck with no ammunition. I was in Korea two weeks before I had a bath, and that was out of my helmet. My job was to repair telescopes on Long Toms. The last Sunday I was there, a friend and I decided to go to the other side of the parallel to see what was going on. Fortunately, we turned back.
I saw a USO show over there, but I don't remember who was in it *(Oscar is three days older that water.)*. I also had a five day R and R in Japan in Kyoto, Nara, and somewhere. One of those days I was sick in bed all day.

Bill Powe spent a little time over in the beautiful Korean countryside, too. Bill remembers his participation in this way :
I was a cook/baker with Company C, the 8069th replacement company. I went in after Pusan in '51 and went up to Kyongsong. One day I had a run in with the chief cook. He asked me to do something, and I told him I didn't do that. The next day I was in the MPs. This was after 9 or 10 months.
One night I was on guard duty; it was about 11 o'clock. Some guys came in on a truck. I grew up with coon-asses, and so I recognized some coon-ass language. I couldn't see 'em, but I called out "Hey,

279

coonass, where you from at?" A guy came up and told me he was from six miles up River Road. He married a girl I knew. I met him once when I was back in the States.

Funny thing about the Koreans, they used human waste for fertilizer. You'd see them walking and carrying honey pots on sticks. They sold the contents to farmers. One time I was on a truck with two other guys. We made a weekly run to Taegu for supplies. One of the guys had bought a squirt gun and filled it with "High Life." This stuff burned like fire. We were coming down the side of a mountain. The roads were skinny. A honey wagon being pulled by an ox was ahead of us. When the wagon pulled over so we could pass, this idiot shot the ox in the rear with the squirt gun. Well, that bull outran the truck, ran into us, and dumped the contents of the honey wagon all over the truck! The commander made us drive the 6x into the river and wash it good before he would let us into camp.

Here we are shown that no matter what you are trained for by the military, they can always find something else for you to do for any reason whatever. Bill said that Korea was cold in the winter, and about like here in the summer. He should know; he spent 18 months over there.

James Ladner served in the 631st Armored Field Artillery Battalion. From late '51 to late '52, he was on border patrol between East and West Germany. James says there were no incidents where he was.

ACKER

Sherman Acker was a truck driver for the 2nd Field Artillery Battalion during the Korean War from 1951-53. Both of his sons were in the Air Force. Sherman Jr. was in Vietnam and Anthony served during peacetime. Nephew Danny was in the Navy for Desert Storm.

Rayford Lee was in the 6th Marines as a gunner on a tank from 1951 to 53 (courtesy his wife).

Jack Tyndall had several interesting assignments during his tours with the Army:
From June '53 to April '53 I was with Company C, 366th Engineering Aviation Batallion around Pusan. We were rebuilding B-26 medium bomber bases. Then I went to Headquarters Company with the 1903rd at Pyongtauk as a tractor/scraper operator. We built a top secret base that was used for a P-51 fighter strip.
The day I got out was the day Queen Elizabeth was crowned, so it was my big day too. I got snockered with the Provost Marshal and had to get on a bus to get out of there in a hurry! I got out just in time to avoid trouble.
After shopping around for a decent job, I went back in the active Army. I went back in to go to Vietnam, but they would only send me to the fringes. I went to Okinawa from April '61 to February '62 and then to Thailand until August '62. I was

a combat engineer there and built a base with some help from the poisonous snakes and monkeys.

I kept trying to get combat duty, but I had a problem. My younger brother had been killed at Pusan in 1950, and I was the sole surviving son. The Army wouldn't give me a combat assignment. My CO told me they wouldn't let me because they were afraid I would be vengeful and get my butt shot off.

I got the Korean Service Medal with 2 battle stars. How? You see, I was underneath the Air Force. That winter and spring they made some big bombing raids, so we got the battle stars, too. I was in the Order of the Flying Purple Shaft. The Air Force didn't want to feed or house us, and the Army wanted to work us to death. We ate cold C-Rations and slept in pup tents while the Air Force slept in Quonset huts and ate hot food from Japan. I guess that's the way it is. No hard feelings.

FLIGHT

I soar through the air as though a great bird with giant wings. I feel the strange wind, not only flowing over my wings but over my entire being. Being powered by a great inner force which propels me, I am tossed and turned in many different directions. Sometimes, by a certain inner touch, I am put into a wide circle. Or, maybe I am put into a sharp, screaming dive, the wind tearing at my wings and nearly shearing them off. At other times I am flipped over on my back. There I see the Earth from an upside-down view. It is

I who is upside-down, being hurled swiftly through the air, turning over and over again and finally returning to level flight. The force which controls my every movement is very gentle, never harsh nor forceful. After being aloft in the clear, blue sky for some time, I am put to earth from where I started to wait among the other great birds and to rest at last.
by Jack W. Tyndall

Derwin E. Spiers, Army, was in the 21st Infantry, 24th Division:
I was there in '52-'53 as a medic attached to an infantry group. I took sick calls and gave shots. We went in at Inchon and then to some island guarding prisoners, only I wasn't doing any guarding. The last three months I was there was spent moving prisoners back to Inchon. We'd put new clothes on the prisoners, but they'd take them off themselves. They just didn't want anything to do with anything we gave them. That was the strangest thing I saw.
Derwin went to a few USO shows and saw Carthel Mitchell from this County over there. He says "I don't know what we were there for. I can't see what we accomplished. I done my duty, and I have no regrets."

Jim Harrison was in the Korean War with the 38th Field Artillery, 3rd Infantry, from January '53 on:
They had just stabilized the 38th Parallel. I spent the first 63 days as a forward observer. Since most of the Class of '50 (West Point) had

283

been decimated, they made me a mustang officer. I was coaching young officers on doing the "infantry shuffle" *(more on that in the Aftermath Section)* to keep them from getting hit with sniper's buffalo guns. The Koreans were so good they could hit you in the hip pocket with a mortar round.

On the breakthrough the ROKs broke down and ran. We were alerted to stand by and be prepared to move on short notice. My battery went into the nose of the thing and got cut off from the rest. There was mass confusion trying to get tanks in. I had to move my guns forward with no support. The only thing that saved my ass was that the Chinks ran out of gas and never crossed the hill in front of us. This was at Kuwah, just south of Seoul. They had made 7 to 10 miles of penetration into our lines, and we were hanging on by our fingernails. I split my battery - took the howitzers and ammo up and sent the motor pool somewhere else-expecting to fight a retrograde action.

The Chinks were doped up before they made these awful charges. When the dope wore off, they were not so crazy. I went through three of those mass assaults. Their sweat smelled so bad from that dope you could smell them charging.

Anyhow, by then I had only six howitzers left, and the 555th had lost 16 out of 18. While the Batallion was getting reorganized, my battery was their direct support.

One time we had a bunch of refugees coming out. My Division was facing another one of ours, and the line was marching straight to the point where they joined. I noticed there were soldiers mixed in with the civilians - dressed in wigs, dresses, and all. I called to the rear to a gunnery officer and told him we needed to destroy that column of refugees. He wouldn't believe me and said "If you're wrong, it's your ass." I told him I had a bunch of kids out on the line and was afraid for them. We clobbered them. There were civilians, but there were also soldiers. I had recognized the "infantry shuffle" even though they were dressed like women!

They were brassy little fellers. I had seen one sneaking behind our lines. He even infiltrated our chow line. I had a Korean first sergeant who walked up, listened to him, and recognized his dialect. We captured him.

A couple of stories. I had a Sergeant Morgan. He almost failed out of ROTC at Texas A and M. He lost an eye and a tooth and was sent home to the States. He wanted to return to the war- to redeem himself, I guess. Well, he came back. One time I told him to take six men and a deuce-and-a-half and "don't come back until you find me some sandbags." Morgan went back to supply and told the master sergeant that Colonel Throckmorton needed some sandbags and damn quick. You know, he even got the master ser-

geant to to load the truck - full.
These guys were pretty scruffy
looking, so I guess he believed
them. Morgan brought back enough
sandbags for the whole battalion!
Then we had no socks. It was a cold
country. I sent Morgan to get us
some socks. He said "Yeah, I know.
Don't come back 'til you get them."
Morgan took SGT Kim, a three-quarter
ton, and a .45 and went to Seoul. He
went straight to the black market,
took out his .45, and jumped over a
counter. He got us two bales of
socks. Morgan came back grinning.
We got a Presidential Unit Citation.
My Sergeant Kim again recognized
some Chinks in the area. It was in a
valley. We set up and called for a
tank battalion to come across the
valley parallel to our artillery
fire. We wiped them out.
I turned in my Purple Hearts. One
night "Bedcheck Charlie" came over
in his Piper Cub. One of our guys
jumped in a foxhole and skinned his
knee. They gave him a Purple Heart.
The next morning I turned mine in.
It doesn't mean what it did a few
years ago. One of our men was in the
hospital with gonorrhea. A General
came by and gave him a Purple Heart
- gave one to everybody in the
hospital. No, sir, I turned mine in.
One time we got hit when I was a
forward observer. The platoon leader
and the platoon sergeant got killed.
I brought all the men out safely.
They wanted to give me a CIB, but I
was in artillery and couldn't get
one. Then they tried to transfer me

so they could give me one. I told them "No, thank you."
I don't believe they've ever screwed up a Medal of Honor or a DSC.

Jim says that when he left Korea every man in his Company embraced him, and every one of them cried. He had the finest group of men ever. The group was always ready and never got beat. Jim finished Korea, and his son, Bill, finished Vietnam. Bill is still with the Army as a recruiter.

Shirley Lumpkin served in the Marine Corps during 1953 and 54. She recalls her duty:
I was a food service officer- the first female in fact. I put my time in at Camp Lejeune. They didn't let women go to war in those days. I think we stopped too soon on the Gulf War. We didn't accomplish anything.

Several locals enjoyed the sunny climes and smooth seas in the Navy. The seas around Korea were uncontested, so the US forces had the run of the place. Lige Ladner and Bobby East were there. Norman Carey "Butch" Mitchell served on the USS O'BRIAN, a tincan commanded by Chester W. Nimitz, Jr.

Serving in support or front line units were: Johnny Groves, Jake Woodward, James A. Martin, Charles Humphrey, George Rester, William D. Smith, Walter Floyd, Billy Glenn Sherrer, Van Smith, and Paul Seal. Roger W. Smith was with the 24th Infantry Division.

WILLIAMS

Brothers Johnny Frank and David Henry Williams were in Korea. David was in the 138th *(see previous)*. Johnny Frank was in the 1st Marine Division, 7th Marine Regiment:

I went over in '54 in the 48th replacement draft. We went in at Inchon and went to the Imjim River. That was right around the 38th parallel. We dug in for a wait to see what would happen. Nothing! The cease fire had already set in, so we were only there 30 days, then they brought us back to Camp Pendleton, the whole Division, and replaced us with Army.

I was in charge of the ammo dump. We stored mortar rounds, M-1s, 30.06s, and grenades. We normally packboarded ammunition up the hills as resupplies. One time I was offered a ride up on a helicopter, but I turned it down because I was so used to walking. Good thing, too. The helicopter got to within 100 yards of the top of the hill, developed mechanical trouble, and crashed. Fortunately, nobody was hurt. I'm glad I didn't take that free ride.

We also took some 26-mile "hikes," some through mine fields. When we had a chance, we went pheasant hunting. Korea had a lot of pheasants. Those mine fields assured me that I would stay on the roads. The Koreans *(peasants)* would plow up the mine fields with water buffalo and defuse the mines themselves.

We were stationed with some Turks and Brits, the Black Watch as a

288

matter of fact. We'd go hang out in their "Nappy House" and have tea and crumpets. They had canned chocolates. We'd razz each other and listen to bagpipe music.

After that he joined the Air National Guard in Louisiana and is still in the Reserves. He continues:

At 55 years old, I'm back on active duty. I retired in November '90. The military can bring you back in any time until you're 60. I am now the Senior Enlisted Advisor for Louisiana and am a Chief Master Sergeant. I've been one since 1 April '67. We've stayed pretty active in the New Orleans area ever since the Cubans flew in under our radar and landed at Belle Chasse NAS.

His son, John Fountain Williams, is in the Army now and did a tour in Germany in '83.

Floyd Croney had one of the grizzlier- but most necessary- jobs in time of war. He was in the 392nd Graves Registration Unit and spent 16 months in Korea during 1953 and 54:

I didn't ask for this duty. I guess, because of the time I went in, they needed deceased personnel handlers *(my euphemism)*. We disinterred troops from their temporary graves, bagged and stored them, and sent them home for a proper burial. We found lots of MIAs in the DMZ after that last big battle they had. We dug up a lot of mass burials, including some North Koreans and Chinese, which we sent back to their government *(One would think such a precedent in humane treatment of the enemy would have carried over from their side into the next war, but we'll see otherwise. Still, Floyd is to be considered an ambassador of good will more or less!)*. Some of these guys were pretty ripe by the time we got to them because they had been there a while, and of some we just found skeletons we tried to jigsaw back together. If they had dogtags, it made the job of registration easier. We had many search-and-recovery missions to find or even check on reports of isolated burials. We took care of any of our people who died then, such as by stepping on a mine or from accidents. In short, we took care of the dead. But, I'll tell you one thing, Korea was the coldest place I have ever been.

Imported entertainment has often been available for the troops, and Floyd tells us:

Marilyn Monroe was there to get the boy's blood boiling even more! Of course, I had a view from behind 20,000 other craning necks, so I got this picture.

Floyd thinks we handled it all well, but that we could have used a little more air power. We definitely needed more manpower to handle the Chinese push. He has nothing good to say about the country, and that it was 40 years behind the US.

***** COWART *****

Richard C. Cowart had ten sons, five of whom served in WWII. The boys from

that generation are Ray and Truett in the
Army, J.T. and Chester in the Marines,
and Jimmy in the Navy. Two of the other
brothers had veteran sons, Richard A. and
John T., both in the Marines, both in the
Korean era. From Richard A. we get this
recollection:

> I was in the 4th Troop at Camp
> Lejeune in '53 and '54. We kept
> training in those tanks; but the
> Lord saw fit to make me be born too
> late for the action. I was only 17,
> so I stayed in the States. One thing
> you may not realize- we Marines paid
> for the Iwo Jima monument in
> Washington DC. That's right. I
> personally had $480 deducted from my
> pay to help pay for that monument.
> Have you ever wondered why the
> veterans always have to buy their
> own monuments? (Sounds like the one
> here. Deja vu?)

The next generation of Cowarts is well
represented by: Richard A., Jr., in the
Picayune National Guard; brother John
T.'s sons, John Russell, David Lyle,
Wayne, and Ken, are all in the Poplarville Guard. To fill in the gaps, another
brother of the WWII generation of this
5-star family, Richard "Mack'" had three
veteran sons. James Earl Cowart was
killed on board ship just before Vietnam
started, Doug was in the Army in 'Nam,
and Donald was in the Guard.

Jack Blackburn went to Korea in
1954. Jack tells us:

> I got there on the 1st of January.
> The ceasefire had just taken effect,
> but we went up to the front. I was
> with the 25th Division, Army, in an-

291

ti-aircraft artillery until August.

Interregnum (Even Colder War)

In 1954 military advisors were sent into southeast Asia: Laos, Cambodia, and Vietnam. Never mind that the French had never been able to solve any of the regional problems, which seem to have been the same as industrial vs. agricultural or religion vs. religion.

Then we backed a military response in Guatemala in 1954, a brief occupation of Lebanon in 1958, and totally blew the Cuban invasion at the Bay of Pigs in 1961. President Kennedy also allowed the Russians to build the Berlin Wall in 1961 *(not a very good year for the home team)*. In 1965 we occupied the Dominican Republic. We sent Marines to Beirut from 1982-83. In 1988 we went to Panama, and in 1990 we went to Saudi Arabia.

Bill Beacht was in the 3rd Marine Division. From '55 to '58 he was stationed in Japan, Okinawa, and the Philippines. Dick Murchison was in the Army for several years in the '50s, as was Lavern Snodgrass. Both were in the Combat Engineers. Frank Marchant was a Navy aviator. Lavern:

I was in the 37th Engineering Group, 5th Corps. In '62 I was in the same barracks Elvis had been stationed in in Hanau. Two guys showed up one day. One of them was named Presley. We asked him if he had brought his guitar with him. He said "No, but I brought my music." Sure enough, the man with him was named Music!

Paul MacInnis, another Navy transplant, got drafted in '57 after he had

293

finished college and been working for a year and a half:

I was in the 34th Artillery and got sent to Munich to babysit Germans as part of the NATO forces. Twice a year we went up to shoot the guns for field training. I took leave for two weeks before going over and got married, so my stay wasn't too bad. I was on a survey team because of my training. We surveyed out launch points for Honest John rockets. They were ballistic missiles.

I actually met a decent officer, a major. I had been working professionally with a theodolite for a while before I went in. One day we had an argument about its use. The major got mad and pulled out the manual. Sure enough, I was right. We did it my way from then on!

Once a month we had batallion reveille; raise the flag, blow the bugle, shoot the howitzer. We put a roll of toilet paper down the barrel to see if it would make snow or come out in one piece. It made the neatest streamer you ever saw and came down in a nice pile. It answered our question, and the whole batallion cracked up!

Paul's first daughter was born in Germany. Now, her first born was also in Germany. Paul says he missed Elvis when he went in, and also when he was on a field mission in Germany.

Adron Hall was in the Navy doing his thing from 1959-63. One of those things goes as follows:

I was on the ENTERPRISE in its glory days as the only nuclear carrier in

294

the world. My highlight came in 1962. In October our squadron was called to go aboard. I was an aviation electronics technician/navigation working on A1H Skyraiders. We didn't know what was going on, but found out a few days out at sea. After going south at flank speed for a while, we guessed. We were there for the Cuban missile crisis.

We sailed around south of Cuba for 50 days, contributing to warding off the missiles. All that time we had our planes loaded to the hilt. We had two or three nuclear weapons loaded and guarded by the Marine guards. We set up a good blockade. Only one freighter with missiles got through, and one of our destroyers got him. Primarily, we were there to keep the missiles out. I believe we did.

We returned in the middle of December after seeing Jamaica from the sea- but only occasionally. Later on the tour we had holiday routine on Sunday. We all got to go to the steel beach. We even had a band of conga drums and bongos.

Thomas I. "Tommy" Stewart was with the Marines from 1960 to 1964. Tommy made the most of it:

I started as an admiral's orderly. I was with four admirals on five carriers in two years. I was all hyped up when I went in and made "honor man" in our platoon. I wanted to be in the Fleet Marines, but I got drafted to do this. I was with the 7th Fleet on the USS TICONDEROGA, RANGER, KITTY HAWK, CONSTELLATION, and BON HOMME RICHARD. I was really a bodyguard and messenger. Once I was with Admiral Connelly in Hawaii. He called me "Bulldog" because I had a bulldog tattoo. The Admiral says: "Have you got the keys?" to which I reply "Yes, Sir." So he says that we're going to tour the island. When we got to an Officer's Club, he asked me "Do you want to go swimming, Bulldog?" I reminded him that I wasn't an officer. He got me trunks, and we went swimming anyhow. Then I got sent back to Camp Pendleton and had to put on a pack and a helmet. Two years of that and I got out. That was a real comedown! Once we loaded up the plane and were on the way to Cuba for the missile crisis, but we were diverted before we got there.

Tommy says he met Lana Turner and Bob Hope in Subic Bay when he picked him up at the airport. He also met Anita Bryant. He really had it made- at least for two years.

John Andrew McDonald was in the Navy from 1960-64. For a non-war veteran, this guy was in a lot of action *(I guess that's why it's called the Cold War!)*. John was on the USS GHYATT (DDG-1) for the Cuban blockade. Then he was with MSTS in Vietnam on the USNS CARD and the USNS CROATAN. John survived the sinking of the CARD by a North Vietnamese mine in 1964.

GLYDEWELL

Maynard Joseph Glydewell was in the 4th Marines. He started WWII at Pearl Harbor and fought all the way through Iwo Jima. He earned a Purple Heart and a Presidential Unit Citation among his many distinctions. Maynard got out after the war, then joined the Army for Korea. After that war he joined the Air Force. His son, Jimmie was an Air Force electrician from '61 through '64 in Germany and North Dakota. Jimmie volunteered to go to Nam, but they told him he would have to extend his service, so he got out. Brother, Larry, was in Germany for two years and Vietnam for one with the Army.

Harvey Eugene Shoemake served in the Navy from June 61 to August 68. He was stationed in San Diego; Port Huaneme *(Whoneedsme)*; Davisville, Rota, Spain; combat duty in Gitmo *(Guantanamo)* Bay, Cuba, and Vietnam. His citations include the Armed Forces Expeditionary Medal and the Navy/Marine Corps Expeditionary Medal.

Lyndon Johnson escalated his philosophy of how to make money during this police action into an experimental playground for the mighty military-industrial complex which had not been dismantled since World War II to try out its expensive new toys. Apparently, the only way to support a "Great Society" was to have a wartime economy, and that is about the only historical significance of Vietnam, excluding population control and dope peddling.

Vietnam

DANANG-TET OFFENSIVE-KHMER ROUGE-FNG-LUKE
THE GOOK- HO CHI MIN-SAIGON-DIEN BIEN
PHU-BLOW-SMACK-WEED-M-16- PUFF THE MAGIC
DRAGON-JOLLY GREEN GIANT -PHU BAI -HUE-
FRAGGING-HENDRIX-AGENT ORANGE-HUEYS-HANOI
HANNAH. *Our Pearl River County lads did
their patriotic duty and did it well. To
the strains of "Purple Haze" and the
scent of burning weed, they fought all
over South Vietnam and other untold
places. The Vietnam War for America
lasted 14 years, from the first attack by
VC at Bien Hoa in 1959 that killed two to
28 January 1973 when the ceasefire became
effective. During 1962 we increased participation to 11,000 troops. This included Special Forces (Green Berets) to train
Vietnamese.*
*There were actually three wars in one. We
provided convential advisors. We also had
special operations. Then, there was the
actual helicopter war. Interestingly, our
soldiers had to sign an oath of secrecy
on their return from the Far East until
1962 because this action was not recognized as a war until then. Getting stories
from our veterans before this time has
proven to be almost an impossibility.
However, the "times they are a'changin'.
We started "advising" in Laos in 1955.
The first 107 Special Forces there were
dropped from the military rolls just so
they could serve there from July '59 to
October '62. They went in with hunting
rifles and civilian clothes. One dozen
eight-man teams served six month tours in
Laos. They even invaded Cambodia after
the Pathet Lao. It is reasonable to*

assume that the earlier Green Berets took part in this action. (This newer information has been gleaned from the VFW magazine for January 1992.)

So that we will all know what is meant by the acronyms, I present this list: ARVN (South Vietnamese regular army), NVA (North Vietnamese Army), Viet Cong (came from all over. They were farmers by day and soldiers by night. They were the original black pajama crew.), and ChiComs (Chinese Communists).

Internal politics with their government led to a series of SNAFUs. By 1963 we had 23,000 troops committed. We should have taken our cue then, but the pinko liberals managed to keep us there. The VC were destoying ARVN units to the tune of one battalion a WEEK! In 1965 we had our first big campaign because they attacked our Special Forces bases at Pleiku and Qui Nhon. The Ia Drang valley was the site for the 1st Air Cav taking on six times their number and beating them. Bombing in the north began then and, in 1965, the Marines arrived at DaNang and the MPs got to Saigon. By the end of the year there were 180,000 troops committed with the Marines in the north, the US army in the central region and at Saigon, and the ARVN troops in the Mekong Delta. Not only did we have search-and-destroy warfare, we also decided to take out logistic bases such as War Zones C and D. In 1967 Operation Junction City was begun to locate and destroy the Cong's Central Office in South Vietnam. We stomped them, but they learned a valuable lesson in changing their battle tactics: Don't be a mosquito biting on a sledge hammer. Theoretically, it was forbidden

299

to chase communists into Cambodia and Laos, but I wouldn't ask any Special Forces guys about that. By the end of 1967 we had 550,000 in Vietnam, so the Communists retaliated with the Tet Offensive on 30 January 1968. Attacks came at the Khe Sanh Marine base, Nha Trang Navy Training Center, DaNang, Qui Nhon, Hoi An, Pleiku, Kontum, Bon Me Thout, and Saigon. The greatest emphasis for the attack in Saigon was the US Embassy, where only five guards were on duty. Even though the Cong were hiding in Buddist churches, we counter-attacked and wiped them all out at some loss to ourselves (see Arnold Matthews). The Marine guards were largely responsible for that. The Cong also attacked Tan Son Nhut and Bien Hoa Air Bases, and, the last of January, went into Hue. To save Khe Sanh, the US spent ten tons of bombs and twenty artillery rounds for each attacker killed (from Battles and Campaigns in Vietnam 1954-1984 by Tom Carlhurt). By mid-1969 we began withdrawing troops. Nixon officially turned those remaining loose on Cambodia in 1970 to destroy the VC bases of operation, and we promptly killed 11,000 of them. By March 1972 most of our ground troops were pulled out of Vietnam, having accomplished nothing for the peace of the area or for the US other than to satisfy a few megalomaniacs on the home front.

I am especially honored to present several old-timers left over from WWII and Korea: Rayford Vaughn, Duwaine Laib, Bud Hughes, Benny Crocker, Charles Humphrey, Arnold Matthews, and Aubrey Lumpkin. Their stories follow. James B.

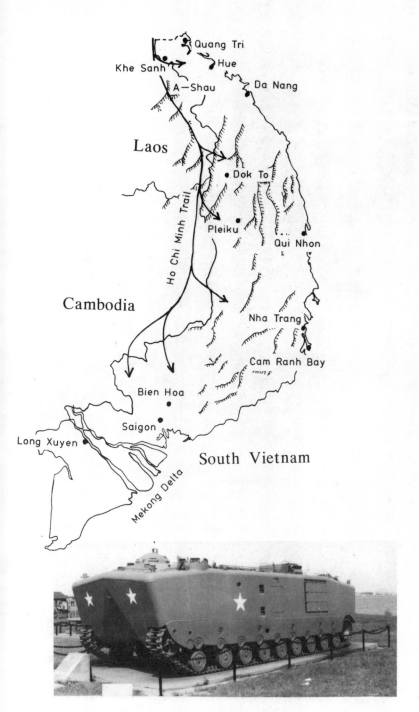

Quang Tri
Khe Sanh
Hue
A-Shau
Da Nang

Laos

Dok To

Ho Chi Minh Trail

Pleiku

Qui Nhon

Cambodia

Nha Trang

Cam Ranh Bay

Bien Hoa

Saigon

Long Xuyen

South Vietnam

Mekong Delta

301

Dave Diamond's first aid station

Suzanne Pleshette's well-wishers, especially thos at the rear. They wish they could see her at this USO show (Dave Diamond).

China Beach, home of Phil
Nameth at times.

Somebody's been hand feeding
these babies- or else feeding
them hands (Phil Nameth).

303

Phil Nameth walking his dog.
You can tell how helpless the
dog is, because Phil is
protecting him with a gun.

304

305

Ed Stevens. Yes, folks, this is his battle attire after a week on the trail. What a snappy dresser!

John Napier.

Smith, a Medic, served in Korea and Vietnam. Clifford Boyd Mitchell and his brother, David Keith Mitchell, were both fighters in Korea and Vietnam.

James Ira McGehee was a helicopter pilot and earned the Vietnam Service Medal, Vietnam Campaign Medal, Cross of Gallantry with palm, the Air Medal, and the Air Medal with one oak leaf cluster. He had plenty of practice because he was in Korea too.

John "Pat" Evans spent a lot of time in SE Asia. In fact, he helped re-write the history of that area through his work in the Special Forces. *(The standard Special Forces A-team consisted of a dozen men. There was a captain, a lieutenant, a master sergeant, an intelligence specialist, two medics, two radio men, two demolition experts, one skilled with individual weapons, and one with crew-manned weapons. The A-teams were sent to Vietnam to train a bunch of rice farmers and villagers to defend themselves against the communists.):*

> I was in Nam for four tours; '61-'62, '63-'64, '65-'66, and '67-'68, all with the 5th Special Forces Group, 1st Special Forces. I was a Green Beret working out of our main base in Ha Trang. In the early days we were "strictly" advisors and weren't issued arms. Of course, we'd go out and kill a few NVRs and take theirs. I wasn't going to have somebody shooting at me and not be able to shoot back.
> We were all over the place. On one 14-day patrol we were searching for

downed pilots. We found a colonel and a major from B-52s. After seeing all the destruction they had wrought and actually having to see the faces of the enemy on the ground on the way out, the colonel's black hair turned snow white, and the major's red hair turned a mousy grey. They both swore they would never fly again. In fact, the colonel is now a missionary in South America.

We didn't get to shave or bathe, so I was pretty ripe when I got back to base camp. There was a chopper sitting on the pad. The troops said "That's yours, Sarge. You're going to see the General." I got in the chopper looking and smelling so fine. When I got there, General Westmoreland said "You passed OCS in basic, and Colonel Coe has asked you several times to accept a commission. You keep turning him down. Now, are you going to refuse a General?" Westmoreland reached into his desk drawer and pulled out a set of First Lieutenant's bars. Then the General said "That's good. Now go downstairs and get your ID made. Your orders have already been cut." Marble Mountain was another of our episodes, but it will remain there.

On my last tour we were on a 14-day patrol when I saw a large tank buildup in Laos and Cambodia. I went to everyone in charge I could find to tell them, but they wouldn't believe me. Sure enough, the next time out we got hit by tanks.

Interrogation. We had an easy way to do that. We'd capture a general, one

of his aides, and a grunt. We'd take
them up 1000 feet in a helicopter.
First, we'd ask the general what we
wanted to know. When he didn't
answer *(which apparently they never
did)*, we'd throw him out. Then we'd
ask the aide. Same thing. By the
time we got to the grunt, he'd tell
us anything we needed to hear. Then
guess what? You got it, out he'd go,
too. We didn't take prisoners.

Pat Evans gave his all, including his
right leg and the use of his left. He
says he just happened to be in the right
place at the right time, except when he
lost his leg. Pat earned-the hard way-27
different medals in Nam: Silver Star,
Bronze Star with three oak leaf clusters
and a "V," a Purple Heart with 19 oak
leaf clusters *(Pat must have kept a
platoon of medics with him!)*, an Air
Medal, Vietnam Campaign Medal with six
bronze stars, Vietnamese Cross of
Gallantry with palm, Vietnamese Medals of
Honor (1st and 2nd Class), Combat Infantryman's Badge, Master Parachutist's
Badge with combat jump star, Senior HALO
Badge, Presidential Unit Citation with
bronze oak leaf cluster, Meritorius Unit
Citation with two bronze oak leaf
clusters, and a Jungle Expert Badge. Pat,
like most of the 'Namvets, has absolutely
no use for that "communist traitor, Jane
Fonda. If she walked into my yard, I'd
shoot her." Pat adds:

We were the finest fighting force in
the world. We had to pass jump
school, know how to use all weapons,
pass intelligence schools, SCUBA,
jungle warfare, desert survival,
HALO night jumps (jump from 40,000

309

feet and open the chute at 600), be
bilingual, and have a Top Secret
clearance. But the Special Forces
were also the "Armed Peace Corps."
In our time in 'Nam we did many
projects like: shelter 600,000 refugees, sponsor 35,00 educational projects, dig 7000 wells, build 1000
bridges, do 50,000 aids projects,
36,000 welfare projects, 15,000
transportation projects, plus build
markets, classrooms, churches, dis-
pensaries, and hospitals.
Entertainment? I didn't get any.
There was a price on Bob Hope's
head. While the rest were enjoying
the show, we were out on search-
and-destroy patrols around the perimeter to protect the entertainers.

LEE

The Lee family from the central part
of the County has made many contributions
to the elite group of patriots from one
generation. Alvin W. Lee was in the Navy
from 1954-58. Carlos E. Lee was in the
Army from 1959-60. Youngest brother,
Douglas N., was in a calvary unit, Army,
in Vietnam in 1968-69. He earned the
Bronze Star. Curtis C. Lee is the last of
these brothers. He was with the 5th
Special Forces Group in Vietnam, twice:

My first tour, I was at Pleiku. My
job was to build a mountain commando
(lots of training for that in South
Mississippi) post and train moun-
tainyard (Montagnard) people in
tactics. That post was in Pleiyet. I
was working under the auspices of
the CIA instead of the Army. Another
one of my jobs was to infiltrate

across the Cambodian border for intelligence purposes.

My second tour, in '64, was in the Mekong Delta, also on the Cambodian border. Our mission was to sweep the enemy out of the region and gather intelligence. We had 200 Cambodian mercenaries and Vietnamese Special Forces working with us.

For my part, our program was going very well until we expanded our operations. If we would have kept up our guerilla tactics, we would have fared better. It was a mistake to escalate, especially with one hand tied behind us. I agree with Bush now. We're not international policemen. We are, however, the strongest nation in the world, and it is our duty to push the Iraqis out of Kuwait *(interviewed 1000hrs 7 February 1991)*.

Curt earned the Combat Infantrymans Badge, Paratrooper Badge, and the Bronze Star. He has two sons in the military. Curtis Patrick Lee is in the National Guard in Poplarville. Other son, Matthew H. Lee, is in the 82nd Airborne Division in Operation Desert Shield as of this writing. *We'll pick him up later.*

A DAY IN THE LIFE OF A GRUNT
Here we are in one hell of a place;
While gives not peace nor grace.

Charging through the jungle with hearts depressed;
Hoping soon that we will find rest.

Suddenly, our hopes and thoughts shatter
As we hear the sound of an AK's chatter.

GIs are down with chins on chest
Popping caps and doing their best.

GIs crawl through earth's wet soil
As the blood from our leader begins to
boil.

Let's kill those Reds is what he said;
So up from the mud sprang 37 heads.

Charging through the woods, crashing over
a tree;
Stumbling and falling over battle's
debris.

A bloody red tear falls from our cheek
As the muscles in our legs get tired and
weak.

As soon as it had started, it had come to
an end.
And to us GIs it had seemed a sin.

We leave the scene, singing a song;
And behind our backs lie 40 dead Cong.

We were lucky that day 'cause none had to
die.
Now victory is ours to hold real high.

South Vietnam is our soil, the Cong our
foe.
Soon a dream will come true as home we
go.

                                        -Kenton

     The Green Berets had one of their
best-known fights on 6 July '64 at Nam
Dong. The Group, along with 371 Vietnamese allies, held off 800 Main Force Viet

*Cong for about five hours until rein-
forcements came. The action was so bloody
and heroic, that the unit leader earned a
Medal of Honor. There were two Distinguished Service Crosses awarded posthumously, four Silver Stars, and five
Bronze Stars. The County was represented
there by a man who wishes to remain anonymous.*

Marlon Stockstill arrived in Vietnam
12 August 1965 as part of the 1st
Batallion, 503rd Infantry Airborne Group.
He was wounded in the hip by a hand
grenade (8 Oct), a shoulder (28 Nov), and
a leg by another grenade (21 May). Marlon
was part of the group to take Hill 175.
He received the Purple Heart with 2 oak
leaf clusters, the Vietnam Campaign
Ribbon with 3 battle stars, and the Army
Commendation Ribbon. He says: "I was
proud to be over there, but it was all
political and for nothing. We took Hill
175, turned it over to the Vietnamese,
they lost it again, and we had to retake
it. We didn't accomplish anything."

Larry Spooner served two tours with
the Special Forces. He was with B-team
from '65 to '67 "out on Rt. 1 at Pleiku."
Larry was with the 101st Airborne at
Mekong during 70 to 71. Once he was at
Fire Base Charlie on seek-and-destroy
missions. He saw nobody from Pearl River
County and no Bob Hope.

We need to catch up with John Napier
again *(see photo)*. Between WWII and 'Nam
John was in on the occupation of Japan,
in the Korean War, and in the occupation
of Germany. He switched from the Marines

313

to the Air Force. He was on General Westmoreland's staff in Vietnam during 1964-
65 as part of HQ, USMACV, Saigon:

> I missed Bob Hope in Saigon in 1964
> on Christmas Eve. The US BOQ, the
> Brink Hotel, was bombed by the Viet
> Cong, which I narrowly missed. I
> barely missed being bombed in Saigon
> twice more, when the US Embassy was
> bombed in the spring of 1965 and
> that summer, the Me Kanh floating
> restaurant.
>
> Also, I have met many national
> figures during my military service
> including Omar Bradley, Bull Halsey,
> Lyndon Johnson, George Bush, and the
> Duke of Edinburgh among others.

John went on in his career to serve as a
special assistant to the Secretary of the
Air Force, Staff Director of the US House
of Representatives Select Committee on
southeast Asia in Washington, Laos, Cambodia, and Vietnam. He was also on the
faculty of the Air War College, and command historian of the Air University.
John wrote many of the articles I used as
background information on The War Between
the States. For all this service to his
country, John earned the Legion of Merit,
Meritorious Service Medal with oak leaf
cluster, Joint Service Commendation Medal
with combat "V," Air Force Commendation
Medal, Order of St. John of Jerusalem
(Great Britain), Vietnam Cross of
Gallantry with palm, plus 14 US and
foreign campaign and service medals.

Ed Stevens was in the 173rd Airborne
Brigade, 503rd Airborne, 2nd Battalion,
Co. C Infantry in '65-'66. The 173rd was
stationed on Okinawa when the U.S. enter-

ed the Vietnam conflict. They were the first group sent over, and Ed came along just after that as a replacement:

I was stationed at Bien Hoa. My primary fighting areas were War Zones C and D, the Iron Triangle near Cambodia. I was trained for the Special Forces and was with an airborne group. Unfortunately, the terrain in Nam would necessarily preclude our winning a war there in 1000 years. *(Remember, the French never could control the area.)* War Zone D was a multi-layered, all-age, mature jungle going up mountainous terrain. The Iron Triangle had been cut over and was just new-growth underbrush that was so thick you couldn't enter it. The area was controlled by the Viet Minh, and the South Vietnamese army had never even tried to take it. I got wounded in the left side (arm, chest) and was sent back to a M*A*S*H unit (Mobile Army Surgical Hospital). It was small, and I'd rather have been there than in a big hospital. At 1630hrs the beer tent would open for business. All of the doctors and patients who could would congregate there in a small sphere of cameraderie. There were some nurses who would put "Hot Lips" Houlihan to shame! I was there three weeks before returning to action.

People I saw I knew? Robert Stewart and I trained together in the States and got back together over there. Marlon Stockstill and Robert Roper and a guy named Keen were all in my company. We had a time together.

315

Christmas '65 the Bob Hope show came to see us. We got to see Joey Heatherton and Anita Bryant. Hmmmmm. All in all, we shouldn't have been there. But, we should be in Iraq *(interviewed 1200 hrs 18 January 1991)*. Saudi Arabia has been a moderating influence in the Middle East. Its like Roosevelt said: "Your neighbor needs a fire hose, you loan it to him."

Brothers Henry and Howell McCormick were in Vietnam-at the same time. They even saw each other. Henry tells his story first:

I served two tours. I was in MCB8 in October '65-'66 as a Naval Construction Battalion *(Seabee)* working with the Marines. In fact, my whole time in the Navy I was never on a ship. In 1966 I went back and stayed until the end on 1967. I was stationed first at DaNang and Tam Ky, then at Tu Lai. I was out on detachment building roads, runways, control towers, hospitals, whatever needed building.

While I was there I saw Bob Hope, Eddie Fisher, Rosey Grier. Man, he could sing like a bird! An Australian girl, Shirley Simmons, was there. It was nice to see a girl out in the bush. I would support the USO just for that.

The war? I hope they don't let it become another 'Nam *(interviewed 28 January 1991)*.

Brother Howell McCormick went to 'Nam as part of MCB8 too, in January 1965:

I was there until May '66. I started

316

in DaNang and went to Phu Bai. I was a pole-climbing electrician. We built camps for Marines. In fact, they were living in the mud until we got there. We also mainly built hospital operation and recovery facilities for them. I was part of Johnson's 500,000 man buildup.

It was quite interesting- especially when I saw Raquel Welsh. Man, did she look good! The war now? I think we're going the right way *(interviewed 29 January 1991)*. We should have done the same in 'Nam.

CROCKER

Benny Crocker and the Crocker family. What a group! Three brothers did a number on the rest of the world during the mid-century. We have Paul J. Crocker in the Army for both WWII and Korea. We have Harold L. in the Navy during WWII with 20 more years in the Army before retiring to the Postal Service. We have Benny devoting 20+ years of his life to the country's service. Benny:

My first night in Vietnam set the mood for the rest of my career. I was in the 1st Air Cav's 11th General Support Company. It was August '65. I was supposed to be the Division Standardization Pilot. The Cong hit our camp right on the perimeter. It had just been carved out of the jungle. We got into a helluva fire fight, and many of our guys were wounded. I was selected to make the MED EVAC. First night in the country. No maps. No in-country orientation. I succeeded in extracting a load of wounded personnel, one

shot through the neck, and got them
back to safety. They found me a
bunk. When I woke up the next
morning, our mess sergeant was dead.
Got hit by a snake in the night.
Good Morning, Vietnam!
The rest of that tour I was stationed at An Khe supporting the command
General and his staff. The generals
were out for a lot of glory. They
flew a lot more than they should
have. In all of our fire-fights, my
unit was in the middle of them. In
June '66 I received an order to give
a captain a check-ride. After flying
with him for an hour and a half, I
found out he was from Poplarville,
too. It was Ed Bass. I had already
been gone in the military for 16
years, so I didn't know him before
then. I finished that tour and came
home September '66. Oh, yes. I won
the Bronze Star for that first
night.
My second tour was from April '68 to
December '68, with the 478th Crane
Company, 1st Air Cav at DaNang. I
was the Command Standardization
Pilot. My baptism by fire this time
came in the A-Shau Valley campaign.
We lost a crane and a crew to combat
action. It was the only one lost in
Vietnam. We carried mostly heavy
weapons and bulldozers. We also
dropped heavy bombs, the WWII
"blockbusters," to build LZs (landing zones). This bomb would explode
a few feet above the ground and not
only create an LZ but also secure
the area. Five minutes after we
dropped the bomb in a triple canopy

318

jungle area, the place was ready for occupation. I got hurt in October and left Vietnam on a litter 2 December.

My third tour was from October '71 through April '72 *(Remember, this guy had just done Korea and two tours in 'Nam. He even went home on a litter after the second and is getting close to retirement.)* in Udorn, Thailand, flying fixed wing aircraft like U-21s and P2Vs. I flew classified missions for the Army Security Agency over Laos and North Vietnam.

Interestingly, in the late '50s I was involved in the early experimentation of arming helicopters. I have lived to see it grow from H-13s and .60 cal. guns to the present. It is mind boggling to see what we have created during my career.

As far as the return trips to CONUS, I came home twice under my own power and once on a litter. They were all bad. I still have nightmares about that- the treatment by the radicals. They'd spit on you and shove you off the sidewalk. I finally quit wearing my uniform home.

Benny Crocker earned over his career a Meritorious Service Medal, a Distinguished Flying Cross, the Bronze Star, 37 Air Medals, the Purple Heart, and the Combat Medical Badge among others. Benny's son, Johnny D., just got home from Iraq. He earned the same Combat Medical Badge. Benny is going to present Johnny his same medal he earned almost 40 years ago *(This has been appropriately noticed along with the father's pride in his voice on 16 May*

319

'91).

I talked to Ed Bass, a two time Vietnam vet:

I don't really have any comment on what I did. I am happy to see that this war is being fought the way Nam should have been *(interviewed 2000 hrs 17 January 1991)*.

Waylon R. Smith was in the Army a platoon leader in the 1st Cav Division. He was in on the initial invasion of A-Shau Valley, Ho Chi Minh's private domain. *(On 9 March '66 a before-dawn attack was made by NVAs on a large force of 17 Green Berets, some LLDBs, three CIDG companies, and a Mike Force. Our guys held them off for one day with the help of some Hueys, a few Jolly Greens, and the apparent forerunner of Puff. The next morning the NVAs poured over them. They were joined by traitorous VCs in the CIDG units. The Vietnamese "fighters" proved worthless; the Green Berets got all shot up with every one of them getting wounded, and an evacuation was made. Again the 1st Cav was there to help. Some of them got shot up pretty badly, too. A-Shau proved to be indefensible.)* When he was over there exactly 30 days, he took a sniper bullet through the middle. Waylon was brought back to Walter Reed Hospital and then to Fort Benning, where he spent a year on convalescent duty. Then he went back to 'Nam for a year as an advisor in the Mekong Delta. He earned a Purple Heart and the Vietnam Campaign Medal.

Michael O. Horn. Mike Horn. Mike.

Mike started in the 25th Infantry Division and ended in the "Big Red One," the 1st Infantry Division. He spent 42 months and six days in Nam starting in November 1965. Mike earned a Distinguished Service Cross, a Silver Star, a Bronze Star, the Vietnam Cross of Gallantry with palm, Vietnam Campaign Medal, nine Purple Hearts, and was put in for a Congressional Medal of Honor. Mike's story in his own words:

I was 18 when I went over, which was good. It was a war like nobody had tangled with before. It was geared that way. South Vietnam had a landmass the size of West Virginia and we had three-fourths of a million troops there. We could have joined hands and marched through the entire country. Instead, we left 57,000 fatherless/ brotherless/ cousinless families in the US for nothing. I hope a war like that will never be fought again. I lived in terror the whole time I was over there because of 102 mm rockets. We couldn't stop them. The gooks could launch them with three bamboo sticks. It was unreal.

One time I picked up a radio to call for artillery fire. My cousin was on the other end!. I had another cousin who was a caretaker at Long Binh jail.

On the morning of 4 September 1967 I went on patrol with 205 men. At 8 o'clock that night, there were nine of us left, and we were all wounded. Even the Battalion Commander was dead. We called in air strikes from ships in the Gulf of Tonkin, seven artillery batteries, and Puff the Magic Dragon to save us. When we got out in the morning, we had a head count of 600 dead gooks. I walked away from two of these battles.

I had a pet monkey named "Charlie." I used to carry him on patrol with me because he would warn me of danger at night when I was asleep. This went along great for a while. One time I happened on some mines. I made up a C-4 bomb with a detonator cap. That night Charlie tried to eat it. Almost wiped out the rest of the platoon along with himself.

One time, I was sent out on patrol with three other guys to try to find a gook hospital down in the Iron Triangle. It was hot-nasty. We squatted down to take a break. One guy got up to look around and got shot through the chest. The gooks were pouring out of a hole in the ground. I forgot myself and charged the hole *(shades of Viking Berserkers!)*. When it was over I had killed 13 of them. The last one I dragged out of the hole by his hair and cut his head off with my knife. And that was the entrance to a seven-story underground hospital. That's how I earned my DSC.

Loc Ninh *(on the Cambodian border)*; I spent a lifetime there. 12 November 1968- my 21st birthday. This area was on a mountain about three-fourths of a mile long, and most of that was runway. The rest was an old French rubber plantation. We were helping build a C-130 runway and had a lot of fuel bladders around. I was living in a foxhole when the gooks started a mortar attack. The shells blew up the bladders, which spilled all over the place-including filling up my foxhole. When it was over, I just dug another hole right beside it and moved in. The JP-4 fuel finally evaporated, but not before we got nervous about somebody having to light a cigarette.

Christmas, 1968. Same runway. A human wave of gooks tried to overrun us at the crack of dawn. They threw 10,000 North Vietnamese regulars at us. We only had a company of engineers, one battalion of infantry, and one artillery battery, six pieces. I remember the hill was red mud. We repulsed them by breakfast and buried 3400 of them by bulldozer to keep from stinking up the place.

One time we got a "90 day wonder," *(a new lieutenant)*. Bear we called him because he was so big. Bear had ideas of glory. We surrounded a village and were going to sic Private Zippo on it. Bear decided to charge a hootch and throw a grenade into it. He ran out and put his back against the wall. Bear went home with a tail full of shrapnel *(Hootch walls are bamboo.)*

Entertainment. Man, we got entertained by Ann-Margret, and she was looking good. I mean, back then she was looking real good. She came out in the field one Thanksgiving to entertain 300 of us *(Floyd Croney, eat your heart out.)*. We also had a real dinner flown in to us by helicopter-turkey, dressing, cran-

berry sauce, everything. We figured
we were being set up for some kind
of you-know-what detail, something
extra because we were being treated
so well.

It was also at this camp I got my
mail straightened out. I was
standing knee dep in mud when I met
the other Michael Horn. He was in a
mechanized infantry group. Our mail
had been switched for quite some
time. But that Ann-Margret was
looking good-no FLAK jacket either!

Dave Diamond had an interesting tour
with the Navy as a hospital corpsman:
I was with the 3rd Amtrac Battalion,
1st Marine Division in DaNang from
July '66 to August '67. We had one
doctor and eight corpsmen to man a
battalion aid station.

We had a USO tour come through with
Ann-Margret. She was very nice! (I
told Dave about Mike Horn's boots
and flak jacket statements.) Oh,
yes, she looked real nice. We also
had Suzanne Pleshette come spend
about a half a day with us, just
making the rounds.

The experience? It was a waste of my
time. I volunteered to go and even
extended for six months, but I
didn't feel like I had done anything
worthwhile while I was over there.
The amtracs didn't have much to do.
They made five knots in the water
and about that on land. They were
too slow to be useful. We did have
one company of rocket launchers.
They'd put C-4 charges in them and
use them to level villages.

Paul Blocker. I saw a "Speakout" in the Picayune Item (19 March 91) by Paul Blocker about Marines, Vietnam, and Russians, so I called him. Awesome:

I was in the 8126th Marines in 'Nam for 13 months during 1966-67. I was a grunt, and my mission was to search-and-destroy. I fought pretty heavy near about every day and usually had one good battle a week. I had three good years of training before I went over, and made a beach landing in the Dominican Republic in '65. I made another one at the DMZ in 'Nam. We had a pretty stiff fight there. We landed and went in five or six miles that day. Remembering that the guns on the ships only had a range of 21 miles, we hoofed it on in ten to twelve miles the next.

Keep in mind that just before I got to 'Nam, there was a blood bath here, and only two Marines escaped. Anyway, that night the gooks surrounded us. We called for the Navy's long-range guns, and they softened them up. About 3 in the morning we started fighting and fought 'til about 11 in the morning. We would have been wiped out except for the Navy guns. I was in hand-tohand fighting three times. We killed a whole division of gooks. *(This battle in not in the literature, nor will we say where it was fought.)*

'Nam was horrible. Shit. I saw things that were so horrible, it tore your insides up. I saw a lot of Russian "advisors" laying on the side of the road, dead. They weren't

325

supposed to be there, but I saw them. They taught the Cong all that nasty stuff. It almost taken away your mind. They skinned our guys. They were still alive. They skinned them down below the ears. They hung our guys upside-down and gutted them. They gutted you just like a hog. They staked one guy out and cut out his groin. Just like in the Indian movies, they staked him out. Another time I found a guy staked out with sugar, I think rice sugar, poured all over him. The bugs were eating him alive. We had to kill some of those guys. They were beyond hope. I saw this four times in 13 months. It was horrible.

You know what makes me even madder. The damn press. If they would have put some of that on TV, what they were doing to us, the country would have been behind us. the press always got down on us *(This is discussed in more detail in the Aftermath Section.)*.

I was in Operation Tuscaloosa. My last outfit I was in was H25. They based a movie on that unit, "Full Metal Jacket." When my tour was over, they tried to get me to ship over. No f---ing way, baby. I came home.

Paul Blocker has been to hell and back. He says the Marines did not give many medals, but that he was put in for a Navy Commendation for saving his whole platoon one time.

Kenny Hendrix, Headquarters Company, 1st Battalion, 28th Infantry, 1st

Infantry Division, went to Nam in January
'67. In July '67 he was killed by a
mortar attack on his base at Phonc Vinh.
Kenny was posthumously awarded the Bronze
Star and the Purple Heart. His wife,
Alma, was on the way to Hawaii to meet
him for an R and R when she found out.

LUMPKIN

Aubrey Lumpkin did his duty to his
country. He worked his way up in the
Marines. Just to acquaint the civilian
reader with what it takes to make the
military a career, we will follow
Aubrey's, which goes like this:

I was drafted and sent to Fort
Bevins during WWII. I became a
medic, and was sent to Valley Forge
PA Hospital. I stayed there until I
was discharged in '47. I enlisted in
the Marines in '50 and was sent to
Parris Island SC for training. Then
I was sent to Portsmouth Supply
Depot until January 1953. I was
commissioned in February '53. Then I
was with the 8th Marines at Camp
LeJeune for several "brush fires" in
the Caribbean in '55. Then I went to
the 4th Marines in Hawaii, and to
San Diego in '57. In '60 I went to
the USS ROCHESTER to command the
Marine Detachment. After that I went
to Corpus Christi as XO. In '62 I
became CO of the Marine Barracks
Naval Air Station. In '63 I was sent
to LeJeune again. In '64 I came to
New Orleans at the Headquarters of
the 8th Marine Corps District.
In December 1967 I went to Nam as
Logistics Officer for the 26th
Marines at Khe Sanh Combat Base

327

(almost on the Laotian border) until October '68. We were under seige for 60 days (January-April '68) by the Cong. We had to be resupplied by choppers because fixed-wing planes couldn't land. They would be shot up before they could leave. Then I became G2 for the 9th Marine Amphibious Brigade.

In February '69 I came back to the States to the National Security Agency at Fort Meade. In the summer of '71 I went to San Antonio and retired in '75.

For all that Aubrey was awarded the Legion of Merit with combat "V," Combat Action Ribbon, and Vietnamese Cross of Gallantry. Familywise, his great uncle from North Carolina, William D. Graham, was in the CSA Army. Aubrey's wife, Shirley Wolf Lumpkin, was in the Marines in food services from '53-'54 *(see Korean War)*. His opinion: "The war is going okay now, but it's going to be bad as far as ground action goes" *(interviewed 28 January 1991)*.

Herman Walker *(see Walker family in WWII Section)* was in the Army, 1st Cav, Mechanized Infantry, in Nam from July '67 to July '68:

I drove a full-track armored personnel carrier, 8" self-propelled howitzers, and M-60 tanks. I was in Saigon for Tet (Feb '68) guarding the perimeter of Ton Son Nhut Air Base. I fought from the Mekong Delta to the DMZ. My home base was at ------ at first, and I spent the last three months escorting ammo convoys from Long Vey.

> I saw Harry Wayne Herrin from Roseland Park right after I got there and haven't seen him since. I got sent on TDY to Bien Hoa loading VIPs for 15 days.

Herman says that all he wanted to do was survive to come home. He feels like he got revenge because the sorry treatment he got over there and on his arrival back in the good old U.S. of:

> That damn Lyndon Johnson. He kept us over there so he could make money. I think he had Kennedy killed because he didn't have enough men committed to the war effort. Well, Lyndon Johnson can't even buy a glass of iced tea with all that money now. I'm sure he needs it in Hell. I just wish I could pour more coal on the fire.

Herman earned the Bronze Star and was adamant about not having any "hero stuff" written up about him.

Leman "Dennis" Roberts pulled two tours in 'Nam with the Army. He says:

> I was in intelligence on the first tour in '67-'68 at Tay Ninh. On the second tour, in '72, I was attached to the 196th Light Brigade as an advisor to ARVN at Bac Lieu in the Mekong Delta. During these tours I ran into a few ambushes and mortar fires, but nothing serious. I ran into a Spiers from Picayune over there. Entertainment? None.

Dennis earned the Legion of Merit, Bronze Star, Meritorious Service, and Army Commendation Medal with oak leaf cluster. He says of Desert Storm *(interviewed 28 January 1991)*: "This war is going the way

329

it should be, keeping the politics out.
We can take the best clue from Bush'
statement about not going in with one
hand tied behind us."

Ernest Lee Rees III was a Navy
Corpsman attached to Hotel Company, 2nd
Battalion, 5th Marines, 1st Marine
Division in Nam. He tells us:
I was shot in the left shoulder on 6
November 1967 while trying to patch
up a comrade in the middle of a rice
paddy. I was 20 years old. Our whole
battalion was wiped out that day. We
had to call in the 3rd Battalion
and, in a few hours, they were
mostly wiped out. We then called in
the 101st Airborne. Over the next
few days, they secured the area.
This was operation "ESSEX" in
Antenna Valley.

Randy Scheel started at Uben, Thailand, for six weeks. Then he moved to
Mukdaharn as an aircraft controller.
Randy is a transplanted Texan, and has
this to say about it all:
I was living in a hootch in Mukdaharn, Thailand. I was directing long
range air defense and strikes to
Vietnam. While I was there the Bob
Hope/Raquel Welch USO tour came
through. That was when Raquel looked
good in white hot pants and boots. I
didn't feel like riding 80 miles
over gravel roads to see her (*The
man must have the constitution of a
saint.*), so I manned the scopes so
the rest could go (*the very epitome
of altruism*).
Then I transferred to Saigon as an

offensive air coordinator in March 1968 just in time for Tet. My job was to coordinate radar, Navy strikes, Dustys, Sandys, Jolly Greens, and air refueling. I was catching hops all over 'Nam- paving the way. I got shot at, ducked rockets, was at DaNang under seige a few days, and never got hit. I was a lucky man.

My opinion? We were all so irritated by Jane Fonda, we thought she was a traitor. *(He still has not gotten over that jerk. Most of the other interviewees brought up the same subject.)* A lot of people badmouthed our troops for not fighting hard enough, but the limitations we were operating under were too restrictive.

(It was about 1968 that President Johnson decided in his infinite wisdom to stop bombing North Vietnam. This opened the Ho Chi Minh Trail to supply lines for the Cong operating in the south and made the war an even unholier nightmare for the US troops. Many feel this is the reason the war and politics turned sour; and, in fact, cost us a victory. Once again, politics and military. Other things were happening on a global scale at this time, not the least of which was the PUEBLO incident. That writeup is at the end of this Chapter.)

Louis Jones had a nice time in 'Nam escorting convoys from Pleiku to Dok To in the highlands where the "mountain yard" people lived during 1968 . Louis survived the Tet Offensive as a tank commander. A partial list of events leading up to a letter in his jacket that recommends him for a Silver Star and much more includes:

> The Commander's tank was hit by a rocket and men were wounded. I pulled up beside it and saw the town overrun by "Sappers" *(Vietcong suicide squad)*, so I tried to retrieve the wounded. All this time I was out of the tank from the waist up. First I took care of the immediate problem of three gooks hiding behind oil drums. I correctly guessed the drums were full of gas, got the loader to put in tracer bullets, shot the barrels. They exploded and set the gooks on fire. I had to put them out of their misery with my 50 cal. machine gun. More fire on my second attempt at rescue, this time from a ditch. Ordinary 105 shells go too far over the target, so I had the loader put in phosphorus shells. A few judiciously placed shots in front of the ditch yielded what seemed at the time to be about 150 more burning gooks. *(Jones does the only humane thing one more time and kills all these.)* With everyone retreated but my tank, I got a call from the rear about some mortar fire they are taking; so I scoped in, fired 20 105 rounds, and the convoy has smooth sailing until the next time.

These convoys were always being attacked. Once, the convoy got trapped on a hummock in a rice paddy that had been reflooded on them. The troops had to fight all night against a batallion of VC "Sappers," which were promptly wiped out.

Jones obviously had something to do with this as he earned during his tour two Purple Hearts, a Bronze Star, Vietnam Service Medal with two bronze stars, National Defense Service Medal with 1st oak leaf cluster, Army Commendation Medal, Republic of Vietnam Campaign Medal, and Expert with Tank, Pistol, and Rifle. You wouldn't want this guy hunting your favorite squirrel stand. Louis goes on to tell me:

> My CO told me he'd give me my Silver Star if I would reenlist and stay in 'Nam for an extra tour. They really needed tank commanders. I told him I was going to retire *(Sarge already had 19 years three months in when he went to Nam)*. He still insisted and ordered me to go to HQ and reup. I came home from Nam as a civilian and, to this day, still don't have my Silver Star. I'd rather be alive.

Note added later (31 October 91): These kids coming back from the Gulf don't know what a war is. They didn't do nothing. The airplanes and tanks did it all. I'm getting disgusted by the treatment they're getting. Most of them never even fired a shot.

James Stockstill retired as a Sergeant-Major from the Army MP Corps:

> I got to Cam Ranh Bay check-in on 16 January 1968. There was a football game on, the Super Bowl I think. On 19 January, I was sent to my unit, the 272nd MPs, to help maintain security for a 3-star general *(Peen)*. I had been there in a sandstone-walled compound for three or four days when we were one of the first to hit by

the Tet Offensive. The gooks were
coming in for our general. A rocket
hit our yard near me, and I saw a
bunch of what I thought to be
Koreans running down the street
about a half a block away. If I had
had some experience, I would have
realized they were Cong and opened
fire. Then I would be dead now,
because 58 of them crowded into the
second story of a building across
the street with a .51 cal. machine
gun. Man, I would have been a goner.
As it was, about one or two in the
morning we had surrounded that house
and made it look like the one in the
movie, "Gauntlet." We killed them
all. I had written a letter to my
wife from Cam Ranh Bay saying I
would be in the 272nd. She got the
letter the same day she saw a
Memphis paper saying the 272nd was
under attack, and that two MPs had
been killed. That was a mess until I
got in touch with her!
The war now *(interviewed 1830hrs 22
January 1991)*, I agree with it. I
think it's going to mushroom. The
"smart" weapons are not so good, and
Saddam is going to pull something
out. If it turns into a total war,
some retirees will have to go back
in and finish their 30, but I hope
not unless they get a grade raise.
James Daniel Stockstill was awarded the
Meritorious Service Medal (1st oak leaf
cluster), Army Commendation Medal (4th
oak leaf cluster), National Defense Service Medal, Republic of Vietnam Campaign
Medal, Valorous Unit Award, Meritorious
Unit Commendation, and Republic of

Vietnam Gallantry Cross Unit Citation. His grandfather, David *(the one sent home to "requisition" food)* was in The War Between the States.

Edward Earl Bankston was in 'Nam in 1968 with the Marines. The Marines had a rule that, if you were wounded three times in succession, you were pulled off the line and sent somewhere safer to finish your tour. Bankston got three Purple Hearts and finished his tour in Hawaii. Bankston, Sr., went to Iwo Jima in 1945 (January) and just missed the battle. He was sent to North China after that. Sr. was a Marine.

Arnold Matthews has led a multi-facceted life, to say the least. For the purposes of this book, his military exploits:

I was in the third wave of the 1st Marines to hit the beach at Inchon *(see Korean War)*. Then they sent me to guard the US Embassy in Berlin without any ammunition. That was interesting!

In January 1968 I was again on embassy duty, this time in Saigon. One time we were short of personnel for fighting, so the guards not on duty had to go to the line to help us. That was Tet.

I went back to 'Nam for a second tour. The only reason I went back was because I didn't want to listen to my old lady fuss at me. I was at DaNang and Hue. We got rescued by the 11th Airborne at Hue. I was captured, but only for five days. I got away in the streets. *(We had to*

retake Hue in late February 1968.
The North Vietnamese had taken it
and executed 3000 South Vietnamese
including many civilians and
executed them. The Marines entered
Hue from the north. The city was
littered with burned out cars,
trucks, and tanks. Dead bodies and
their stench were everywhere. The
Marines attacked the Citadel in a
full frontal assault that lasted
about two weeks. By the time the
Marines had retaken Hue, 150 of them
were dead. We also know one who was
wounded; though, for the life of me,
I can't see why the Marines would
send a man who had just been through
Tet at the Saigon Embassy all the
way up to Hue to another nasty
battle just one month later.)
Arnold received for his devoted service
during Korea, as an unarmed guard at the
US Embassy during the Berlin crisis, and
for his action during Vietnam, two Purple
Hearts, a Bronze Star, and the campaign
medals by his first admission. (After Pat
Evans told me what he had really done, I
found out more about my old Scouting
buddy of 12 years. You camp with these
guys, eat and travel with them, and think
you know them. HHHHMMMPH! That toothless
old goat.) Arnold also earned by his own
admission after some coaxing a Distinguished Service Cross and a Bronze Star
at Saigon, a Silver Star and a Purple
Heart at Hue, a Bronze Star at Seoul, and
a Purple Heart at Ch'osun. Arnold is
really proudest of his three Marine Good
Conduct Medals, though. (Some men are
born fighters, and some are born lovers.
And, folks, let me tell you. Arnold ain't

336

no lover!)

MARTIN

Alfred "Buck" Martin was in the 8th Air Force in the Philippines when he got called to Vietnam in 1968:

I was in communications control at Cam Ranh Bay, working with supplies. We could hear and feel the shells going off about a mile away, but I was never in any action to speak of. We had a theater of sorts, little wooden benches outside. One night, a cobra crawled up the arm of a man sitting beside me. He never knew it. The guy on the other side saw it and- you'll never believe this- called in a snake charmer. That snake crawled off and never bit the guy *(I didn't think to find out how the movie ended. The story was exciting enough!).*

I saw Brian Watkins over there. He's from Pearl River County. As for this war *(interviewed 31 January 1991 exactly two weeks into Desert Storm),* I think we're right on top. This is one of the best presidents we've had...

Buck's son, Alfred "Ronnie" Martin, was with the Navy on the USS GUAM. He was in Nam twice in 1970 and '71 at Tonkin Gulf. Ronnie also participated in the invasions at Grenada and Lebanon. Buck's other son, Paul, was in the Marines, and is now with our own 890th. Oh, yes, Ronnie's wife is also a nurse in the Navy Reserve now.

Jim McCain was in the Navy over in 'Nam in '68. He recollects:

I was on ships, the RANGER, CONSTEL-

LLATION, and MIDWAY in DaNang harbor. I was a jet engine mechanic,
standing 12 hour watches, seven days
a week for the duration. We had no
attacks and no casualties. We even
went over on the beach at times to
repair planes.
Bob Hope and the Golddiggers with
Joey Heatherton came to our ship. On
the war? At first I thought we were
right. I wish we had the same
freedom they have now; we would have
saved thousands of lives.

Richard Terry Smith was on the USS
FORRESTAL. On 29 July 1969 there was a
fire and explosion that killed 134
sailors. Smith was one of them.

Cecil "Gene" Walker was a Huey pilot
in a '68-'69 tour. He spent his first
three months at Bung Tao with the justice
system before becoming part of Detachment
4 Corps in the Delta Section. Gene's jobs
were to provide air support for gunboats
on river patrols, scramble fire teams,
and help Vietnamese outposts on the Viam
Do Trong River. His 'copter was armed
with several .30-cal. machine guns and
rockets. Gene tells about "One Shot
Charlie":
When we were out on patrol, someone
would fire at us from a village to
make us attack. One Shot Charlie (a
Cong) would sneak into a non-taxpay-
ing (to them) village, provoke us to
attack, and sneak away before the
action started. We would blow the
place to pieces, not knowing about
"One Shot" in the early days. This
tactic would assure that the

villages around would pay extortion taxes to the Cong the next time or be attacked by us. It took a while for us to catch on to this tactic.
For his work, Gene received three Air Medals, a Navy Unit Commendation, the National Defense Service Medal, Vietnam Campaign Ribbon, Vietnam Service Medal, and Meritorious Unit Commendation. He says it was a "BS" war; but, when you're in the military, you're a hired gun. You go where they send you.

Kenneth Kirkland was a Navy gunners mate assigned to the 7th Fleet on the USS BON HOMME RICHARD, an aircraft carrier. He was all over the Far East in his two tours at Vietnam. Kenneth went over in 1968. His group mined DaNang harbor. He was on line during Alpha Strike when US troops moved into Cambodia. He was also sent up to Korea to assist in the release of the crew of the PUEBLO *(Tuck, are you reading?)*. Kirkland received the Vietnam Service Medal, Vietnam Combat Medal, National Defense Service Medal, and the Expeditionary Forces Medal.

William "Bill" Eck. Personable sort of fellow- moved here from Pennsylvania, works a lot with Picayune on Stage. Bill: I was in Nam with the Navy from June '68 to June '69 attached to a Navy communications station at Market Time, Cam Ranh Bay. Our little station was designed for 35,000 messages a month. We handled 135,000. It was a hard duty, and we stood port and starboard watches for the entire year relaying messages from shore to offshore for gun support.

We also ran a point-to-point circuit
with the Air Force and Army.
I volunteered for duty in 'Nam because I thought we had a purpose and
mission. I thought it could have
been handled better without the
politics. I was also ready to go to
Desert Storm, but I would have to
have had bungee cords to hold my
coat together!
I saw Bob Hope once, but we mostly
had the smaller USO shows down where
we were.

Bill earned his silver dolphins and was
assigned to several submarines over the
years. He says:

I was first on the USS CROAKER, a
pigboat *(diesel)*. We had two after
showers. One was full of potatoes.
The cooks and corpsmen used the
other. We washed in the sink, if we
could get water. Habitability
increased on the nukey boats
(nuclear subs). I was on the JACKSON
(SSN-605) and the TULLIBEE (SSN597),
fast attacks. I was also with
SUBDEVGRP-2. The one true deterrent
the US has always had to global war
has been the nuclear subs. I feel
that they are responsible for ending
the Cold War.

Bill says there are two kinds of ships in
the Navy, subs and targets.

M.C. Vickers spent a year in 'Nam,
eleven and a half months in the field as
a radio operator for the company commander of the 1st Air Cavalry Division,
Company B. M.C. was at Bong Son and
participated in the six day battle for
Dai Dong. The NVAs entrenched themselves

within six miles of the 1st Cav's main supply complex. A patrol was sent to check out antennae protruding from huts, and soon reinforcements were called for. The NVA had trapped themselves into a purely defensive position, and the Americans poured it to them. Final count-400 dead gooks. M.C. says:

> At one time I got separated from my platoon and got into an area where I shouldn't have been. I ended up capturing seven enemy soldiers and brought them all back alive for interrogation. I was scared to death, but I did it anyway. I got a Bronze Star with a "V" for that one. I am proud of my opinion about being there. While I think we should not have been there, this is my country. I'll serve her as she wants. I'd do it all over again.

M.C. also earned another Bronze Star, the Vietnam Service Medal, Vietnam Campaign Medal, an Air Medal, and the National Defense Service Medal.

Ernest Barnett can recall nothing good about Vietnam except his dog:

> I was in the 50th Scout Dog Platoon, 4th Division, from October '69 to October '70. I was a scout dog handler at Ankei and Pleiku in the Central Highlands. It all started at NCO school at Fort Benning. The last week of school they asked me what I thought about it. I told them I didn't think anyone out of this school was qualified to go to Vietnam, especially as a leader. They should be under someone. The next day they kicked me out. I was

given a dream sheet with three
choices, so I picked dog handler.
We had to walk point- always point.
I was a professional point man. My
dog had been there eight years. He
was alert to all of the sights and
sounds and smells of a patrol. These
dogs were special. They even had
priority over the GIs. If one of
each was wounded and there was only
room for one on the chopper, the dog
was supposed to get priority. We
never did that, but that is the way
it was supposed to be.
My dog was a shepherd. We also had
tracker teams of labs *(Labrador
retrievers)*. We had a dog in our
platoon that had a Bronze Star. He
killed two Dinks in a bunker during
Tet by himself. No, we couldn't
bring any of our dogs home with us.
In fact, none of them came back.
Mine probably ended up on some
slopehead's table, skewered.
The mortality rate was not very high
for us *(contrary to popular opinion)*. The dogs were really good. Our
job was mostly to find booby traps,
spear traps, and grenades with trip
wires. The dogs never set the trip
wires. They were good. Only two guys
got wounded. Unfortunately, one was
me. We got a hand delivered "to whom
it may concern" grenade or bomb one
time. Me and another guy dove for
cover while the rest just stood
there picking their noses. Sure
enough, the two that jumped got hit.
The worst treatment I received was
by my own people. My platoon leader
told me he was going to get me

killed. I believed him. He said he wanted a dead Southerner to name his camp after. I stayed out on patrol. When we came back in, we were supposed to put our name on the bottom of the list. I always put mine on top so I could stay out in the bush. The longest I stayed out was six weeks at a time.

Coming home was a bad trip, too. A girl in the New Orleans airport spit in my face and called me a baby killer. I'd have torn her head off her shoulders if I could have gotten to her. The whole Vietnam experience sucked.

Ernest earned a Purple Heart and an Army Commendation Medal *(It sounds like he deserved more.)*. As for the Gulf War: "I'm proud of 'em. They handled it so well" (27 October 1991).

Tom Mullins was with the Army as an air cavalry scout. He was part of a hunter/killer team. For his action he received a Bronze Star, Vietnam Cross of Gallantry with palm, Vietnamese Campaign Medal with one battle star, National Defense Medal, and Army Achievement Award. He was in a unit over there with another man from Picayune, Charles Cale. It took several years at home for the two to find each other. Charles originally came from Alabama, and the two met in Vietnam. As Tom was the scout in a Huey, Charles was the pilot. These guys job was to find an enemy concentration, send in Cobra gunships, and rise above to watch the action. If infantry help were called for, they would go back for the troops and bring them back to the fight. One of their camps was called LV Betty, located just outside Phan Thiet. *(A comment here is appropriate. Phan Thiet is just east of Saigon, and these guys were using short-range choppers. Why are they fighting in the heart of South Vietnam instead of in the north like Korea?)* Charles provides us with a clue: "We were sent there to protect a people who didn't care for anything except where their next bowl of rice came from. They didn't care who the government was. To sum up my experience: I wouldn't take a million dollars for the experience, nor would I take a million dollars to go back."

Robert Richard Miller, 5th Special Forces/Green Beret, served tours in Bu Prang and Quon Loi during 1969. He won two Bronze Stars, one with a "V" and one with an oak leaf cluster, Purple Heart, Vietnam Service Medal, National Defense Medal, an Airborne Medal, and a Commendation Medal. Miller was killed in action near the Cambodian border.

John T. Dobson was a combat engineer with the First Engineer Battalion, First Marine Division, for a tour during '69 and '70. John swept roads for mines to make them safe for our transportation units. That was at Marble Mountain, a rather large rock landmark outside DaNang. *(This must have been a popular place. Pat Evans was there, too.)*. He earned the Navy Achievement Medal with combat "V," Combat Action Ribbon, National Defense Service Medal, Vietnam Service Medal, Republic of Vietnam Cross of Gallantry, and a Vietnam Campaign Medal. John must have done some strange

Cleveland Amacker
Korea
Army

Hershel Amacker

Air Force

Raymond Amacker
Vietnam
Army

Sollie Amacker
WWI
Army

J. Hollie Blackwell,
Jr.   WWII
Army

George T. Burks
WWII, Korea
Air Force

Gregory Burks

Air Force

Ronald T. Burks
Vietnam
Air Force

Willie A. and George
Burks   WWII
Army Air Corps

Billy Frazier
Korea
Army

John E. Geames
Vietnam
Air Force

Aubrey Graham
WWII
Army

Richard A. Heath II   J. Hallon James   Jerry Kellar
                      WWII
Navy   Navy   National Guard

Louis W. Kennedy, Jr   Roy L. Kennedy   Wilford W. Kennedy
Korea   Korea   WWII
Army   Army   Army

347

Shirley Wolf Lumpkin
Korea
Marines

Thomas H. Moody
Korea
Marines

Joe Ben Rester
WWII
Army

Jack C. Richardson
Vietnam
Army

Louis A. Saucier
WWII
Army

Donnell Shehane
Vietnam
Air Force

Dorman "Red" Smith
WWII, Korea
Army

Bill Spiers
WWII
Navy

J.W. Spiers
Korea
Navy

Kenneth W. Spiers

Navy

Albert Earl Stewart

Army

Hezzie Williamson
WWII
Army

Victor L. Williamson
WWII
Navy

Louis Woodward
WWII
Army

Zora Elaine Woodward
Air Force

engineering to have been in so many
fights *(and he's such a peaceful guy
now!)*.

   James Madison "Jim" Young was with
the 475th Tactical Fighter Wing, Air
Force, at Ton Son Nhut Air Base. Jim is a
hard man to reach. It must have something
to do with all the good he's doing this
town by cleaning it up. Jim:
   I was an aircraft mechanic. We
   worked 10 to 12 hours a day repair-
   ing all sorts of planes with a lot
   of battle damage. We had to work so
   hard, we had our own defenders so we
   wouldn't have to stop. We had a real
   affection for them. They did a great
   job of protecting us when the base
   came under attack. Fortunately, that
   only happened a few times.
   The things I remember most? In
   August '69 we saw them put the first
   man on the moon. This made our
   position extremely frustrating in
   that we could do that, but we
   couldn't get along with our fellow
   man. The second was of immediate
   help. Nixon ordered the bombing in
   Cambodia, and that marked the
   beginning of the end of the war. We
   felt so abandoned after Tet. Over
   half of our casualties occurred that
   year (1968). There had been no
   progress being made, so we felt like
   that was the light at the end of the
   tunnel.
Jim made a very inspired speech during
the Operation Homefront festivities at
Picayune on 6 April '91. The gist of his
speech was that a bunch of old men, the
President and the Senators, put the young

men, the soldiers, in a war in a no-win situation *(kinda like letting your alligator mouth buying something your hummingbird butt is going to have to pay for)*. Then they retired to the ranch and left the young men out on the proverbial limb.

We also had at least one landscape architect who didn't much care for the scenery, Pete Wentworth. He helped build the Ho Chi Minh Trail so the rest could see the beautiful countryside more easily. Several countians enjoyed the place so much they served more than one tour. John Allen Wilbanks, Army, was at Pleiku and Quinuan the first tour and at Saigon the second with the 716th MP Battalion. He earned the Bronze Star, Army Commendation Medal, and Vietnam Service Medal. Ed Pinero was there in 63 and 66 with the 3rd Marines, 3rd Recon, 1st Marine Batallion. Jerold W. Spiers was a master diver with the Engineers. He earned a Bronze Star, National Defense Medal with oak leaf cluster, and Vietnam Service Medal with oak leaf cluster. William Misenheimer was an air traffic controller at Cam Ranh Bay. Ron Burge served in the Special Forces and received three battle stars. Rueben Wayne Carroll was in the Air Force. Donald Eugene Carroll was in the Army. Clarence Ashley Byrd, Army, was with heavy artillery. Charles J. Koster was in the 173rd Airborne Brigade for one tour. He earned the Combat Infantrymans Badge, Vietnam Commendation Medal, Vietnam Campaign Medal, Air Medal, and Bronze Star. Kenneth Harold Boudreaux was in the Navy. Jimmy Dale Boudreaux (brother) drowned in DaNang harbor trying to effect a rescue. William F. Leaumont, Air Force intelligence, received numerous decorations including seven Air Medals and two Air Force Commendation Ribbons. David Lee Watson was in communications intelligence. James R. Davis was in Co.A, 3rd Btn, 506th Inf, 101st Airborne. He earned a Combat Infantrymans Badge near Phu Bai.

NAMETH

Phillip Nameth. Now let's see. Big Phil's family has a long history. His father, Carl, was in the Navy on a destroyer in WWII for just about the whole Pacific campaign. Phil's son, Joseph, is in the Navy at this writing at boot camp in Orlando. Phil himself?:

I went to Nam in September '69 to September '70 with the 981st MP Battalion. I pulled duty guarding the ammo dump at Cam Ranh Bay, on the perimeter of Army and Air Force bases at Nha Trang, and the outport at Son Dong as a dog handler. There weren't very many of us. We had several skirmishes and rocket barrages, but nothing serious. I was in the barracks all the time, so I had a radio and all the other neat things. We even got to go to the real China Beach for incountry R and R.

The dogs were treated just like humans. They had personnel jackets, shot records, everything except a pay record. The dogs even earned medals. Unfortunately, they all contracted a disease and were destroyed rather than let them bring the disease back to the States.

I went through basic with four or five guys from Picayune: Glen Tate, some Pentons. We all went to Nam, but to different places.
Phil earned several awards, one of which was the Army Commendation Medal.

Daniel E. Goynes was in the 101st Airborne Division. On 10 May '71 he earned a Silver Star for: "serving as assistant pathfinder team leader during an aerial assault in Thu Thien Province.. Upon arriving at the landing zone, Sergeant Goynes immediately silenced an enemy soldier firing at his position, and then crawled across the landing zone to join his team commander. Through an entire day of enemy contact, he administered first aid to wounded friendly troops and assisted in protecting the perimeter. In the afternoon, he led a patrol through enemy fire to secure a resupply of ammunition and water. Sergeant Goynes gallantry in action..."

JONES
Somebody had to keep the supplies flowing. Charles E. Jones was in a C-130 Herc crew flying high in the sky carrying WRISK kits. Chas was in and out of Turkey, Vietnam, Greece, Vietnam, Korea, Vietnam, and parts unknown and don't care to remember. Always on TAC bases for four years, Chas never had a moment's rest. He earned a Meritorius Unit Citation. Let me digress here to describe the Jones family ties to the wars of the 20th Century. The Jones family has lived in Pearl River County for many years. Chas' great uncles, John Henry and Dan Harrell, fought in WWI where John Henry lost a

kneecap. His father, Johnny Will Jones, was already 32 when he was drafted to fight in WWII. He fought in the ETO. Charles' brother, Johnny Will, Jr., fought in Korea and Vietnam. And, that brings us back to Chas.

If you are able
Save for them a place
Inside you
And save one backward glance
When you are leaving
For the places they can
No longer go...
Be not ashamed to say
You love them
Though you may
Or may not always
Take what they have left
And what they have taught you
With their dying
And keep it with your own
And in that time
When men decide and feel safe
To call the war insane
Take one moment to embrace
Those gentle heroes
You left behind...
            -Michael Davis O O'Donnell
            Dak To, Viet Nam

McLAURIN

In relation to families, an appropriate letter has been submitted that gives insight on much of the state of war. The McLaurin family had five Vietnam era veterans, four sons and a daughter. The letter is written by Cornelius Hamilton "Sonny" McLaurin:

"I was sent to Vietnam in the spring of 1970, trained as a weapon specialist but assigned in DaNang, South Vietnam in the Fire Dept. Bud *(brother Willie James)* was stationed in Saigon as a military advisor.

"After he learned that I was in Vietnam, this was against his wishes. We had several communications by mail. I told Bud in one of the letters that I had signed a waiver, volunteering for Vietnam duty. Bud, after a few months, wrote me and said that he was missing his family and wanted to see his girls. He also noted that it was just too much for our mother to worry about, having two sons in that stupid war. Thereafter, all arrangements were made for him to return to the States.

"Before he had a chance to read my letter telling him that I wanted him to go home, he was killed...

"Having to reminisce on this part of my life is indeed difficult.

"After Bud's death I again volunteered to go back to Vietnam with much hatred in my heart. God saw fit for me to return. Moments like this I wish it was Bud, not I, who had returned..."

After Sonny came home from his second tour, his brother, Johnny Charles, went over. Then his brother, Shirley, and his sister, Josephine McLaurin Turner, joined up.

Rayford B. Vaughn, Sr., was in WWII, Germany during the Korean War, and Korea during the Vietnam War *(not too shabby for a country boy)*. Rayford B. Vaughn, Jr., was in 'Nam for a tour in '71-'72 with the 101st Airborne at Phu Bai and the 196th Light Brigade at Da Nang. He says:

In the 'Nam war the military was not separated from foreign policy. If you objected to foreign policy, then you objected to the military *(presence in SE Asia)*. This one will be a different, much shorter war *(interviewed 28 January 1991)*.

Vaughn says he missed all the entertainment because he gave his tickets to his men.

Van Bolden. Most of us have heard of him through his "Speakouts" in the "Picayune Item." Well, Van Bolden is also a veteran with some very definite ideas about his war:

I was in the Navy for Vietnam. During 73-74 I was sent on patrol duty in the eastern Med with the 7th Fleet on the USS TRUCKEE. We were a tanker/refueler for the Fleet. Most people don't even remember the Arab-Israeli War, but we were there. Since we were the energy source for the Fleet, we were very uncomfortable all that time. We used to get spotlighted. I saw it one time. When the light went off, there was nothing there. We never knew if we would be attacked. It was scary.

I don't know if we should have been as involved as we were in the Gulf War. I don't think they've done any more that we did. These guys were confronted with a Star Wars. They never even saw anyone they were shooting at.

J.L. Wells shows up one more time to add these words:

All I remember about Korea is that

we anchored off Inchon, I think. I was on two different aircraft carriers, the CARD and the CROATAN. I was in MSTS at the time. We hauled planes to DaNang, Saigon, and Cam Ronh Bay. My brother, Bobby, retired from the Air Force. He was in Korea and Vietnam, but I don't know what he did.

LAIB

Duwaine Laib was in Navy intelligence, so he can't say much; however, he spent a career in the Navy:

I was in and out of 'Nam in '69, '73, and '74, and went to Thailand just before we pulled out. I was a Navy casualty officer in Saigon at the end for POWs and MIAs. It was the most traumatic, but most rewarding, job I ever had. There is no question we've still got guys over there.

There are several good points about being overseas all this time *(Europe and SE Asia)*. I was never in the US, so I didn't have to put up with US yellow journalism about the war. Also, my kids were able to grow up in Europe, so they missed all the social problems of growing up in the US ten years ago. It was also a different school system.

If we could have done the job they're doing now, we could have been successful. We won't come home from the Gulf empty handed.

Duwaine's daughter, Jami Laib, is an intelligence specialist in Russian language with the Air Force in Alaska now.

Fortunately for all these Purple Heart winners, we had a medical staff- by all accounts, a pretty good one. Ronald W. "Ron" Kelly was with the 44th Medical Brigade, 3rd Field Hospital. Ron flew "dust off" missions picking up the wounded. Let him tell it:

We brought two guys in that had white phosphorus burns. One died en route, and the other died about a week later. They had a pet monkey. He found a phosphorus grenade and pulled the pin. We also brought in a lot of VC. For some reason, they never made it back to the lines.

I found out a guy from Picayune was there, David Farrell, and paid him a visit. James S. "Jimmy" Porter came to see me. We had a lot of visiting "dignitaries" come to see the patients: Ron Ely, Tab Hunter, Sebastian Cabot, Ricardo Motalban.

Elwin "Doug" Lee was an assistant chaplain at Pleiku. He was also a bodyguard for the head chaplain with the 25th Infantry Division. Doug:

I prepared for a month before going to Nam by getting hymnals, music on tapes, Bibles, and printing supplies. We went from platoon to platoon holding services. Each soldier had the opportunity to attend weekly. We also held memorial services for those who were killed. We even had a 21-gun salute on tape. We also printed bulletins with songs for the services and bulletins for the memorials. It was a horrible experience, but I was glad I could

359

be of some assistance.
Doug is one of the writer/singer/publishers of the song, "Freedom Isn't Free."

In making a good account of themselves our young men have earned Bronze Stars, Combat Infantryman Badges, Purple Hearts, Vietnam Combat Medals, Vietnam Crosses of Gallantry Vietnam Service Medals, Silver Stars, and all kinds of commendations. Even though we encountered much reticence for various reasons in the interview process from veterans of this war, we certainly don't see any reason for it. These guys did the best job they could under the circumstances and have nothing to be ashamed of.

PUEBLO INCIDENT
In retrospect, 1968 was a bad year for the home team all over the world. Not only did we undergo the Tet Offensive, we also suffered the national ignominy of the PUEBLO incident. The North Koreans captured the PUEBLO in international waters. Its contingent of men included a Pearl River Countian, one D. Richard Tuck. Dick recalls:
On 23 January 1968 the PUEBLO was captured by North Koreans in international waters. They blindfolded us and made us walk the plank. Fortunately, it ended on a dock instead of in the water. They drove us in a bus, where we underwent beatings by the populace at every stop. I must have resembled one woman's ex-husband, because she took a vengeance on me. I finally had to push her aside.

Our really severe beatings and interrogation took place inside "the barn." We learned how to bend the truth to survive. I finally convinced them I was an oceanographer and, if that proved to be a problem, I still had a dime and would call President Johnson and get this matter straightened out. Some guy jumped over the table and hit me on the chin with his rifle butt.

After the beatings and interrogation stopped, things got boring. We went out for exercise for an hour at night. We bathed twice a day and ate three times a day. It was either sheer fright or sheer boredom.

Once we went through a world-wide Communist press conference. After going on for a while, the East German sighed in beautiful English: "I wish you guys would knock off the crap so we could go home." It broke us up on our side. He knew what a sham show it was.

During Hell Week we started getting beatings again. It seems they had been taking pictures of us, and we had been giving them the finger in every one. Somewhere back in America some old fogy got the idea we were spelling out HELP. "Time" and "Life" ran the story, and we got the beatings. This was just before our release (courtesy Picayune Item of 28 August 1988).

I spent the same time as a POW as the military on board and was treated the same (rather rotten and certainly not within the spirit of the Geneva Convention). At any rate this disgrace was perpetrated by the area commanders who did almost nothing to prevent our capture and the top brass that placed the ship in such a vulnerable position in the first place.

After everything else the military finally recognized Tuck with a POW medal in 1990. Tuck also earned a Purple Heart for his beatings. That shows how severe they were. The whole gang got beaten with 2"x4"s for the finger episode. Tuck's middle finger still looks a little crooked. *I don't know what a civilian is supposed to do with a medal, but so be it.* Tuck had been a tank commander in the Army before he held this job.

Interestingly, Vietnam Special Forces were allowed the leeway on occasion to select their next targets. I'm sure Tuck and the boys were never aware of it, but a contingent of Special Forces was on the way to North Korea to take the base before the PUEBLO landed. They were going to wreak havoc and effect a rescue before the politicians had a chance to interfere. Talk about timely action!. The guys were almost there when General Abrams ordered them back to Vietnam under threat of court martial. The group included Pat Evans. We'll hear more about Abrams later.

Along this same story line we have another "almost" rescuer. Barney Lampp was in and out of Vietnam from '65 to '69 with the Navy's 7th Fleet:

I was a machinists mate on the USS DAVIDSON. I essentially had three tours in 'Nam. On one of them we started up the river to Saigon and ended up having to back out. Can you imagine backing a ship out of a channel? Fortunately, we weren't very far up. I was there when Saigon was attacked during Tet. *(Now here comes the pertinent part.)* We were there when the PUEBLO got captured. I was within 15 miles *(less than the horizon)* and saw them take the PUEBLO. We had orders not to fire on them *(Koreans)* unless we were fired upon. We just sat therethe entire 7th Fleet - and watched them capture and drive off with the PUEBLO. I couldn't believe it. Barney says he's glad this war is over. Of course, he had a vested interest in it, a son named Tommy. We'll pick him up in Desert Storm. Barney also says he liked the way everyone supported the war and his family while Tommy was gone. "Thank God he got home alright."

USS SCORPION

Strange happenings were all over the place in '68. The World's nuclear submarine force was reduced by at least three. One of these, the USS SCORPION, belonged to the US. It went down in April:

In late May I was on the USNS BOWDITCH to do my normal 8 to 5 job when we were diverted. After almost running over a non-NATO sub on the way down, we arrived at the beginning search point, roughly the last reported position of the SCORPION. By the end of the cruise we had found the missing sub. A few weeks later a task force set up on station and dragged a sled through the area for some bottom photography. Even a non-nautical engineer or explosives

expert could see that the SCORPION
did not implode of its own accord.
It exploded. You could see the whole
conning tower, the screw, large
pieces of the decking. It looked
like it had been shot amidships. We
on board figured that a game of cat-
and-mouse with the Russkies had cost
the SCORPION its life, along with
that of the entire crew. Perhaps
we'll never really know.

Interregnum (The Final Straw)

In the years since 1973, the US military has participated in policing the world for peace and has emerged as a frontrunner in the science fields of navigation, mapping, ocean-bottom coverage, guidance systems, stealth bombers, smart weapons, etc. Many Pearl River Countians have been on the front line of these efforts.

Let's start with J.P. Rester. He spent a long, illustrious career in the Air Corps/Air Force from 1942 to 1976. In WWII J.P. earned the EAMETO Medal with 4 battle stars and an Air Medal with 1 oak leaf cluster. Then he went into the Air Force Reserve, serving as instructor at Keesler and Fort Rucker. Now, here's the kicker. The Air Defense Identification Zone Facility at Dobraburg, Germany, was named the Rester Center after J.P. died. That shows what high esteem he was held in.

Robert Miller of Millard served a long tour of duty in 'Nam *(see that section)*. VFW Post 9103 in Spring Lake NC is now named in his honor. The football stadium in Carriere at Pearl River Central is likewise named after Kenny Hendrix.

WILSON

The Wilson family was very well represented in the Armed Forces in the early '70s. Rayburn "Ray" Wilson tells us:
I was a machinist's mate, first on the COLUMBUS (a guided missile cruiser), and second, on the INDEPENDENCE (a carrier). I did two Med cruises, and they were basically very peaceful.

Vietnam ended while we were over there. I enjoyed it, but I wouldn't want to make a career of it. The sea duty was too long. I was on the INDY with Don Spikes from here.

Ray's brother, James Thomas Wilson (deceased), was in the Air Force in 1972. His wife, Rosemary, was also in the Air Force at the same time as an enlistee. She went back in as an officer in 1979 and stayed four or five more years. Uncle W.J. Wilson was in the Korean War. First cousins, Chalmus and Stanley, were in: Chalmus went into the Navy in 1970 and will retire soon. Stanley went into the Marines in the early '70s

WOODSON

Ronald L. Woodson was in the Navy in the mid-'70s. Ron was on the USS ORISKANY as a crypto operator and the USS POINT LOMA as a radio operator. The ORISKANY was an older flat top, the last of the ESSEX class. Ron was in the western Pacific fleet operating out of Hong Kong and the Philippines in 1975:

We were having a changing of the fleet one time at 180 degrees. The Russian Bear *(name for a recon plane)* always came to take pictures. This time we were changing with the RANGER, and she had scrambled six F-4 Phantoms. Well. the Bear came in escorted by one on each wing tip, one front and rear, and on top and bottom. That must have felt weird for the pilot!

In 1976 I was on the POINT LOMA, the mother ship of the TRIESTE II. We were all over the world doing research and sending raw data to oceanographic institutes *(Who said the military never returned anything to the civilian populace?).* We had a renowned oceanographer, Bob Ballard, with us. He was on board for all our dives- to look at the submarine, THRESHER, and picture "safaris" of the Mariana, Puerto Rican, Panamanian, and Cayman trenches. I remember old Ballard had never seen a sea bat *(tsk, tsk, too bad for his tail!).* We introduced him to one, and I lifted the bucket.

Ron said they would fill the POINT LOMA with ballast and sink it to a level that the "little pig" could float off *(I hope the ship had plenty of freeboard).* The best part was on deck forward of that. There was a permanant basketball court set up where we had tournaments. Ron's brothers, Donald and Ricky, were in the service. Donald was on the TICONDEROGA as a communications expert. Ricky is in the Army Reserve.

Other Cold War incidents occurred during the interregnum to keep the coals smouldering. From 12 to 15 May 75 we went to Cambodia and took back the SS MAYAGUEZ. In '80-'81 we had the great Carter debacle, the Iran hostage situation featuring the aborted OPERATION EAGLE CLAW. On 19 August Khadafi (a petty tyrant in Libya) tried to take on the whole Med fleet. Two of our carrier based F-14A Tomcats aced two Libyan Su-22s. We had some trouble in Lebanon in 1983. There was an assault on mighty Grenada in 1983 because of its radical tendencies and arms stockpiling. URGENT FURY took care of that. In December 1985 we had to put up with more terrorist activity in an abortive hijacking attepmt by the Palestine Liberation Front on the SS ACHILLE LAURO. Khadafi tried to plan a retaliation, so we blew up his camel track and several other strategic places in April 1986. That was OPERATION EL DORADO CANYON. Unfortunately, we missed him. In 1990 another terrorist raised his ugly head.

On 10 November 1990 the Career Womens Club Brick-by-Brick Committee unveiled its monument in front of the City Hall in Picayune. This gave major memorials at each end of the County- a war memorial in Poplarville and this one. During the unveiling ceremonies attended by 3 to 4000 people, a rather scruffy-looking guy came backstage lurking around. He walked with a limp, had long, greasy hair in a ponytail, a black leather jacket. Just the kind you don't want to be in a dark alley with on a dark night. Wrong guess! Everyone backstage was getting nervous when Bobby Rushing went over to find out if she could help:

The man was almost in tears. He told me his best friend, a man in a wheelchair, had just committed suicide last night (9 November). He was really close to tears. Then he gave me a medal *(a Special Forces Medal from Vietnam)* and asked me to place it on the monument for the unveiling and dedication. I asked him whose it was and when I could give it back to him. He said he didn't have any use for it any more. They had been in Vietnam together, and he wanted me to keep the medal after the ceremonies. I have it mounted now and will always honor it even though I don't know who it belonged to.

FREEDOM ISN'T FREE
"To those who served our country and those

who gave their life.
You loved our land and trusted God
To defend our stars and stripes
With pain and death and dignity, you bore
our country's name,
And fought in foreign lands and sea
So freedom here could reign.

"We lift you high and so with pride, we
commemorate this day
With engraved brick and granite stone,
We would like to say;
It's those like you fighting side by side
Some gave their life for me,
The freedom America now enjoys is freedom
that isn't free.

"Heroes do not come to be because they win
or lose.
They're honored for their sacrifice and the
pathway that they chose.
To you- our veterans- who walked that
second mile;
It is to you we give this honor; you are
America's child.

"We salute to give our heroes praise;
You are Pearl River County's pride,
We honor you for all you gave in claiming
freedom's prize.
We unveil this memorial-
A symbol for all to see;
Thank you- our veterans- Freedom isn't
free."

-Doug and Diane Lee
copyright

We were all sitting around congratu-
lating ourselves - fat, dumb, and happy
about world events. No wars were going on,
the Russians had pulled back and were

falling apart at the seams, and only a madman named Sodamn Insane, I mean Saddam Hussein, acting up a bit in Iraq. He had taken some little old place named Kuwait and was facing a UN resolution whereby all the armed forces in the whole world were aligned against him. The man would have been a fool not to back down. At 6:00 PM CST on 16 January 1991 he became just that.

Operation Desert Storm (The Gulf War)

SCUD MISSILES-SMART WEAPONS-SAND-TANKS-
WATER-MORE WATER-EVEN MORE-RESERVES-
NATIONAL GUARD- HELICOPTERS-ISRAEL-ALLIES
*What a turkey shoot! The war started off
with softening runs by the Allied Air
Forces. The object was to knock out
rocket bases, tanks, Republican Guards,
communications, supplies, everything.*

We had a rather large naval force
present at the war. I was able to
interview several crewmembers just after
the war. Danny Acker, cousin of Sherman
and Anthony *(see WWII section)* told me:

> I was with the 7th Fleet in the Red
> Sea for the whole thing on the USS
> DETROIT. The DETROIT is a resupply
> ship: oil, ammunition, whatever you
> need in the fleet. I was over there
> until 5 March. Tempers really flared
> on our ship. We were supposed to
> have been relieved earlier than we
> were, so there was a lot of
> bickering and fighting.
> I don't think we should go back
> *(interviewed 8 April 91)*. The Iraqis
> are only killing more Iraqis. Who
> cares?

I saw Danny at the homecoming parade
sponsored for the early veterans, and he
was among the first to get back.

Shawn Palmer was on the USS SARATOGA
in the Red Sea. He reported:

> I was plane captain of an EA6B, a
> "Prowler." Prowlers jam radar, and
> ours did their share. Our ship also
> fired 26 Herm missiles. These sought

371

the radar and blew it up. I only wish we hadn't waited so long to start the war *(interviewed 8 April '91)*. I was over there from August '90 to March '91.

Shawn created quite a stir in the local press:

One day I was on watch, getting a plane ready to go. My watch supervisor came and told me to come with him right away. When I told him I was busy, he insisted and took me to the watch shack. The XO was there, looking rather stern. I thought I was in deep trouble. Then he grinned, stuck out his hand, and congratulated me on the birth of my son! I was shocked and relieved. They even let me make a satellite phone call. What a homecoming!

I was on the ship with Tim Cunningham from Picayune, but I never saw him. *(Shawn was also on board with the following seaman.)*

One of the men responsible for the most excellent bombing runs was Robert "Wayne" Littles on the USS SARATOGA. Wayne is an airplane bombing specialist. He's the one who loads them up for their daily runs *(I wonder how many personal messages he sent Sodamn?)* from the Gulf of Oman.

The Allies flew 110,000 combat missions in 43 days of the war, losing only 36 planes. And, Boy, did they soften them up!

Curtis Shoemake was a flight control technician with the F-15 Eagles of the 33rd Tactical Fighter Wing, Air Force.

His unit had the most air-to-air kills in the battle, with 16. Curt said he had to give up a lot of his freedom to help the Saudis *(courtesy Picayune Item)*.

The ground war against the vaunted Republican Guards lasted 100 hours. Schwartzkopf's opening act employed the largest helicopter strike ever. It totally surrounded the Guard. In the grand finale the largest tank battle since WWII clobbered them and left Sodamn with only one Division, and them not equipped. It would be hard now for the Iraqis to go to war with their grandmothers.

We have a brother-sister combination: the Burnetts. I talked to Calvin after the homecoming parade:
I'm in Bravo 55ADA, the Air Defense Artillery. I was in Korea on standby for the whole thing. One interesting thing, Schwartzkopf was my base commander when I was stationed at Fort Stewart *(Calvin shows a lot of pride in the military. This is quite a switch from the last war.)*.
What we accomplished was a great thing, but it was scary because you didn't know what would happen at any given time. It was a pick and choose situation.
Calvin says he has already earned nine medals in seven years of active duty. But, he really beams when he talks about his sister:
"Sandra" Denice has only been in the Army for two years. She's in the 843rd ADA, Patriot Missile Battalion *(You all remember the SCUD missile*

attacks). Sandra fired 8 of the 41 Patriots sent up. Five of them hit! Not only that, but she captured an Iraqi prisoner while on guard duty one night in Dhahran. A full bird colonel gave her the Army Achievement Medal in March for that. I wish she could be here for this *(homecoming activities)*, but she got extended.

Tommy Leinbaugh, 313th Military Intelligence Battalion, 82nd Airborne, was in Saudi Arabia from 28 August '90 to 30 March '91:
I studied guerilla warfare for a lot of people at one time as opposed to the Special Forces. I qualified on all types of equipment, especially generators. We were stationed outside Dhahran. Hot? It was 122 degrees when I got off the plane. It was so hot, we wore our long uniforms with the sleeves rolled down just to soak up the sweat. Then, maybe a breeze would cool you off somewhat. We learned that from the "Hajis."
We lived in a self-contained unit with three Kuwaiti linguists and practiced our desert training while we were awaiting action. When it came, it was short and sweet. My group convoyed north into Iraq and then east toward Basra. In less than two days we established our position. Saddam was scared of us "Red Berets," so his troops surrendered before they got to us. I personally had an M-60 machine gun and an M-16 rifle waiting for them. The Iraqis

could probably have taken us because we were only one Division, but they surrendered instead. So, we just held our position until they sent us back to Dhahran and home through Germany.
Food? We ate T-rats and MREs. Some of the MREs had M and Ms and chewing gum. They may have been old, but I always ate all of mine.
Tommy says he feels great about the war. *(These guys are all full of spit and vinegar. They could have kept going with no problem.)* The Iraqis did not want to fight after having been at war with Iran for the past eight years. Tommy also says he's waiting to see what the Israelis will do for retaliation. He says you don't mess with them *(It sounds to me like you don't want to mess with Tommy Leinbaugh.)*.

"Little" Larry Spooner found an interesting way to get to the action in a hurry:
I went over with the 3673rd Army Maintenance Unit from New Orleans because I could get there faster. When I got there, I was attached to the 24th *(Mechanized)* Infantry at Logbase Echo about five miles from the Iraqi border. I was in on the big sweep *(From 24-27 February 1991 the 24th was travelling just east of the 101st Airborne with the 3rd Armored Calvary Regiment. They headed north toward the Euphrates River to block the roads. Then they headed east to face the vaunted Republican Guards.)*.
The Iraqis just threw down their

375

guns and surrendered. The only action I was in was when I got hit in the head by a stray piece of shrapnel. This was before the sweep. It was nothing serious. I got a concussion *(Nothing serious! This County needs more men like him.)*.
Our food was okay. You just buried the MREs in the sand. It was like an oven.
Larry feels like they executed the war well. There was no Stateside BS to hinder them. *Larry's father was in Vietnam and appears at the end of the book in the Afterword section.*

STOCKSTILL

This information was related to me by Tommy, Jr. His grandfather, Theodore, was in WWII. His father, Tommy, Sr., was in Vietnam in '69-'70. Tommy himself:
I was in the 1st Marine Division, 1st Light Armored Division for Desert Storm. August 1990 found me at home for my first leave in an year. I got to enjoy four days. We went over on 3 September '90. I went ten days later because the shortage of transport aircraft had units camped out on the runway and nearby abandoned roads hoping for an opening to go. We landed at Al Jubail at midnight on a C-5, and were sent out in the field as first unit behind the Egyptians, Saudis, and Kuwaitis. Our unit was the standby in case the Iraqis came across. When it was hot, it was 138 degrees during the day. When it was cold, it was about like winter here.
I was in communications in a mobile

unit of light armored vehicles (LAV). They had big guns on them. Sometimes I drove them, but I never got to fire a shot. We slept under the stars because we had to be ready to move in under a minute. When it was so cold, sometimes we'd sleep in the vehicles.

Hours after arriving in Saudi, many of us headed straight into the field to form a screen-line defense directly behind the Saudi, Egyptian, and Kuwaiti forces.

Our unit was the first to receive enemy artillery fire. My unit had moved from the coast of the Persian Gulf westward to an area on the Kuwaiti border called "the elbow," near the castle of Um Juhl. We conducted patrols and psychological operations to provoke peaceful surrender of the Iraqi troops. *(It was a great success as it later proved.)*

One night we were attacked by a brigade en masse of T-72 and T-55 tanks and armored vehicles. Our two companies faced them. We were supported by Cobra helicopters and A-10 Thunderbolts, and we defeated them and turned back the attack. The Iraqi commanders were so frightened by our ferociousness and firepower that they halted the entire attack and stopped their own reinforcements. They would have outnumbered us ten to one and defeated us instead. We lost two vehicles that night and 13 personnel. One of the vehicles fell to a T-72 main gun round and one fell to friendly fire.

This was understandable, since we were only 25 yards apart!

There are three things I remember about the ground war. The surrendering Iraquis. There were thousands of them with anything white they could lay their hands on, marching forever unfalteringly south. The noontime smoke and the ever present blackness of it. And third and most, the look of joy, relief, and happiness on the faces of the Kuwaiti resistence fighters when we, the first coalition forces to enter the city, rolled in. I'm afraid no amount of words can describe that moment. It almost made it all worthwhile- the killing, the bloodshed, the misery, fear, and loneliness of the last six months for us. Anyone who claims to describe that moment is a damn liar and is wasting your time.

After liberating the airport the following morning, the war was over for us. Thirty-six hours later it would be for everyone else except for the natives. They are still recovering, and I guess they always will be.

When we started up through the burning oil fields, I spent two days in them. We had no equipment for breathing, so I'll probably die at 40 from all that smoke inhalation *(he's 22 now)*. The oil fields were like nighttime all day long. We had to use our night vision devices, but you still couldn't see beyond the front of your vehicle.

I don't think, now that I've been home for a while, that we did what

378

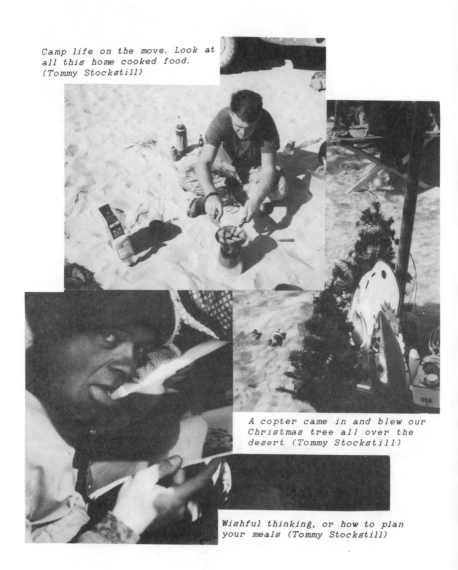

Camp life on the move. Look at
all this home cooked food.
(Tommy Stockstill)

A copter came in and blew our
Christmas tree all over the
desert (Tommy Stockstill)

Wishful thinking, or how to plan
your meals (Tommy Stockstill)

Marine Corps Commandant Al Gray
(Tommy Stockstill)

A visit by Pearl River County's
"Major Dad", Gerald McRaney
(Tommy Stockstill)

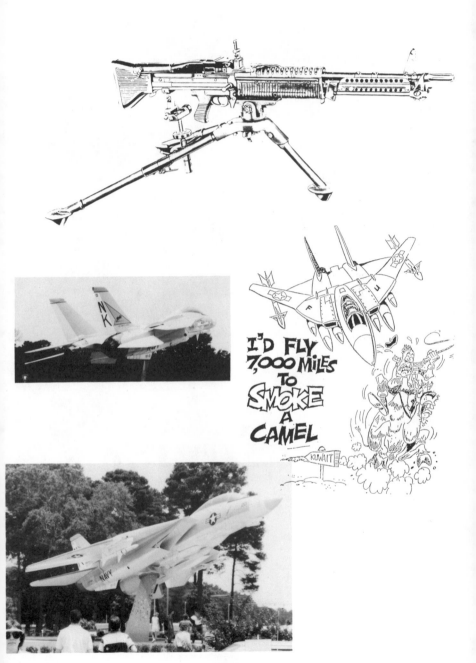

I'D FLY 7,000 MILES TO SMOKE A CAMEL

KUWAIT

USA TODAY

NO. 1 IN THE USA ... NEARLY 6 MILLION READERS A DAY

THURSDAY, JANUARY 17, 1991

NEWSLINE
THE GULF WAR AT A GLANCE

THE ATTACK: With a historic, lethal air strike, troops of Operation Desert Storm rain bombs on Iraq, 3A. President Bush: "Just the way it was scheduled." 4A.

MARKETS REACT: Japan's Nikkei shoots up 1004.11 points to close at 23,446.81. "What happens in Tokyo follows in London and then the U.S." 1B.

PAYING THE PRICE: U.S. officials deny it, but Iraqi leader Saddam Hussein, left, also may have been a target. 2A. Connoisseur of violence. 8A.

NO RESISTANCE: U.S. and allied forces met "no air resistance" from Iraq, USA says. 4A.

EARLY TARGETS: Iraq's air force and chemical, nuclear plants took a pounding. 3A.

Agence France-Presse
SADDAM: Said to instill fear in enemies.

UNITY URGED: Democratic leaders of Congress who voted against war urge support from all in United States. 4A.

MEDICAL AID: No clear view exists on number of military casualties. 4A. Hospitals ready. 9A.

THE DISPUTE: A look at the issues and answers surrounding the gulf crisis. 8A. Peace marches. 5A.

DESERT FIGHTERS: Twenty-eight nations have sent ships, aircraft or personnel to gulf. Airplanes total more than 1,800; ships, 167. Ground forces total 745,000. 9A.

U.S. BOMBS BAGHDAD
Iraqi air force 'decimated'

President Bush :
" Tonight the
battle has
been joined.
"

"
When the
troops we've
sent in finish
their work, I'm
determined to
bring them
home as soon
as possible.

By Bill Nichols
USA TODAY

U.S. missiles and bombs struck Iraq and Kuwait in massive, pre-dawn raid today reportedly decimating the Iraqi air force and knocking out nuclear and chemical weapon facilities.

"The battle has been joined," President Bush said Wednesday night in a TV address. "The world could wait no longer. ... We will not fail."

Iraqi President Saddam Hussein replied in a radio broadcast five hours after bombing began: "The mother of all wars has begun." Iraq, he said, would crush "the criminals

LAV-60 scout vehicle looking over oil fields in Kuwait (Tommy Stockstill)

Stinger crew with captured Iraqi helicorter (Tommy Stockstill) We were going to bring this helicopper home, but Swartzkopf commandeered it

Inside a bunker hit by a smart bomb (Larry Spooner)

Iraqi bunker after a visit by an F-15 smart bomb (Larry Spooner)

EPW camp in southern Iraq (Larry Spooner)

"....and the rocket's red glare." (Larry Spooner)

Devastation Alley...Iraqi vehicles (Larry Spooner)

US propaganda sheets dropped all
over the Iraqi army and populace
(Tommy Stockstill)

Liberated Kuwaitis (Tommy
Stockstill)

The oil field disaster from the
inside. This is actually at high
noon (Tommy Stockstill)

SATELLITE   THE NATION'S NEWSPAPER   50 CENTS

USA TODAY

NO. 1 IN THE USA . . . NEARLY 6 MILLION READERS A DAY

THURSDAY, FEBRUARY 28, 1991

NEWSLINE

GULF WAR SUMMARY, INDEX

WALL STREET: Dow rises 24.51 points to 2889.11 as investors begin bargain hunting, relieved that the gulf war is virtually over. Peace and defense stocks. 1,3B.

BRITISH CASUALTIES: Nine British soldiers – seven of them teen-agers – killed by "friendly fire" laid down by a U.S. A-10 Warthog tank-killing jet. 3A.

RESERVISTS DIE: Christine Mayes, left, is among the first female soldiers killed in war since eight nurses died in Vietnam. 1,8A.

HEALTH PROBLEMS: Iraq, Kuwait may be on the verge of malnutrition, diseases. 2A.

A FREE KUWAIT: Kuwaitis shower allies with gratitude on first day of freedom. 2A.

MAYES: She just wanted to serve.

MANY LOSERS: Iraq isn't only loser in the Persian Gulf war: Soviet weapons, military doctrine fail the test. 4A.

WAR LOG: Day 43. 3A. State of the war. 11A.

EQUAL ROLES: U.S. leaders in the gulf acted with "deference and respect" for their Arab hosts. 4A.

OVERESTIMATED: Iraq's military might was a lot less fearsome than described by the media. 4A.

WAR CRIMES: Allied forces in Kuwait are preparing to prosecute Iraqis for atrocities against civilians. 4A.

HOPES DASHED: Iraq's retreat from Kuwait is met with a sense of mourning by Palestinians. 5A.

POSTWAR CONCERN: U.S. officials are rais-

> 66 We've accomplished our mission, and when the decisionmakers come to the decision that there should be a cease-fire, nobody will be happier than me. 99
> — Gen. Norman Schwarzkopf

By Greg Gibson, AP

HOW THE WAR WAS WON
DAY-BY-DAY, 6, 7A

BUSH: 'VICTORY' IN 100-HOUR WAR

Iraq given 48 hours to surrender

By Jessica Lee and Tom Squitieri
USA TODAY

President Bush Wednesday declared a "quick, decisive and just" victory in Operation Desert Storm and suspended military action at midnight EST.

"Kuwait is liberated. Iraq's army is defeated. Our military objectives are met," the president said on national television. He also listed the terms Iraq war:

we needed to do. We knew Saddam was waxing people. From the time we quit fighting, the Kurds started coming out of the woodwork and fighting. Our leaders wouldn't let us fight with them *(We are all familiar with what has happened to the Kurds.)*.
Tommy said he looked all over for Chad Burchfield, but never found him. Tommy earned a Combat Action Medal, a SW Asia Medal, and thinks they're all going to get a Kuwait Liberation Medal.

SONES
We are presented three generations of Sones males in the Armed Forces. Their philosophy is that, according the Steve, "I hope my grandson will not let the chain be broken. That is, if I have one!" In the interest of keeping these patriots together, I include them all with the youngest warrior. Starting with WWII, Harvey Sones, Sr. was in the Army Air Corps from 1942-45. Harvey started as a fueler for bombers and fighters, went on to communications, and ended his tour as a PT instructor on Lake Pontchartrain for sailors going to the Pacific. He was also stationed on a rescue cutter. All this training was done on Lake Pontchartrain because it was similar to the Pacific environment *(Boy, it sure must have been different back then. Look at it now!)*.
Harvey's son, Stephen B. Sones, retired from the Air Force. Steve says:
I was a telecommunications expert in Belgium with NATO from '66 to '70. This was just after DeGaulle kicked us out of France. That's where Ben was born *(coming up)*. My family lived there while I went to Vietnam

during 1972 and '73 at Ton Son Nhut
Air Base.
I don't know what some people think.
If they would have sent me to Hanoi
with my backpack and a slingshot, I
would have tried to do it. I've
always believed my superiors gave me
instructions for the good of the
cause. Sometimes, though, military
people want to become political people, and sometimes political people
want to become military. The decisions get crossed up, and the military
guys pay the price for the bad
decisions.
When I came home from 'Nam, we
changed planes in Houston. The
civilians there moved to the other
side of the waiting room. Nobody
would speak to us. You felt like you
had the plague.
Then, along comes Steve's son, Benjamin
"Ben" Sones, Marine Reservist coming
home from active duty deployment who took
part in the fracas in the dunes. Ben:
I went over in November; it took one
and a half months to get there. We
stopped off in Oman and Yemen to do
some practice maneuvers for about
three weeks. There were about 102
ships. We had a full regiment of
Marines. *(Ben tells me for general
interest that a platoon is 100 men,
four platoons make a Company, four
Companies make a Batallion, and four
Batallions make a Regiment.)*
We slipped up on the horizon off
Kuwait one night. The fleet Admiral
wanted to parade all the ships as a
show of force, to give the Iraqis
a last chance before the go-ahead.

Nobody knew we were there. They didn't take the bluff, so that night we went back and landed. I was in the 4th AAV out of Gulfport. We made a half-moon back into Kuwait- 428 miles in four days on no sleep. We lived on the coffee from the MREs to stay awake.

(The BLT 3/5 scrapbook outlines the participation of the Batallion Landing Team during DESERT SHIELD, DESERT STORM, and OPERATION SEA ANGEL. On 1 December 90 they embarked from San Diego aboard five amphibious ships. On 27 December they took part in OPERATION QUICK THRUST in Subic Bay. Then they participated in SEA SOLDIER IV amphibious exercises in Oman with the 4th MEB Marines. On 4 February they passed through the Straits of Hormuz, ammunition was passed out on 23 February, and the war began on the 24th. That afternoon BLT 3/5 made an unopposed amphibious landing on Blue Beach at Al Mishab, Saudi Arabia, while some of the force remained at sea to continue the deception that the Marines would land elsewhere. Ben's A Company, 4th AAV joined there with other groups. The movement started 25 February to an area inside the Kuwaiti border. After establishing a defensive position they conducted route and security operations to Al Jaber air field. On 28 February the ceasefire came. The BLT cleaned enemy bunkers of weapons and received an order to clear southwest Kuwait of Iraqis. Still no contact. On 2 March they received enemy fire, so they breached an obstacle belt and began clearing operations in the Al Wafrah Forest, known as the "Waf" to us. The AAV used bangalore torpedoes

*and satchel charges in and around the oil
field and secured the area. That evening
they were told to gather their assets and
leave Kuwait. Then the Marines had to
spend two months on a ship before being
ordered back to CONUS. On 17 May BLT 3/5
went into Bangladesh to help with
OPERATION SEA ANGEL. They were there
until 29 May.)* Ben continues:

In my opinion, nobody joins the service for nothing. We did our job. We
were told to do it, and we did it
right. I ran into some other guys
from around here: Chad Burchfield,
Kevin Dedeaux, Robert Wendell Smith,
and Lynn Rowell- all members of the
4th AAV in Gulfport.

Tommy Lampp was sitting at home
getting ready for college in the Army
Reserves when he got a letter that
changed things a bit:

I was in the 344th Maintenance Group
out of Bogalusa. In December '90 I
was sent to Hafral-batin, about 30
minutes out of town. It was about
like the French Quarter without any
of the frills. We had 120 to 150
tanks come in from Germany that we
had to repair and send to the front
lines. We had one month to do it in,
and we did. They were M-1 and M-1A1s
(Abrams).
I ran into Chad Lenoir and Michael
Lamonte over there. The bad thing
about our war, make that battle, it
certainly wasn't a war, was we kept
hearing over the radio that Saddam
was dead, and, three days later, the
CIA was looking for him. I don't
think the media should have spread

394

the rumors. We didn't have anybody
high enough around us to quieten
them down. I also think we should
have kept bombing and fighting until
we were sure Saddam was dead.

Tim Gerstner was activated at Ft.
Polk in the 812th Medical, National
Guard. He was a crew chief on an air
ambulance helicopter in Saudi from 12
February to 28 May.

Patriotism is running high in the
country right now. Johnny Baker dropped
out of college to join the Marines in
October. He says:
> Unfortunately, I got out of boot
> camp too late or the war ended too
> early *(Johnny was home for the
> homecoming.)*. I'm on my way to Camp
> Lejeune for combat training now.

We lost 81 troops in action and nine
POWs. We lost 33 planes. Check this out.
We captured over 150,000 and killed even
more. We destroyed 4000 of their tanks,
141 planes, 2140 pieces of artillery,
1856 armored carriers, and 33 ships *(from
USA Today)*.

*Interestingly, the interview process
was ongoing during this battle in the
Gulf. I was able to ask questions of
about 25 of our older veterans about
their feelings on the battle and will
show them in chronological order. The
original interviews are scattered
throughout the book for the reader who
cares to reconstruct.*
On the day the war began, 16 January
'91, our guys thought this was a most

necessary war and a nice way to handle
Saddam. On the 17th, Saddam was felt to
be an analog to Hitler and that we should
have already hit him. One was happy about
the 50 tanks surrendering. On the 18th
someone was worried about Saudi Arabia
and our helping them. He quoted FDR:
"Your neighbor needs a fire hose, you
loan it to him." There were some
reservations about this becoming another
Vietnam. All felt we were doing the right
thing. At this time I noticed that nobody
had expressed any concern for oil or
Kuwait, and that the primary concern was
Saddam.

By the end of January our veterans
thought the "pushbutton war" was going
just fine. Some thought the smart weapons
did not pack much of a wallop and were
just so many expensive toys. One was
worried about ground action against the
Republican Guard *(Who could have predict-
ed they wouldn't fight?)*. Keeping politics out of the war and not having "one
hand tied behind us" seemed important.

By the first week in February, we
felt that we were starting to lag some;
but that, as international policemen, we
had an obligation to rid Kuwait of
Saddam. The idea of giving dates and
times about the conduct of military
action seemed out of place. In late
February Schwartzkopf was being hailed as
a hero. There was also doubt we would go
after Saddam. *(Sure enough, we didn't.
Look what it's costing us now not to have
killed him. I think maybe the politicians
will never learn to stay out of it.)*

At least one expressed that same
fear in March, and he proved to be right.
Saddam is still running around roughshod,

and I wouldn't want to be among the last troops to leave the country. We did not finish our job.

Unfortunately, our goal was not Saddam Hussein. The master terrorist is still around to fight another day- possibly with sticks and stones, possibly with terrorists. Now, I'm not a capitalistic war monger, but I have been accused of being a little to the right of Attila the Hun. I think we should have marched all the way through Iraq, gathered up prisoners, and given them to the Israelis as payment for the Scud attacks. That's justice. Then they should have taken a lesson from history, gathered up Arafat and Khadafi, and done the same. We could have solved all the Middle East problems at one time.

Historically, there have been two perfect battles by Americans, Cowpens in the Revolutionary War, and Lee's Wilderness Campaign. This one will undoubtedly go down as the third. Schwartzkopf was able to pull it off because of the heavy technical training of the fighting man and because President Bush did not interfere.

Aftermath

When I had finished gathering all the material and interviews, I realized there were several gaps, and many heart-rending facets of war. I also found many discrepancies between the "book learning" philosophy of all wars and the eyes of the beholder, the foot soldier. After much head scratching, I decided that the interviews had done so well that maybe a super-interview- a round table discussion - would do even better.

Accordingly, on the night of 28 February 1991 a group of veterans and myself met. I prepared a general outline for discussion, and the guys took the ball and ran. They chewed it up, digested it, and spit it out. After all that soul searching, Rusty Penton, Burt Pearson, Larry Spooner, Pat Evans, and Tom Mullins came up with the following. There are also some anonymous comments enclosed. Interestingly, this was the night peace was declared in the Middle East. We covered such topics as (1) why people go into the military, (2) the training they received when they got there, (3) pertinent facts about their tours, (4) their treatment by the military populace, and (5) their treatment on their arrival home by the civilian populace.

The concensus, or my editorializing, will always start on the far left margin. Any time one of the guys soared on his own, his comments were treated like the interviews and indented. The names have been left off as being superfluous. The guys just wanted it to be a discussion with real facts. It would not be hard to cross reference if the reader so desired.

We felt that the people went into the military for the longest time after WWII because it was the only job they could get. They were not even qualified to do that, as witnessed by the various test scores and general falling off of discipline in the military. The military at one time was even given equal billing with penal confinement; a judge would give a criminal a choice- jail or the Army. This is no longer true.

The recruiters are guilty of getting caught up in the fringe benefits with no mention ever of the possibility of having to go to war. The college aid (GI Bill) is now one of the best recruiting tools. It is also going to raise the overall I.Q. of the Army to where it can function again at a higher level than it did in Vietnam. The fighting is the stickler. Recently, there was a man interviewed on TV at Ft. Polk LA. In his interview he said that he had not joined the Marines to fight! *(What did he think Marines did? Sit around knitting?)*

The training that recruits receive elicited much response from all the participants. On basic training:

A recruit gets 16 weeks training now between basic and AIT. There was no AIT in WWII, only 13 weeks basic. In some fields such as engineering, there was no infantry training.

I went through the obstacle course in 1940. There were no top soldiers, only "band aid stripers," who were non-coms off duty. We had dead level machine-gun fire going 18 inches off the ground as we crawled through and under barbed wire, up a hill, through tires and a buried enclosure, a trench.

I went through the same for 'Nam. We were on the infiltration course when a rattlesnake popped up. One guy threw him over to another, who did the same. The third guy got scared and jumped up. TAT-TAT-TAT-TAT. The machine gun sawed him in half. We lost two just in AIT.

Well, then, they're not doing basic like they used to. Our machine gunner was up in a tower firing over our heads.

We were taught never to question our orders and to say "I will." We started with a can-do attitude. The miraculous may take a few days, but we could take care of the impossible immediately. We lost a lot of kids in 'Nam because of a breakdown in this philosophy. Discipline started fading by the time I got out in '69. If you don't have discipline, you don't have a fighting force. In Nam guys would say "huh" or "what," and they are the ones who got killed. You can't question your leader. Bill Calley is a perfect example. The Army spent $40,000 to make him a soldier. They taught him to follow orders. He was following orders at the My Lai massacre. One of his men wrote to his mother about baby killing, and she got in touch with a Congressman *(politicians and war again)*. Now Calley lives at Ft. Benning, never to be free. He's on compound restriction. Did he take a fall for his superiors? You bet your ass he did. I think they should give him his back pay, pat him on the back, and release him.

Training definitely says you will not attack women and children or kill the civilian populace:

In Korea we got sent out on patrol, looking for snipers. I led my platoon up to a village where we suspected sniper fire to be coming from. I sent half straight in, and I led the other half in from across the other side. All the women and children were standing over there on the other side waiting for the patrol and didn't notice us. When the other guys got there, I saw a little girl unwind a hand grenade from a bun of her hair. Without thinking I sprayed the area with my Tommy gun. We found all sorts of grenades, knives, and weapons on them. A photographer from a Detroit newspaper was with us. I told the men to blow the village. He asked "Why?" I told the men to blow the village again. We killed 23 North Koreans, fully armed with AK-47s. They were hidden in false basements. I was trained never to kill women and children, to be a gentleman in war. One time I was on patrol in 'Nam and ran up on a 9-year old boy. Since I had kids of my own, I just stared at him for a while. I figured I'd just go around him. That was my first wound. The kid shot me right below my heart and knocked me back about six feet. It's a good thing I had on my flak jacket, but I still

got a bullet in me. I was a little
more careful after that.
Training for the Special Forces seems a
little more intense than for the regular
grunts:

About 1955 when the Special Forces
started, we were taught espionage,
intelligence, combat, to go in and
disrupt a government such as Chile,
Nicaragua, and El Salvador, and then
set up a government with key personnel. We were taught to use all types
of weapons. Our jungle training was
in the Okefenokee Swamp. By the way,
that McKuen who was training those
Marines in that South Carolina
swamp, he was right. He was trying
to make Marines. I agree with him.
We started out as Rangers. Then we
dyed our clothes black and became
the aggressor force. If you were
already a paratrooper, you still had
six months training. We were also
taught how to destroy or set up a
water supply, sanitation, and CPR.
Our test was that we were given a
piano wire, a trench knife, a .45
with seven rounds, and a first aid
kit. If we got back after two weeks
with all the bullets left, they were
real happy. Rattlesnake doesn't
taste too bad. Boa is better *(and
they wonder why people call them
Snake-eaters)*.
The Army was pretty smart in its
training. I was from the swamps of
Louisiana. The war in the Pacific
was in the jungle, much the same. My
CO was smart enough to realize
that's where I belonged. Each of us
had his own specialty, so, one day,

an E-6 might be answering to an E-5.
No problem. We were taught discipline. In WWII our group covered UDT
(underwater demolition team) operation on small islands. We would
establish a beachhead of sorts, the
UDT guys would wipe out all the
anti-tank and personnel mines, and
we'd go back to the subs in our
rubber rafts. We either beat the
Japs or got the hell kicked out of
us.
Three times in the Army I was told
to forget everything I had ever
learned; once when I went in, once
in the Rangers, and once when I went
into Special Forces.
Special Forces training for Vietnam
was six and a half months of training. Then you got tested. If you
passed, you got 21 more weeks of
training and tested again. Then you
got more training and, if you passed
that, you got Special Forces
training.
Now, the ground-pounding Marine in
this war *(Gulf)* knows as much as a
field-grade officer did in WWII. Not
only that, but he's also qualified
to lead other troops.

The concensus seemed to be that the next
war would be fought in space. The troops
would have to have a college education
just to operate the equipment. Speaking
of which:
WWII rifles would kill at 1000
yards, but they were slow. But then,
it was a slow war. God, it was slow.
The M-60 machine gun would blow the
1919 air-cooled away. It's like

comparing an M-1 to a carbine. The
M-60 is faster, has a bigger load,
the bullets go straight forward.
It's like a buzz saw. By 'Nam the
M-16 rifle bullets were tumbling.
This was not supposed to kill as
many, just wound them.
We had "starlight" in 'Nam. It
allowed us to make out shapes at
night. The tanks had infrared peri-
scopes. They could see in the dark-
somewhat. You could tell if there
was a ditch, but not how deep it
was. Now they don't even have anyone
up in the turret. The tank would run
at night easily. I stood behind a
tree and watched tanks on night
maneuvers. They just charged through
the woods and never hit anything.
The planes now, they're plastic and
wood. Radar can't detect them. The
pilot doesn't even shoot the guns
anymore. When the sight comes on, he
may still be ten miles away. Some
ships are the same way. The
technology is so fast now, my wife
already has a tape of the first
bombing runs in Iraq- a book, too. I
couldn't even fight any more.

That presents a short history of the
training and technology involved in
ground war. Now we're going to try to put
it all together and see what happens with
it. We're talking about war here; pure,
unadulterated war:

What you're doing in your own little
unit was the whole war. You didn't
know anything else about anybody
else (That is the reason I asked for
units in the interviews. Some of the

history has been recorded accurately.). There were a lot of bastard units you won't ever know anything about. I personally know of 200 you won't ever know about from 'Nam. I fought beside an outfit in WWII for two years, the 534th Infantry Regiment. They were attached to the 96th Division for rationing and quarters, but you won't find them in the history books. *(Asked when we could expect any of this information to be made available in the literature, the replies were:)*
Some of that will never come out. The Geneva Convention went out the window. If a General wrote it in his memoirs, they would kill him. It would never be published. Even if he did, he only knew about his little area.
You wanted to bond with the new guys and replacements as soon as you could because you needed to able to depend on them and they on you ASAP. In the Special Forces we have clubs. The skull is on the left side of the entry. When you walk in and take a drink from that, that created the bond of cameraderie. As soon as you saw someone in a beret, you knew he was a brother.
I asked about trip wires and booby traps:
We walked very carefully. We had to learn how to walk. Your eyes never left the ground. You were aware of what was in front, but you looked at the ground. It's almost like you felt with your toes. As quick as you felt something touch you, you froze. You had to wait for someone to come

405

help you out. You more or less had
to drag your feet. It was not that
hard to find the trip wire; you had
to find the one that tripped that
one and the one that tripped that
one. You didn't trust anything that
looked normal. You'd see a bunch of
bananas and reach up to get one.
You'd probably lose an arm.

Bamboo was great for them. Any time
you have orientals, you have to deal
with bamboo. They had punji sticks
and Malayan gates. The Japs would
put punji sticks in the rivers. The
Marines would get hung up on them,
and the Japs would sit on the other
bank and machine gun them. We got
wise and started grenading the
rivers before we crossed them.

The Japs would tie two nooses across
the trail. They were attached to
saplings bent over the trail. Some
poor soldier would step into them,
trip the trigger, and the trees
would spring up and rip him apart.

They've got automatic shotguns now.
You hold the trigger down, and 18
rounds of 12 guage 00 buckshot come
spewing out. I used to commandeer
shrimp boats with one. You call
everyone out, point it down the
hatch, and spray. It would take care
of anything.

I had a CO in Korea. He woke up with
a bottle of "Crow." The last thing
he touched before he went to sleep
was a bottle of "Crow." He bought a
shotgun in Japan, brought it back
with him to our armorer, and had him
cut it off just in front of the action. This gun was strictly against

406

the Geneva Convention. He'd go bunker busting with us. We'd grenade and spray a bunker. If anyone came out, the CO'd put that shotgun to their head and pull the trigger. The man was crazy even though he was a Medal of Honor winner from WWII. I got to where I was afraid to go out with him (This reminds me of Goshie Burks' story about the use of shot-guns in Korea.).

There are no breathers in war. We learned to survive by assuming we were dead before we ever got there. We accepted that fact, and that's how we stayed alive. To the Special Forces a 14-hour break would keep us going. You'd see guys in 'Nam get-ting ready to leave the clubs. They'd start pouring drinks in their fatigue jacket pockets. It might be the last they'd ever have. Later on they could wring out their pockets for a taste in the field. The Air Cav would have a periodic standback. Otherwise, you got your replacements while you were on line and hoped they learned fast.

War is hell. I reminded the group of that line, and this is the response:
The history books are wrong about how WWII was won. Here's how it was. There'd be six men on a patrol. We'd sit there and tell every man what his mission was. If he got killed, the next one knew exactly what to do. If he got killed and so on. That's what won WWII- communication. In WWII I had a 90 day wonder show up. He had a brass badge on his

right shoulder, on his left shoulder, and on his helmet. When he asked what he could do, I told him to take off the badges. He said "but I'm an officer," I said "Okay, we all know that. Now take off those damn badges." "Why?" "Because they make a perfect triangle with your face in the middle." We had a bunker with a tunnel out through the hill. That way we didn't expose ourselves when we went out on patrol. We had some trap doors to go through so, one night on patrol, I told the Lieutenant to let me lead. He said "No, I will." He was the first one to stick his head out that tunnel with all those brass badges on, and a sniper put a bullet right there *(points between his eyes)*. I went to report after the patrol, and the Old Man asked where the Lieutenant was. I told him he stuck his goddamn head out and got killed. That just goes to show you the idiocy of command. What cost us 'Nam was dope...ineffective training...poor command. That's basically it. In fact, that's pretty close to what cost us Korea. I can't make it any plainer than that. We took Old Baldy three times in three days and finally napalmed it. In 'Nam we took and retook a hill outside Hue ten times. The CO was trying to build up his body count. I got a 90 day wonder one time. The CO told him to listen to me and he'd be okay. First thing we got out, and he stood up and yelled "Gung ho." They shot him in the head. We lost three of them in 14 days. The last one, we were on the perimeter. Remember we talked about how to walk in Nam? I'm on guard, hear some noise, and yell "Halt!" in English and Vietnamese. No answer crunch crunch crunch- I asked for a pass word crunch crunch CRUNCH nothing, just like an NVA- CRUNCH CRUNCH CRUNCH -still no answer. I grabbed my flash suppresor and hit him in the head. Sure enough, it was our 90 day wonder. He tried to court marshall me, but the Old Man wanted me to court martial him. After the next mission I got sent to Westmoreland for my commission.

We have two stories on the bonding, or cameraderie, that we discussed earlier:

In Korea we had a valley to sweep. There was a road up the valley and rice paddies up the side of the mountains. We had a fire base on top of one of the hills in a paddy. They started lobbing mortar rounds in on us. I had to get my guys off that hill. I did, but they got in a good round.

In 'Nam we had a medevac chopper. Ours was going off with the wounded, and I was still on the ground. That chopper was shot down. I didn't even think. They were my guys. I grabbed a weapon and bandolier and went to that helicopter. I got hit six times, but all my guys got off that ship. By the time Mike force got there to relieve us, they were all saved. When they asked me why I did it, I said "They were my guys." No regulation can hold that bond.

In 'Nam you didn't know who your
enemy was. From 1962-68 we didn't
know anything about Agent Orange
other that the fact that it was a
defoliant. Chester Nimitz's own son
died from it. Then they looked into
it.

We sometimes operated out of the
sphere of normal operation. The
Special Forces would be out on "vacation" trips or two month R and Rs.
You know, sometimes the vegetation
would obscure the view or you'd get
lost *(see Vietnam Section on PUEBLO
capture)*.

We had a lot of insubordination in
Nam. The troops didn't like stran-
gers coming in. We also didn't get
the proper support. Once on a forward fire base we called for LAWS
(light anti-tank weapons). The
Marines sent us 100. Ten worked.
Other times we were on sterile missions. We had nothing on to identify
us as Americans. They would dump us
500 miles from our home base. We'd
do our job and call for a pickup.
Nothing. It's like we were being
sacrificed. We had our weapons and
maps. We knew how to get back,
although it may take a few months. I
had a CIA SAC up against the wall
one time like this *(holding him up
off the floor by his neck)*. I would
have crushed his trachea if someone
hadn't saved him.

The bane of every soldier is getting
captured. Our round table had some views
on that:

I got captured in Kwajelein. We were

going in to get an Aussie shore watcher. These people would watch the Jap navy going by and report it to us. Well, we had a fresh lieutenant commanding the companyfresh out of the States. We went in, and he stood up and fired a flare so he could see where everybody was. The place lit up like Canal Street. The Japs overran us. Several of us were captured and the rest were killed. Talk about a stupid officer!

I got captured once while I was on "vacation." Fortunately, aside from the piano-wire boot laces, we also had two-edged pieces of steel sewed into our field jackets. They were great knives. I got away after being detained for about three weeks.

The serviceman's diet got better as time progressed. You recall Job Foxworth and his two biscuits and molasses just before Corinth. By WWII they had K-rations. "They would keep you alive, but they tasted like shit." They had hot coffee every day. By Korea they had one hot meal a day. The best you could say about that was that nobody ever starved to death in the Army. By Vietnam they had C-Rations, which may not have been tasty but were nutritional. Now the troops have MREs. Considering the generation: "They aren't McDonalds, but they'll do."

Medical wise, the big problem in WWII was water and dysentery *(just like the War Between the States)*. Every GI got issued seven pairs of socks, so if he got "jungle rot, it was a personal problem." Malaria was also big in the Pacific.

About 40 percent of the wounded died. In 'Nam hepatitis and malaria were the biggies because the guys would not take the pills. By this war, there were helicopters, so the wounded got taken care of faster and only about 10 percent of the wounded died.

The conduct of war has been a moot point, depending on whose history you read or listen to. You could really get confused as to the issues and even who the bad guys were. The media seems to have been able to control the outcome of some action even more than the generals. The round table took a look at each and drew these conclusions:

Roosevelt started the Manhatten Project in 1940, before we were in a war. A lot of people didn't give him credit. He was smart. He left MacArthur alone in the Pacific. Then Truman took over. He was caught between a shit and a sweat after the first nuclear bomb. He didn't do anything, and they dropped the second one. If Hitler had been able to find a detonator, he would have armed the V-2s with nuclear warheads and won the war. Saddam had the same problem, but the FBI caught that boatload of detonators going to Iraq.

In Korea we should have never stopped at the Yalu River. We had the morale, the arms, the materiels. MacArthur was gung ho. He had aspirations of being great. He was going through Manchuria to Moscow, but Truman brought him home and busted him. He was lucky: Patton wanted to

do the same, and they killed him.
The same thing happened to Westmoreland in 'Nam. Johnson brought him home and replaced him with Abrams, who set up fire zones. That worked against us. If they'd left Westmoreland alone with our 30 Special Forces teams in Laos, Cambodia, and North Vietnam, we'd have won it in short order. But we had a candy-ass President who wouldn't let us do that.
If we'd had the support in Korea and 'Nam they *(Desert Storm)* have from Bush, we'd have done better. The country would have been behind us, more patriotic, and we'd have had less casualties. Instead, we had a chicken shit President, chicken shit politicians, and chicken shit commanders. Every one of us would have followed Westmoreland to hell.
Schwartzkopf is a great general. He had great backing, and he fought a great war. This one will go down in the history books. Bush is a smart President. He left him alone.

The media involvement in the fighting of wars and the course of history:
There was too much press in 'Nam. The media forecast all our moves, so were always pre-empted. We'd have a planning meeting two days before a strike and have two enemies to account for. The press, with all its freedom, was right there in on the sessions and then busting their butts to scoop each other. Ho (Chi Minh) had television sets and co'ld read.

At Long Vinh our house boys were spies *(This was a strange war. House boys?)*. I caught one pacing off the distance to our bunker and reporting it. The Major didn't believe the house boy was measuring artillery coordinates for a barrage. Sure enough, that night we got one.

Another time all but three of us in my team got wiped out. We were walking along another time and found a peeled GI. His skin had been peeled back, and he had been burned to death with cigarettes. The press didn't report that.

Yet another trick was for the <u>mama-san</u> to stroll up to a populated spot and ask a GI to watch her baby carriage while she went shopping. The carriage would blow up, baby and all, killing the troops around it. The press didn't report that either. There was too much press in 'Nam, and it was all negative. They'd report our plans in the papers and on TV. The Cong knew what we were going to do before we did it. They were a bunch of do-gooders who didn't know what they were talking about. If they could find a negative, they'd report it. If you went out on patrol with 20 rounds and killed 19 gooks, they'd want to know what happened to the 20th round. Never mind the 19. If they could find a kid with his head blown off, they'd show that. I don't know how many times I've seen that same little naked girl on TV- I think about 1500 times. I just saw her again in this war.

414

The first day of this war some idiot on CNN was showing 15 of our jets taking off from Saudi to Baghdad. This idiot was showing Saddam exactly what was happening. Then a miraculous thing occurred. The general called Bush, and Bush told him to run the war any way he wanted to! Presto, no more press. One time they did try the negative approach by trying to place civilians in front of a bombed bunker, but the public wasn't buying it.

Coming home. If you take all this good training and put it to good use, and if you are lucky and things go right, you've got a good chance to come home. We all know about the ticker-tape parades for the returning heroes of WWII. We also know about the negative press of the returning Vietnam vets. Let's hear it from them.
I was with a wounded friend at Ft. Lewis WA, helping escort him back home. He was on a stretcher. When we went out the gate, an American civilian hit him with a brick and called him a baby killer. The brick split his head so that he had to have some more stitches to go along with his wound. Welcome home, hero.
I came home to Ft. Lewis. The military wouldn't take me from there to a civilian airport so I could go home. Because I hadn't been paid for a while, I couldn't take a taxi. I had on my uniform and had to hitch a ride through all those protestors. Welcome home, hero.
I'm not so sure a professional soldier

can handle all this. I know an 18-19 year old can't. What has our country done?

The country wanted some heroes. President Johnson had us all on stage one time in Washington after one of my tours. It was all a publicity stunt. A reporter came up to me and asked me how it felt to be a hero after Johnson pinned the Silver Star on me. I said "I don't. I just stayed alive." It was a goddam publicity stunt to get people to support Vietnam. One guy got a Congressional Medal of Honor, two more got Distinguished Service Crosses, ten more Silver Stars, and a handful of Purple Hearts. It was all a publicity stunt. It made us all feel cheap. Don't call me a hero. I'm not one. I was just in the wrong place at the right time. If I could have been somewhere else, I would have.

One time I came back from 'Nam to go to Ft. Bragg. Then the Army sent me to the Capitol in Washington. It was surrounded by concertina wire, and we were on guard duty. Hippies were coming up and throwing human excrement on us. They were peeing on our boots. I finally had to call my colonel aside and tell him to pull us back in 30 seconds or we'd start killing civilians. We had to put up with that in Nam. We weren't going to put up with it here. He pulled us back.

I learned my lesson. Another time I came home from 'Nam and didn't wear my uniform. When some tourists asked me if I was returning from 'Nam, I replied "No, I've just been vacationing in Hawaii." You got to the point you didn't want to answer because you didn't know what kind of reception you'd receive.

Speaking of coming home, check this out. The US Government unintentionally was the largest dope dealer in the world at that time. They transported much, VERY much, dope back into the good old US of. How? Would you believe in body bags. Guys working each side of the pond. The ones in Nam would split a corpse up the middle and load his insides with dope- heroin, weed, whatever; southeast Asia was full of it. Then they'd put the guy in a body bag, put it on the C-3s, and send him home for burial. Guys on the US side would receive the body, take out the dope, and sell it. Nobody was the wiser. What about that for a homecoming?

Let's end the round table on a good note: I came home through Oakland. Everyone kind of looked at me, but didn't say anything. When I got to the New Orleans airport, my wife was not there yet, so I sat down. An older couple just returning from a vacation started talking to me. Then they offered to give me a lift to Picayune. Since my wife was on the way, I declined. They sat there and kept me company until she got there.

Enlistment. Training. War. Coming home. This is what some of the ground pounders from Pearl River County thought about it all. You may agree or disagree. That's fine. It's what they fought for; and, until you've been there, you don't have anything to say about it at all. Period.

An even better welcome by Major Dad's wife, Delta Burk (Tommy Stockstill)

Veterans Memorial in Picayune

Veterans Memorial in
Poplarville

Conclusion

During the Cold War Pearl River Countians have also been stationed overseas in many places and in the rest of the good old U.S. of: Key West (rough duty), Norfolk, Seattle, Crouton AFB, Italy, France, Keesler AFB (also), Hawaii (terrible), Forts Dix, Leonard Wood, Bliss, Bragg, Sam Houston, Ord, and Hood, Japan, Okinawa, Goose Bay, and Clark AFB. There have been many incidents such as the MAYAGUEZ, the USS LIBERTY, the Libyan cat-and-mouse games, Granada, the Iran hostages, Operation Desert Shield, and so on.

Wherever the young people of Pearl River County have been sent they have done so honorably and have brought much joy and pride to the rest of us. It is not much, but this book is dedicated to them with a big "THANK YOU."